THE CONCEPT OF DEITY

THE CONCEPT OF DEITY

A COMPARATIVE AND HISTORICAL STUDY

*The Wilde Lectures in Natural and
Comparative Religion in the
University of Oxford*

by

E. O. JAMES

D.LITT., D.D., PH.D., F.S.A.,

*Professor of the History and Philosophy of Religion in the University of
London, Fellow of University College.*

1950
HUTCHINSON'S UNIVERSITY LIBRARY
Hutchinson House, London, W.1

New York   Melbourne   Sydney   Cape Town

Holy, concepts of

Deity

Printed in Great Britain by
William Brendon and Son, Ltd.
The Mayflower Press (late of Plymouth)
at Bushey Mill Lane
Watford, Herts.

CONTENTS

pomorphism and personal theism in Rabbinic Judaism; The effect
of the doctrine of the Incarnation on anthropomorphism in
Christianity; The analogical method in the Early Church and in
Scholasticism; Butler and "The Analogy of Religion"; The place
of anthropomorphism in modern conceptions of Deity.

PREFACE

THIS volume contains the substance of a part of the material collected for three courses of Wilde Lectures in Natural and Comparative Religion in the University of Oxford at a time when the leisurely pursuit of learning had been disturbed by the conflict and chaos into which the world had been plunged immediately after my appointment to the Lectureship. In the choice of a subject I had been guided by Dr. Wilde's definition of Natural Religion as "man's conscious recognition of purposive intelligence and adaptability in the universe of things, similar to that exercised by himself." And, as it seemed to me, the stirring happenings of the hour certainly had not lessened the importance of an objective inquiry along the lines indicated in the Statutes. If the fabric of modern civilization was and still is tottering under the impact of current events and ready to crumble in the dust, a scientific examination of the system of belief and practice which has acted as a consolidating dynamic of human culture through its long and checkered history, is not without its significance at this critical juncture in world affairs.

For good or ill, most, if not all, of the great institutions which have formed the framework of society have had their roots in the idea of Deity as a beneficent providential order of transcendental reality. In being handed down through countless generations the beliefs, concepts and customs have assumed a great variety of new outward forms in the process of transmission and development. To determine their true meaning and function as a cohesive force and as an expression of ultimate reality, the comparative and historical methods can be employed with considerable advantage, especially if they are brought into conjunction with the more ultimate quests of the philosopher and the theologian in their respective searches for a deeper evaluation of the data in terms of validity and truth.

While a comparative study of religion, as of all other aspects of cultural phenomena, is committed to a strictly scientific approach to its material, it cannot exercise its proper functions in isolation from these other closely allied departments of knowledge. Religion is essentially a human reaction to the ultimate facts and meaning of life, and constitutes a living reality for those who accept its premises and presuppositions. To regard it merely as a branch of anthropology

would be to fail to recognize its true significance as a human discipline. Equally to confine the inquiry to a historical study of the
sequence of events would afford very little insight into the fundamental nature of the phenomenon as a way of life based on certain
deeply laid convictions. Always and everywhere those who genuinely
practise religion must believe in what they are doing, in the reality
of their faith and what it stands for in the deeper regions of their
inmost being. "One person with a belief,' wrote Mill, "is a social
power equal to ninety-nine who have only interests." Hence the
influence of a living faith as the core and consolidating dynamic of
all sound communal life. Therefore, account must be taken of the
philosophic aspects of the data if the full significance of the evidence
is to be inferred.

That Dr. Wilde when he made his benefaction had in mind
such an approach to the subject is indicated, I think, by the designation of the Lectureship as "Natural and Comparative Religion,"
and the description of its purpose as that of promoting "the increase
of true religious knowledge." Like Lord Gifford, he desired to
further the empirical study of religion as a strictly natural science
without reliance upon any conception of revelation. But he was
also anxious for "the modes of causation, rites and observances and
other concepts involved in the higher religions" to be interpreted
and evaluated in relation to the recognition of a providential order
of ultimate reality on which human beings have believed themselves
"to be dependent for their continued existence and well-being, and
with which they have endeavoured to live in harmonious relations."

In drawing a contrast between "the higher historical religions,"
which the expression "Comparative Religion" is to be taken to
mean, and "the naturalistic ideas and fetichisms of the lower races of
mankind," it might appear that any consideration of the beliefs and
practices of peoples in a primitive state of culture is ruled out by the
Statute. In the light, however, of our present day understanding of the
principle of continuity in a world in evolution, it is not possible to
cut off as with a knife the history, philosophy and function of the
higher religions from all that lies behind these developments. Thus,
if we are to discover the true significance of the concept of Deity,
it is not sufficient to analyse the ideas which the more enlightened
and reflective portions of mankind have entertained on the subject
in the past and still maintain to-day. Even the humblest efforts of the
least sophisticated representatives of the human race have to be
treated as relevant to the inquiry after their own fashion.

Since by training, outlook and inclination I am myself primarily
an anthropologist, in honouring me with an invitation to give these
lectures the electors doubtless expected that I should devote the
courses principally to a comparative study along anthropological
lines. It would be a mistake to suppose, however, that the anthropologist is concerned merely with the rites and customs of savages.
On the contrary, his field of research embraces every aspect of
cultural development where his methods are applicable; and clearly
they are appropriate in the scientific investigation of the fundamental theme in "natural and comparative religion" which I have
selected for the purpose of this inquiry. In view of the emphasis laid
on "the higher historical religions," however, I have been careful
to limit the use of material drawn from primitive states of culture
to that which has a definite bearing upon the more advanced
conceptions of Deity, particularly in relation to the idea of Providence.

Again, as it is now no longer possible to keep in watertight
compartments the beliefs and institutions of the lower and higher
cultures, so at the other end of the scale the distinction between
"Natural" and "Revealed" Religion is much less clearly defined
than when Dr. Wilde and Lord Gifford established their respective
Foundations for the furtherance of the objective study of religious
phenomena without reliance upon any special divine self-disclosure.
In Christianity, for example, while the idea of revelation is still
regarded as a fundamental element in the faith, in recent years the
empirical approach to the study of theology has become widely
adopted by theologians with far-reaching results in a critical understanding of the Scriptures and their contents. Moreover, the former
deductive method of interpretation based on revelational presuppositions has been abandoned very widely in favour of an inductive scientific method in which facts are carefully attested and verified
by the aid of all the available evidence, as in any other department
of empirical knowledge, and doctrines formulated, like scientific
hypotheses, as conclusions drawn from the data. Thus, revelation
from being a process through which clearly defined theological
propositions have been disclosed in the form of articles of faith
deducible by reason from explicit and infallible decrees to be found
in the Bible or the official formularies of the Church, has now become
a category necessary for the interpretation of certain properly
ascertained facts. Under these changed circumstances the line of
demarcation between the approaches to Natural and Revealed

Religion has worn so thin that the distinctions formerly drawn are of little more than historic interest, except perhaps in backwaters where earlier modes of thought survive undisturbed. But regarded from the present empirical and historical standpoints, the general principles that govern the idea of revelation as an inductive category clearly fall within the scope of a comparative investigation of "natural religion." Therefore, I have not hesitated to consider their implications in the elucidation of the problem of the concept of Deity, independent of any attempt to establish a unique supernatural authority for specific traditions or dogmas. This clearly lies outside the terms of reference.

Finally, if a serious effort is to be made to promote "true religious knowledge," just as earlier distinctions between rudimentary and developed beliefs and practices, and natural and revealed religion, have had to be abandoned, so the isolation of the comparative method from the philosophical approach cannot be sustained. The ultimate purpose, significance and validity of the empirical data become vital elements in the evaluation of religious phenomena regarded as ways of life and aspects of reality. Nowhere is this more apparent than in the synthesis of ideas which have found a focus in the concept of Deity. In the investigation of this problem it is essential that the "how" of science and the "that" of history should be supplemented with the "why" of philosophy by subordinating cause to purpose, origin to validity and historico-empiricism to teleology. Therefore, the philosophic implications of theism have been considered as falling within the compass of the inquiry, though, of course, to do full justice to this vast subject would require a separate volume devoted wholly to it. Here, however, the available literature is extensive, and all that has been attempted in these pages has been to show the bearing of the relative metaphysical thought upon the comparative and historical evidence under consideration.

It was my original intention to publish the lectures in the form in which they were actually delivered at Oxford. But the abnormal conditions that prevailed in a university in a state of perpetual flux necessitated so much repetition and explanation that they proved to be unsuited for publication as they stood. Before it was possible to undertake a complete revision of the manuscript the cessation of hostilities, which coincided with my appointment to a new Chair, involved me in a welter of academic duties and responsibilities. These disabilities, together with the pressure of other literary commitments, have caused regrettable delay in putting together a section of the material in its present form. Nevertheless, this has had the advantage of enabling me to benefit by the work that has been done by others in the same field during the interval that has elapsed, and so to present what I hope is an up-to-date statement of the position. In conclusion I should like to express my gratitude to my revered university for appointing me as its Wilde Lecturer, an experience which has been at once an honour and a pleasure which I have appreciated immensely. As on many former occasions, I am indebted to my wife for her assistance with proof-reading.

E. O. JAMES.

Oxford.

CHAPTER I

THE PRIMITIVE CONCEPTION OF PROVIDENCE

ALTHOUGH the idea of God has been the subject of critical inquiry since the human mind began to reflect upon the problem of Ultimate Reality in the early days of Greek speculation, the origin of the concept of Deity inevitably lies hidden from view. Whatever secrets the Palaeolithic deposits may yield to the spade of the pre-historic archaeologist, it is not very probable that they contain much evidence on this subject beyond what can be conjectured about the dawning religious consciousness from the few hints given in the available data. The anthropologist makes no attempt to arrive at absolute beginnings. He begins wherever he most conveniently can and works backwards until he is brought up sharply at a certain point by a total lack of evidence. Thus, in the matter of belief in God, all that he can affirm is that religion is apparently a universal pheno-menon in human society as it is known under existing conditions. To go beyond this is speculation and conjecture, but, nevertheless, the principle of continuity suggests that all the more important kinds of vital activity have been present from the beginning. If, as there is strong reason to suppose, religion is one of the funda-mental disciplines of mankind, it is within this general framework that the origins of the conception of Deity must be sought, and the nature and attributes of the concept determined.

Notwithstanding the fact that the term "primitive" is purely relative, having reference either to a mode of life and thought which appears to be earlier in time, or to that which, though late in time, is yet culturally less mature, it covers the field of inquiry where a study of the kind contemplated in this volume must begin. Thus, it is now generally agreed that the customs and beliefs of surviving groups of mankind on the fringes of the higher civilizations, living under conditions of material culture little changed from those which prevailed in prehistoric times, are not far removed in other respects from the notions and traits of Early Man. In the case of religion this surmise is strengthened by the fact that nowhere is the human mind quite so conservative and static as in its attitude towards a transcendent order of reality, if for no other reason, simply because it represents the ultimate court of appeal and absolute source of knowledge, power and existence. The religious consciousness being so essentially an emotional experience of the external world—of beneficence, harmony and orderly creation in conflict with their opposites—it has acquired a very deeply laid traditional and mystical significance which tends to make authority and "feeling" rather than critical reason the ground of belief and practice. Indeed, rational processes hardly play any determining part in the discipline until reflective thought has become definitely established and the question of validity of paramount importance. Therefore, in primitive society the phenomena of the sacred as a consolidated whole are taken for granted without question as a body of esoteric tradition revealed to the initiated under conditions of intense emotional stress and suggestibility, and having all the prestige and weight of an undivided public opinion.

Moreover, the doctrines and practices accepted in the first instance on tribal authority are verified in the experience of the individual and the group because they are not concerned with theoretical speculations concerning such matters as the origin of the world and figments of the imagination going back to a hypothetical "mytho-pœic age," as often has been erroneously supposed by modern interpreters, but with certain practical and pressing problems of daily life. Myth and ritual in primitive society, in fact, are the things by which men live because they enable them to secure their means of subsistence and to deal effectively with the many precarious, inexplicable and uncontrollable situations that confront them on all sides. Being thus vital aspects of continually recurring experiences and of perpetual emotional crises, they are permanent elements in the life of the community so long as the environmental conditions remain stable. It is not until the organic structure and vital rhythm of primitive society begin to collapse that the established beliefs and institutions undergo a fundamental change. As the culture breaks up its myth and ritual lose their essential significance in the life of the community and degenerate into idle tales, conventional ceremonies, quaint and picturesque survivals of a bygone age, sophisticated pastimes, or, in some cases, unedifying superstitions devoid of any serious meaning and purpose, except as scientific data for the recon-struction of the past.

Studied alive as integral elements in a living culture, arising directly out of the religious, social, economic and ethical tradition, the traditional lore and ritual organization of native tribes are a reality lived as expressions of their own subject matter and customary behaviour.[1] So long as life pursues the even tenor of its wonted ways the attitude of human beings towards the ordinary and commonplace is not very different at any time or at any level of culture. It is only when natural phenomena—the sun and the moon, the clouds and the winds, mountains and rivers, earthquakes and storms—arrest attention by striking and unusual behaviour that they call forth a magico-religious reaction. This, however, cannot be regarded merely as an individual response springing wholly from deep-seated individual needs, desires or wishes craving for fulfilment, as the psycho-analysts have contended. Unconscious symbolism may have this in common with primitive thought that in both words are replaced by concrete images, yet myth is no more a day-dream of the human race to be interpreted by the symbols of psycho-analytic exegesis than the behaviour of modern neurotes is a faithful reproduction of a primeval ritual organization. At best any similarity that exists between the two classes of phenomena can only indicate that in both there has been a return to an infantile mentality. But the most potent influences in the shaping of myth and ritual have come from an emotional response to the physical and social environment rather than from individual instincts.

The pressing events in the external world and in the immediate circle of human relationships, the struggle for existence and survival, the innumerable daily frustrations and awe-inspiring experiences, often completely outside human control and beyond comprehension; above all the ceaseless preoccupation with the means of subsistence and continuance of the species—these were and are the causes and occasions of the emotional situation out of which rite and belief have emerged. Around the trinity of instincts—self-preservation, the propagation of the race and the cohesion of the group—which go to make up existence,[2] the religious sentiment has developed a complex growth which has found expression in the idea of Providence, of creative and recreative power, and the transcendental ordering of the religious and social life. But none of the instinctive processes is absolute in itself, or able to provide the key to the understanding of the whole reality within which it occurs. Thus, feeding, breeding and living together in an orderly manner collectively constitute the emotional centres of myth and ritual and give rise to the prescribed techniques for effectively dealing with

[1] cf. Malinowski, *Myth in Primitive Psychology* (Lond., 1926), p. 21ff.
[2] Rivers, *Instinct and the Unconscious* (Camb., 1920), p. 52.

B

unpredictable elements in an intense situation, and for providing a consolidating dynamic indispensable to the integration of the community.

Long before the human mind makes any attempt to explain or theorize about the things it perceives but only dimly understands, it is aware of a distinction between the commonplace and the mysterious, between occurrences it can deal with and those beyond its foresight or control, without drawing any hard and fast line between the "natural" and the "supernatural," in the sense in which we employ these terms to-day. In primitive society every object or event which arrests attention, or is inexplicable in terms of the normal, is assigned to the sacred order and given a transcendent significance, so that the whole phenomenal world is regarded as permeated with forces and influences which, though imperceptible to sense, are thought to be real and tremendously powerful in the control of natural processes and human destinies. Nevertheless, it is not to be supposed that the primitive mind is so absorbed in "pre-logical" mystical thinking and "collective representations," as M. Lévy Bruhl and his collaborators in L'Année Sociologique maintain, that it is unaware of a conception of the natural order, and is incapable of distinguishing one object from another, making a thing what it is not.[1]

In arousing the realization of a super-sensuous transcendent sacredness, or "otherness," beyond itself, society unquestionably has played a very important part by the power it exercises over its members under tribal conditions. But it does not follow that les sociétés inférieures are in a pre-logical stage of mentality in which the "law of participation" reigns supreme to the exclusion of the "law of contradiction" so that a man believes himself to be both a human being and an animal.[2] If he is unaware of any distinction between himself and some other creature, he can hardly be illogical in maintaining the symbiosis. It is not lack of logic that characterizes primitive beliefs but inability to distinguish between agent and act and cause and effect. The things causally related are not identical with those that are so connected by the modern sophisticated mind. Secondary causes with intermediate links in a chain of events are not clearly recognized and no abstract distinction is made between an order of uniform happenings and a higher order of miraculous

[1]Lévy Bruhl, Les Fonctions Mentales dans les Sociétés Inférieures (Paris, 1915), p. 76ff.
[2]Lévy Bruhl, La Mentalité Primitive (Paris, 1922), p. 19.

occurrences. The savage merely marks the difference when it is presented in the concrete and exploits it for his own purposes, interpreting it in terms of remote and recondite agencies.

Nevertheless, these mental reactions, however characteristic they may be of savage behaviour, are not confined to any state of culture. They recur in times of stress at all human levels, just as under normal and placid conditions man always learns from experience and observation, and applies perfectly "natural" and "scientific" methods based on causal sequence in the search for food, the provision of shelter and clothing, and the arts and crafts he invents and develops. When these fail to meet the situation other ways and means transcending the powers of ordinary observation have to be found. As the primitive is more limited than modern civilized man in coping with his environment, he relies more extensively on "supernatural" agencies and transcendental causes, but so far as mental processes are concerned, the difference is one not of logical thought but of material surroundings and mental and technical limitations.

Again, while it is as a member of a social group that the human species has developed its cultural inheritance, fundamental beliefs and institutions, and built up the structure of society, religion is not just the "collective representations" of society in regard to sacred things, as Durkheim has tried to prove.[1] It is not true to say that in "a general way a society has all that is necessary to arouse the sensation of the Divine in minds, merely by the power that it has over them; so that to its members it is what a God is to its worshippers." This conclusion was reached by a study of totemism, the "god of the clan" being regarded as "nothing else than the clan itself," the totemic principle being identified with the Melanesian concept of *mana*.[2]

According to Codrington, who first introduced the native term *mana* into anthropological literature, any object, person, or event behaving in an unusual manner, either for good or ill, is thought in the Pacific islands to be endowed with this mystic quality. "If a man has been successful in fighting it has not been his natural strength of arm, quickening of eye, or readiness of resource that has won success; he has certainly got the *mana* of a spirit or of some deceased warrior to empower him, conveyed in an amulet of a stone round his neck, or a tuft of leaves in his belt, in a tooth hung upon a finger of his bow-hand, or in that form of words with which he brings supernatural

[1] *Elementary Forms of the Religious Life* (E.T. Lond., 1915), p. 47.
[2] op. cit.

assistance to his side. If a man's pigs multiply, and his gardens are productive, it is not because he is industrious and looks after his property, but because of the stones full of *mana* for pigs and yams that he possess. Of course a yam naturally grows when planted, that is well known, but it will not be very large unless *mana* comes into play; a canoe will not be swift unless *mana* is brought to bear upon it, a net will not catch many fish, nor an arrow inflict a mortal wound."[1]

So widespread in primitive states of culture is this conception that for purposes of scientific exposition it has been found convenient to use the term *mana* to cover all manifestations of transcendental power ranging from a mystic force associated with will and intelligence, like the Uroquoian *orenda*, to the non-moral holiness, or *baraka*, of saints, sultans and sanctuaries in Morocco.[2] Therefore, Durkheim is justified in regarding the totem as a sacred object having *mana*. But totemism represents a highly specialized organization of a social group around a common supernatural ally, be it a species of animal, plant or some inanimate object, from whom descent is claimed and with whom intimate and exclusive relations of a sacramental nature exist, uniting the members of the clan or kin in a blood brotherhood.

In the first blush of a new discovery following upon a series of papers by J. F. McLennan in the *Fortnightly Review* of 1869, a former generation of anthropologists was inclined to seek a totemic significance in almost every act of worship or veneration paid to animals and plants. Moreover, the importance attached to the custom by Robertson Smith as a primary feature in "elementary forms of the religious life," led Durkheim—and subsequently Freud—to make totemism the original institution of religion. For this assumption there is no evidence. Apart from the fact that it does not occur at all among such very backward tribes as the Andamanese, the Semang, the Punan of Borneo, the Pygmies of the Congo and the Bushmen of South Africa, or the clanless non-totemic peoples of the North-West Pacific coast of North America, isolated from the focus of civilization, where it is established it seems to combine a number of very different features suggesting a relatively late and multiple origin. Thus, it is closely connected with the maintenance and

[1]The *Melanesians* (Oxford, 1891), p. 118f.

[2]cf. Marett, *The Threshold of Religion* (Lond., 1914), pp. viii, 60ff; J. N. B. Hewitt, *American Anthropologist*, N.S. IV, 1902, p. 38ff.; Westermarck, *Anthropological Essays presented to Tylor* (Lond., 1907), p. 368ff.; *Marriage Ceremonies in Morocco* (1914), p. 360ff.

distribution of the food supply (particularly in Australia) and with the cult of ancestors, the doctrine of reincarnation and the control of the weather. These are grouped together as a complex social and economic system uniting in a single whole the order of nature and that of human society.

In the consolidation of the community religion unquestionably played an enormously important part, and in primitive states of culture the conception of Providence has emerged in relation to the conservation of the food supply and the emotional reactions this has produced, interpreted in terms of *mana*. But it cannot be maintained that the idea of God "is nothing less than society divinized," or that the concept can be explained entirely by "collective" rather than "individual" forces. Behind collective representations there lies a deeper transcendental reality external to man but operative in abnormal occurrences, uncanny objects, exceptional people and any person or thing that has come into direct contact with this sacredness. Before the rise of conceptual thought and clearly defined ideas, "the sensation of the divine" was an emotional response to awe-inspiring phenomena transcending the ordinary and commonplace and outside the range of normal experience and understanding. It was conceived neither in terms of the personal or the impersonal, nor of the social or mystical. As Marett has said, "savage religion is something not so much thought out as danced out, that, in other words, it develops under conditions, psychological and sociological, which favour emotional or motor processes, whereas ideation remains relatively in abeyance."[1]

In the absence of a theology, or indeed of any established dogmatic beliefs, the emphasis is on the things done (i.e. the ritual organization) to control the vital concerns of man—e.g. propagation, nutrition, stability and an orderly life. These rites certainly exercise a specific social function but they are the expression of a sense of dependence on a power outside both man and society, a power that may be described as *Providence* in the sense of the concrete universal good, the sum total of the beneficence and bounty of the world and its processes. The institutions of religion are not "ideas with which the individuals represent to themselves the society of which they are members and the relations they have with it,"[2] but the means whereby communion with and in beneficent abundance is secured, and the evils of want and sterility are overcome.

[1] *Threshold of Religion*, p. xxxi.
[2] Durkheim, op. cit., p. 225.

A combination of reverend regard and fear towards this trans-cendental source of human well-being produces the emotion of awe which is not quite the same as *mana*, since it is a psychological condition rather than a mystic force or influence attached to certain objects. Otto's term the *numinous* as a "category of value," if not "perfectly *sui generis* and irreducible to any other state of mind,"[1] is nearer to the primary and elementary datum required. This "idea of the holy" as a transcendent presence standing over against the individual self-consciousness—the feeling that there is "another" out beyond human consciousness, the social structure and the natural order, which is also within man—may well be the raw material out of which the concept of Deity has developed. Nevertheless, the reaction has not been produced, it would seem, by a real operative entity described as an "unnamed transcendent something" which later developed into a "numen loci, a daemon, an el, a baal or the like," as Otto contends.[2] On the contrary, the notion of Divine Providence as over-powering mystery drawing men towards it in mystical experience and communion, and calling forth the sense of creatureliness by its very power and greatness, is associated with specific abnormal and awe-inspiring phenomena. An object or event producing the reaction may be perfectly familiar except in its manner of behaviour. It is this which connects it with transcendent "otherness" and makes it holy, taboo and the centre of a cultus.

Similarly, it is not true to affirm with Durkheim that "nature as such cannot inspire religious emotion"[3] inasmuch as it is precisely in relation to extraordinary and arresting events in the natural order, and the reliance of man on his physical environment, that the first inklings of Providence are to be found. The notion of the Divine is no "mirage of social facts" dependent entirely upon the "collective effervescence" of tribal ceremonies.[4] It is an implicit theory of the universe essentially cosmological in character, the individual reaching out beyond the confines of the social and natural orders to the sense of mystery and awe at the very heart of all things.[5] Furthermore, individuals are capable of profound religious experiences independent of the collective emotions at such seasonal ceremonies as those

---

[1] *The Idea of the Holy* (Oxford, 1928), p. 15.
[2] op. cit., p. 130.
[3] Goldenweiser, *Journal of Philology*, XIV, March 1917, p. 116.
[4] Durkheim, op. cit., p. 226ff.
[5] C. C. J. Webb, *Group Theories of Religion and the Individual* (Lond., 1916), p. 151.

performed by the native tribes of Central Australia in order to make the totems increase and multiply for the benefit of the whole community.[1]

Since each human being is mystically united to his sacred ally from which he derives his name and descent as the source of his life, on certain occasions he may retire to the bush in silence and solitude to make as it were a "private retreat." There he awaits the appearance in a vision of his secret helper, or *nagual*, to give him the guidance he is seeking. Thus, among some of the Indian tribes of North America, during the initiation of a youth destined to be a warrior, an eagle or bear will appear to him, a serpent will manifest itself to a future medicine-man, or a wolf to a hunter. To complete the bond a portion of the *nagual*, or guardian spirit, is worn about his person as an embodiment of its soul-substance. Sometimes, as among the Déné, a representation of the animal is painted in vermilion on prominent rocks in the most frequented spots.[2]

The tutelary spirit is usually distinct from the clan totem but, nevertheless, both are embodiments of mystic power and constitute the link connecting a human being with the providential world-energy which they symbolize. Neither is primarily "the individualized forms of collective forces,"[3] for the sacred animal is essentially a mystic object representing the primitive conception of Providence around which the social and economic organization has developed under the influence of group-consciousness. In certain communities this has taken a specialized form in totemism as the means whereby a closely knit confraternity owning a common allegiance to a sacred ally has sought the aid of providential bounty and found a unifying dynamic to enable the members to live together in an orderly arrangement of social relations.

In these rudimentary and generalized notions of the sacred, which appear to lie at the root of the conception of Deity on its immanental side, may be detected the beginnings of a long and complicated process which has found expression in due course in what has been described in the trite phrase as being "in tune with the Infinite." Conscious of a vast ocean of life and vitality outside himself and the phenemonal world, yet permeating the whole of creation, satisfaction can come to the individual only in uniting

---

[1]Spencer and Gillen, *Native Tribes of Central Australia* (Lond., 1899), p. 167ff.

[2]G. Morice, *Proceedings of the Canadian Institute* (Toronto, 1889), 3rd series, Vol. III, p. 161.

[3]Durkheim, *Elementary Forms of the Religious Life*, p. 425.

himself to the super-sensible source of strength and power at the heart of the universe. But coupled with this awareness of a beyond which is within and around man, there is also the awe-inspiring and overpowering realization of an "otherness" which is above, of a power awful and mysterious transcending the entire process of creation as its ground and support.

These two fundamental aspects of the idea of God are inherent in the first strivings to express in a ritual technique the most urgent needs of propagation and nutrition, and the sense of dependence on an externalized providential power regarded as the plenitude of bounty and beneficence. This undefined object of veneration and reverend regard is not feared as a source of malevolence, or so completely "wholly other" and "non-rational" as to lie outside the reach and understanding of man. On the contrary, its attraction is its beneficence and its power of drawing the creature to itself through the mediation of carefully prescribed ordinances designed to be at once the channels of supernatural potency and safeguards against the perils of approaching the sacred without due care and respect. Man must walk humbly and circumspectly in the heavenly places for many are the pitfalls and dangers that await the unwary, the immodest and the profane in these lofty and mysterious realms. It is not that they are infested with malign influences, though such may lurk in their secret corners. Rather is it because the sacred is taboo and so is surrounded with ritual prohibitions. Thus, in association with the notion of Providence the birth of humility is to be sought and with it comes the sense of awe that produces the feeling of creatureliness in the presence of the Creator by His very power, greatness and beneficence—all, in fact, that is implied in the term "transcendence" combined with that of "immanence" as attributes of Deity; however crude and naïve may be the modes of expression in these rudimentary stages of God-awareness.

With the development of conceptual thinking, this generalized and undefined notion of Providence has given rise to a complex order of super-causation in the region of the super-sensible in which gods, ghosts, spirits, totems, ancestors, culture-heroes and so on have acquired a place and status. Any attempt at reducing this confusion of ideas, concepts and evaluations to something approaching order encounters at once the initial difficulty arising from the fact that no such order exists in primitive society. The neglect of this all-important consideration has led many modern scientific observers and theorists to divide up into clearly differentiated categories, systems and disciplines, beliefs and practices which the primitive mind is incapable of keeping asunder.

The ritual organization, as we have seen, has grown up around the fundamental realities and necessities of existence which we have grouped together under the comprehensive title of "Providence." This, however, being a composite term covers a very wide field, including such a variety of phenomena as the food quest, sex, marriage, fertility, birth, adolescence, death and the sequence of the seasons. Consequently, when these are interpreted in terms of the activities of spiritual beings, ghosts of the dead, and individualized divinities, inevitably they react one on the other as integral elements in a coherent whole—the order of the sacred. This represents the matrix. What comes out of it takes many shapes and forms, each and all having a common source, but on coming to maturity they all develop their own characteristics revealing anything but an ordered sequence of evolution.

At an early stage in this process, as supernatural potency acquired will and lived a life of its own, it seems that an animistic duality emerged in which the body of a living organism was made subordinate to an independent animating principle. But animism cannot be regarded as a "minimum definition of religion" along the lines suggested by E. B. Tylor.[1] For the reasons that have been considered, the starting point must be sought in something at once wider and vaguer, a sacredness in which the body and its indwelling life are not distinguished or personified.[2] Moreover, at the animistic stage in this development, between the two conceptions of a pervading life enabling the living being to think and act, and the "second self," or phantom-soul, there is a distinction which Tylor failed to perceive. Dreams and visions cannot be made to account for the entire phenomena since they do not explain the idea of the soul as a reflection, a shadow and the breath, or its association with a vital organ of the body such as the heart or head, or with the blood as the life principle.

The doctrine of animism resolves the universe into a fundamental duality of body and soul regardless of the fact that this dichotomy is the product of a long process of conceptual thinking and philosophical reflection which took its rise in Greece in the sixth century B.C. rather than in primitive society. In dividing

---

[1]*Primitive Culture* (Lond., 1871), p. 425ff.

[2]i.e. the phase which Marett has described as "animatism". *Threshold of Religion*, p. 14ff.

Reality into the invisible permanent world of ideas grasped by the reason, and the transient phenomenal order visible to us and known through the senses, Plato developed doctrines which Heraclitus, Anaxagoras, the Orphics and the Pythagoreans had borrowed from an earlier stratum of thought, very much as in their turn Descartes, Leibniz, Lotze and McDougall went back through the scholastics in the Middle Ages to the animistic ideas of Plato and Aristotle. But while it cannot be denied that the notion of soul, ghost or spirit is a genuinely primitive belief, the interpretation placed upon it by Tylor belongs essentially to the philosophy of religion, as indeed he recognized.[1]

If the primitive mind is not as mystical and pre-logical as sociologists of the school of Durkheim and Lévy Bruhl have contended, it certainly is not prone to clear-cut evolutionary sequences of thought which held the field in the latter part of the nineteenth century. Then it seemed reasonable to surmise that starting with animism as "the minimum definition of religion," the development of the idea of God proceeded in an orderly manner either, as Herbert Spencer argued, from the deification and propitiation of distinguished ancestors and heroes,[2] or, as Frazer maintained, by a supposed craving for simplification and unification reducing to localized departmental deities a multiplicity of spirits, souls or wills animating every aspect of natural phenomena, until a further generalization caused the many gods to be deposed in favour of one supreme Ruler and Controller of all things.[3]

Against this hypothesis, however, is the occurrence of "High Gods" among low races who are neither the souls of famous men raised to divine rank after death, nor animistic spirits or departmental gods. This evidence, first brought to light by Andrew Lang,[4] has now revealed as an integral element in the primitive conception of Deity, the shadowy figure of the tribal Supreme Being who is supposed to have existed before death came into the world and to have been responsible for bestowing the laws, customs and beliefs of the people over whom he rules as the great chief in the sky. Among the Australian aborigines, for example, the All-Father is thought to have made himself and to have lived on the earth he created before he retired to his heavenly abode. While usually he stands aloof from

[1]*Primitive Culture*, Vol. I, p. 426.
[2]*Principles of Soci. logy* (Lond., 1885), Vol. I, p. 411.
[3]*The Worship of Nature* (Lond., 1926), p. 9ff.
[4]*The Making of Religion* (Lond. 1898).

everyday affairs, he is regarded as the guardian of the tribal ethic and not infrequently plays the role of the "god of the mysteries," presiding over the initiation rites.[1] It is on these solemn occasions that youths are carefully instructed in the tribal lore and the inviolable customs and institutions, invested with the supernatural sanctions bestowed on them by the supreme divine Law-giver in accordance with the unalterable principles he established in the beginning.

As the personification of the moral order, these unique figures represent the highest expression of supernatural potency and will, primal and benevolent, the givers and guardians of the good and the right, the supreme originators and upholders of the laws whereby society is maintained as an orderly whole. While in these respects, as Andrew Lang and Fr. Schmidt have pointed out, the tribal All-Fathers resemble the God of the Hebrews, it is only within the very limited capacity of the primitive mind to comprehend the concepts and attributes of Deity that the more profound evaluations can be applied to them. Thus, when they are said to have existed before death came into the world, this does not presuppose any conception of time which admits of eternity as its corollary. Or, again, to affirm that they are able "to go anywhere or do anything" does not mean that they are regarded as omnipotent or omniscient except in the sense that such expressions might be applied to a powerful chief or medicine man. Similarly, with regard to their creative powers. These are comparable to those exercised by a great rain-maker and are limited to the restricted cosmological outlook, seldom extending over more than the locality which a particular tribe inhabits.

Moreover, these functions generally are confined to the formative period when they called into being the existing order in nature and society as it obtains in the tribe. Having done their work, they are thought to have retired to the seclusion of the sky, henceforth taking little or no part in the control of natural processes and human affairs. Originally, however, they seem to have personified the conception of Providence in its transcendent aspect and to have been the token of beneficence until this was brought under the control of a hierarchy of independent gods and their earthly embodiment the divine king. When this was accomplished the Supreme Being became virtually functionless so that he was seldom the object of worship, and for practical purposes he was eclipsed by the more popular and intimate divinities. Indeed, All-Fathers, although highly

[1]Howitt, *Native Tribes of South-east Australia* (London., 1904), p. 488ff.

respected and occasionally appealed to as a last resource in times of crisis, have tended to become otiose and redundant. They may figure in the background at initiation ceremonies, but their dissociation from the ritual organization at all other times has caused them not infrequently to degenerate into bogeys to frighten the women and children, as among the Arunta and Luritja tribes in Central Australia, where they are little more than personifications of the sacred bull-roarer, the thunderous booming of which is regarded as their voice.[1]

It has been this isolation of the All-Father from the practical concerns of everyday life that has prevented anything in the nature of a genuine monotheism developing in primitive society. That such a belief ever existed at the threshold of religion, as Fr. Schmidt and his followers have endeavoured to maintain,[2] is highly improbable. In every community, it would seem, there are always a few to whom religion in its loftier, vaguer and more transcendental aspects makes a ready appeal, but in the case of the majority it is only at certain times and under particular conditions—such as at crises in the career of the individual (birth, marriage, death), or those of the community (seedtime and harvest, war and famine)—that the religious sentiment is aroused to any appreciable extent. To the intermittently or indifferently religious, High Gods are too elevated and remote to be popular objects of worship. Being the highest conception of Deity that the mind can conceive in terms of transcendence, they tend to become the "wholly other," the Absolute, unless they are brought into direct relation with the immediate vital concerns and ever-present realities of human existence. To be effective gods must be ritually accessible, efficacious and responsive to man through the established technique of a cultus. Therefore, while the Supreme Being stands alone, head and shoulders above all secondary figures—animistic spirits, lesser divinities, deified ghosts, totems and so on—he never holds the field in primitive society to the exclusion of all other gods.

The recurrence of this conception of Deity in all states of culture and phases of religious development, suggests, however, that it arises spontaneously as a purposive functioning of an inherent type of thought and emotion rather than as an elaboration of a certain

[1]Spencer and Gillen, *Northern Tribes of Central Australia* (Lond., 1904), p. 497ff. Howitt, *Native Tribes of South-east Australia* (1904), p. 488ff.

[2]Schmidt, *Ursprung der Gottesidee* (Münster, 1935), Vol. VI, p. 492ff. *Origin and Growth of Religion* (1931), p. 150.

kind of knowledge concerning the universe.[1] Being primarily a psychological tendency, the monotheistic *idea* is implicit among all races of mankind, and though it has varied everywhere in value and efficacy, wherever it occurs it constitutes the highest expression of the concept of divine transcendence. As an emotional evaluation of the "mysterium tremendum" it is more fundamental than any final product of an evolutionary scheme, and so far from polytheism passing into monotheism by way of abstraction and generalization, simplification and unification, speculation about the universe and its processes has led to the peopling of natural phenomena with a multiplicity of spirits and departmental deities until the High God has become a shadowy figure obscured in the haze of animism.

Although a value is attached to the Supreme Being superior to that of all other gods or spirits, it is most unlikely that at any time or place this expression of a special kind of religious experience and emotion has existed to the exclusion of all other types of belief and practice. On the contrary, as we have seen, the generalized notion of Providence normally is associated with the more intimate and accessible supernatural agencies. Nevertheless, the fact that High Gods are often assigned creative functions as "producers,"[2] and are thought to have been responsible for the establishment of the present order of the world and of society, brings them within the providential cosmological scheme. Hence their intimate association with totemic ancestors and with sky beings in creation stories where often they assume the role of the First Father of mankind, the Earth Maker or the Sun Goddess.

It is doubtless true, as Dr. Radin maintains, that in many of these myths the idea of Deity has undergone a good deal of modification through the influence of the "religious formulator,"[3] but the fact that so often tribal All-Fathers are represented as having retired from the world to the sky, suggests that "once upon a time" they were more closely connected with the course of nature and the actions of men. Thus, not infrequently they are believed to send rain to fructify the earth, or, as in the case of Bunjil in Australia,[4] to animate men whom they have shaped as manikins out of bark over which they have spread clay, and then breathed into their nostrils, mouths and navels the breath of life. Or, again, at a

---

[1] cf. P. Radin, *Monotheism among Primitive People* (Lond., 1924), p. 67.
[2] cf. Söderblom, *Gudstrons uppkamst* (Stockholm, 1912), pp. 149, 166ff., 175.
[3] *Primitive Religion* (Lond., 1938), pp. 151ff., 256f.
[4] R. Brough Smyth, *The Aborigines of Victoria* (Melbourne, 1878), Vol. I, p. 424.

relatively higher level of culture, the Maoris of New Zealand held that a god Tiki, or Tane, kneaded with his own blood riverside clay into an image of himself and brought the effigy to life by breathing into its nose and mouth.[1] Similar stories recur throughout the Pacific and in many other parts of the world,[2] showing how widespread is the belief that the Supreme Being is the author and giver of life. However much these beliefs may have been formulated under the influence of the religious genius, be he medicineman, priest or prophet, it is almost certain that he was interpreting mythologically ideas and actions that were generally accepted by the community as a whole, since religion is rooted in a universal need expressed in terms of Providence, of which generalized conception of sacredness the Supreme Being was an integral element.

It was only when the All-Father ceased to exercise his creative and sustaining functions, or delegated them to lesser and more intimate divinities, that he tended to become a deistic figure in a remote sky world. Providence always must be more than a "Producer" or a "First Cause." Unless the High God is also the ever-present ground of creation upon whose support it depends at every moment of its existence, he fails to supply the most fundamental religious requirement in any effective conception of Deity. It is not enough for him to be "that than which a greater cannot be conceived," for his very ontological transcendence may render him so remote and inaccessible as to exclude altogether a personal relationship with man and the universe; just as to identify Him with "a power not ourselves making for righteousness" may deprive him of any conscious sovereign rule over creation, if God becomes "the whole world as possessing the quality of Deity". To be effective at any cultural level, Providence must be interpreted as the transcendental source of beneficence at the very heart of all existence with whom communion is possible in order that life may be sustained, retained and renewed at its dynamic centre.

[1] W. E. Gudgeon, *Journal of the Polynesian Society*, XIV, 1905, p. 125ff.; R. Taylor, *Te tha a Maui: New Zealand and its Inhabitants* (Lond., 1870), p. 117.
[2] Numerous examples are given by Frazer in his *Folk-lore in the Old Testament* (Lond., 1918), Vol. I, pp. 10-44.

CHAPTER II

THE WORSHIP OF NATURE

In the more developed polytheistic systems the prominence given to the deification of the attributes of nature represent an interpretation of observed facts as these are understood at a particular level of culture. The natural order—the sun, the moon, the clouds, the winds, the seas and the rivers; everything in fact that comprises the material environment—is in a state of flux, and this is interpreted in terms of potency and act, very much as in the Aristotelian concept of motion; the reduction of a condition of potency to a condition of act. The process thought to bring about the transformation or change may be described as one of "personification" inasmuch as it assigns to natural phenomena powers analogous to those exercised by human beings, since only in this way, in the absence of knowledge to the contrary, can the behaviour of the objects in question be explained.

There is nothing mysterious, mystical, "prelogical" or unreasonable in arriving at this perfectly natural conclusion so long as the scientific causes remain undetected. Indeed, prior to the determination of the Newtonian laws of motion, movement was normally regarded as the means by which the "essence" or potency (δύναμις) inherent in the object realized its purpose in act (ἐνέργεια). And in Greece after more than a century of metaphysical speculation on Being and Becoming, the movements of the heavenly bodies were attributed to indwelling souls or spirits in eternal motion as "visible gods."[1] If these were the views held wholly or in part by such profound thinkers as Plato and Aristotle, and subsequently by St. Thomas Aquinas, it is not surprising that a similar interpretation of natural phenomena occurs at the threshold of conceptual thinking.

In the absence of any rigid distinctions between the natural and the supernatural, the animate and the inanimate, the phenomenal order is identified with that of human existence, and the behaviour of the one equated with that of the other. As animistic and polytheistic ideas develop the process of personification includes a great variety of modes of expression with clearly defined anthropomorphic,

[1]cf. Plato, *Phaedrus*, 247ff; *Laws*, 898ff.

31

theriomorphic or naturalistic forms, unlike the shadowy and vaguely conceived potencies and providences of more rudimentary phases of culture. Thus, in contrast to the Numina of Roman religion, the Greek pantheon presents us with an organized world of deities with outstanding personalities and attributes, while the Ancient Egyptians represented their gods either in human guise, like Osiris, Isis, Min and Ptah, or as animals (e.g. Sebek, depicted as a crocodile), and sometimes in a combination of the two—e.g. Horus, Thoth, Khnum, with the heads of a falcon, an ibis and a ram respectively, surmounted on a human body. Each city and nome had its own god, and as in predynastic times as townships grew in power and influence the local gods acquired corresponding importance, so after the unification of Upper and Lower Egypt under Menes (the traditional founder of the First Dynasty), the deities of the succession of capitals—Heliopolis, Memphis and Thebes—gained pre-eminence.

Since the sun is the predominant natural feature in the Nile valley, ripening the crops with its life-giving rays, at a very early period it was worshipped as the chief god in the pantheon, rising, it was supposed, as a falcon, surmounted by the solar disk and cobra (the *uraeus* or serpent), and with outspread wings flying across the heavens as Re-Herakhty, i.e. "Re-Horus of the Horizon." Three other Horuses were stationed on the eastern side of the sky, and at Heliopolis, the original centre of the solar cult, he appeared as an old man tottering down in the west to rise again in the east as Khepri, the sacred scarab beetle, having in the meantime passed through the underworld during the hours of darkness. As it was erroneously supposed that out of the ball of dung which the beetle collected for food and rolled between its legs a new living scarab appeared, the insect became a symbol of the Sun-god holding the solar disk and rolling it across the sky from east to west, apparently self-created. Thus, the Sun-god was regarded as the self-existent transcendent Creator of all things who, as Atum, at the beginning of time existed alone in the primeval ocean of Nun. Either by having sexual union with himself, or with a consort who appeared to him, he begat Shu, the personification of the air, and Tefnut his wife, the personification of moisture. These produced Geb the earth-god, and Nut the sky-goddess; and finally from them sprang Osiris and Isis, and Seth and Nephthys.

The inclusion of Osiris in the Great Ennead of Heliopolis shows that as the process of correlation went on, local gods were given a place in the sun as they acquired eminence. Originally he (Osiris) had no solar connexions, being a chthonian deity and the personification of the life-giving waters of the Nile, renewing the soil after the inundation, whose cult-centre was Busiris in the Delta. But as the new life springing from the fertilizing mud of the river typified the dying and reviving god, Osiris not unnaturally was brought into relation with the Sun-god, both deities representing two essential aspects of the process of vegetation. In the meantime, however, Osiris had acquired a chthonian significance, and as his legend developed, he was regarded not only as the imperishable life of the earth which revives and declines every year with the changes of the season, but also as the king and judge of the dead in the other world.

In the Heliopolitan version of the Osiris myth he was the beneficent king who had been placed on the throne of Egypt by Geb and was murdered through the jealousy of his brother Seth. Isis, his faithful wife and sister, thereupon undertook a relentless search for his body and when at length she found it, Re, the Sun-god, sent his son Anubis, the funerary god, to reassemble the severed limbs of the corpse. Isis having restored it to life, she conceived a son, Horus, who when he grew to manhood avenged the death of his father by defeating Seth in a mortal combat. Horus, however, lost his eye in the fray and on having it restored to him by Thoth, the god of wisdom, he gave it to Osiris to eat to make him "strong in soul." But Seth disputed the legitimacy of his conqueror and a trial was staged before the Heliopolitan Ennead presided over by Re. Thoth pleaded the cause of Osiris and proved that he was "true of voice" and that Horus was his son and successor. Despite protracted vacillation on the part of the nine gods, who for eighty years argued the case before the Heliopolitan council, eventually Horus was vindicated and Osiris appointed Judge and Lord of the land of the dead, where originally he reigned as a sinister figure, a terror to gods and men.[1]

The composite nature of this story reveals the many elements which were combined in the Osiris-Horus myth and its cultus. For ritual purposes, in fact, every divinity was Osiris and every king assumed the role of Horus in life and that of Osiris at death,[2] while

---

[1] *De Iside et Osirides*, in *Scripta Moralia* (Didot, tome i, 429) E. T. by Squire. (Camb., 1744); Breasted, *Religion and Thought in Ancient Egypt* (Lond. 1912), p. 18ff. Erman, *Handbook of Egyptian Religion* (Lond., 1907), p. 32ff. Frazer, *Golden Bough*, Pt. VI, Vol. II, pp. 3ff. A. H. Gardiner, *The Chester Beatty Papyri*, No. 1 (Lond., 1931).

[2] Erman, *Handbook of Egyptian Religion*, p. 45. H. Frankfort, *Kingship and the Gods* (Chicago, 1948), p. 181ff. A. H. Gardiner, Hastings *E.R.E.*, Vol. V, p. 478.

at the same time remaining the physical son of the Sun-god Re.[1] In this dual capacity the reigning Pharaoh was the embodiment of all the life-giving powers so that the throne became the dynamic centre of the nation and its occupant virtually the creator and upholder of the right ordering of nature, making "the verdure to flourish in the two regions of the horizon." As the incarnation of Re he conferred upon the country the beneficence of the Sun-god; as the living Horus he was the personification of Providence as this was understood in the Osiris tradition. Thus, he summed up in his complex personality all that was divine in the Nile valley.

Behind the elaborate polytheism of the Egyptian pantheon lay the all-enveloping sun in its various personifications, and the life-giving waters of the Nile equated with Osiris,[2] upon both of which natural phenomena the country depended for its fertility. Ultimately, as will be considered in greater detail later,[3] this situation represented a plurality in unity, and it is hardly likely that any clear distinction was drawn between the nature and activity of the two gods who were incarnated in the king.[4] In any case, they were brought together in the divine kingship in one complex personality.

Born of an incestuous union between the Pharaoh impersonating the Sun-god, and his consort representing Hathor,[5] he was publicly acknowledged by his heavenly father on the day of his accession when he was purified with "the water of life which is in the sky," to give him "good fortune, all stability, all health and happiness." In the Toilet ceremonies in the House of the Morning he was renewed daily and declared to be like his father Re, who "ariseth in the firmament." By the potency of his words he was a creator, the upholder of justice, omniscient and omnipotent.[6] Throughout his life he was the recipient of the same worship as was offered to every god and goddess in the land, and in theory he was the priest *par excellence* of all the local shrines and their divinities. With the Osirianizarion of the solar theology, since as the living Horus he

---

[1]Frankfort, op. cit., p. 160f. Breasted, *Religion and Thought in Ancient Egypt*, p. 124.

[2]Blackman, *Zeitschrift für Aegyptische Sprache Altertumskunde*, Bd. 50, 1912, p. 69ff.

[3]cf. Chap. V, p. 90.

[4]Frankfort, *Ancient Egyptian Religion* (New York, 1948), p. 88f., cf. 30, 43. W. D. Kristensen, *Livet fra deden. Studier over aegyptisk og gammel graesk religion* (Oslo, 1925), pp. 117f. I. Engnell, *Studies in Divine Kingship in the Ancient Near East* (Uppsala, 1945), p. 7ff.

[5]Frankfort, *Kingship and the Gods*, p. 43f. Sethe, *Urunden des Aegyptischen Altertums* (Leipzig, 1906), IV, p. 219f.

[6]Erman, *The Literature of Ancient Egypt* (London, 1927), p. 280.

was the earthly embodiment of Providence in its beneficent fertility aspects, it was his duty to officiate at the ceremonies upon which the well-being and prosperity of the nation depended.

At the Harvest Festival of Min, an ithyphallic god identified with Amon and Horus, the king made offerings to the cult-image of the god and walked in the procession immediately before it, preceded by the white bull, the embodiment of the deity. On reaching the temple at Koptos he ceremonially reaped the first sheaf of spelt and of barley "for his father" (i.e. Osiris) to insure a plentiful harvest.[1] Similarly, at the Spring Festival in the month of Khoiakh, held in honour of the death and obsequies of Osiris, when the victory of Horus over the enemies of his father was celebrated by a ritual combat, the Pharaoh renewed his royal functions as the controller of the fructifying forces in Nature by assisting at the erection of the Dd-column at Busiris on the last day of the feast, after the burial rites had been performed. This symbolized the resuscitation of the god in the tomb to a semblance of his former life.[2]

If this was the equivalent of the renewal of the reign of Osiris, it explains the choice of this festival for the accession of a new king and for the celebration of the periodic jubilee rites known as Sed, when the coronation ritual was repeated. From the representations of this very ancient observance—probably the oldest religious feast in Egypt—as they appear on the monuments of Hierakonpolis and Abydos, and in the fifth Dynasty temple of Usirniri at Busiris, the Pharaoh assumed the garments and regalia of Osiris and sat in a shrine wrapped in bandages in the form of a mummy, holding in his hands the crook and flail. On the mace of king Narmer, belonging to a very early period of Egyptian history, nine steps are depicted leading up to a shrine in which the king is seated as Osiris with fan-bearers and a procession of standards. Similarly, on a seal of king Zer of the first Dynasty, in front of the monarch arrayed as Osiris is the ostrich feather on which the dead king was supposed to ascend to the sky.[3]

Although the Osirian character of the Sed-Festival has been

[1]Blackman, Luxor and its Temples (Lond., 1925), pp. 179 ff., 182. Mythand Ritual (Oxford, 1933), p. 28ff., A. H. Gardiner, Journal of Egyptian Archaeology, II, 1915, p. 125. Frankfort, op. cit., p. 188ff.

[2]Gardiner, op. cit., p. 123. Frankfort, op. cit., p. 178ff. Moret, Du caractère religieux de la royauté pharaonique (Paris, 1902), pp. 12ff., 255ff. Sethe, Dramatische Texte zur altaegyptischen Mysterienspiele (Leipzig, 1928), p. 156ff. Untersuchen zur Geschicte und Altertumskunde Aegyptins, II, 1905, p. 134ff.

[3]Petrie, Researches in Sinai (1906), p. 183ff.

questioned,[1] it is generally agreed that it was a renewal of the king-ship through a process of rebirth.[2] Petrie and Frazer among others regard it as a modification of the ancient custom of killing divine kings when they were at the height of their vigour in order that the sacred life might be transmitted to a successor undiminished.[3] This is by no means improbable since the life of Pharaoh was bound up with the prosperity of the country and the fertilization of the crops, while the rebirth of the queen as a goddess[4] completed the union of earth and heaven upon which the fecundity of Nature and the recreative processes were thought to depend.

In all ancient rituals in which the king was identified with the sky as the source of transcendental vitality and beneficence, the queen was equated with the earth as the immanental principle essential to the bestowal of providential bounty. Therefore, as the sovereign at his consecration was reborn as the gods he embodied, so his consort was reborn as the Mother-goddess in one or other of her several capacities as the creatrix, like Isis the female counterpart of the primeval abyss from which all life sprang. Thus, in Meso-potamia the king was the son either of Anu, the Lord of the sky and father of the great gods of the heavens, or of Enlil, the "king of heaven and earth", who became the most important of all the Sumerian deities.[5]

Closely associated with these gods as the authors and givers of life and the source of the kingship, was *Dumu-zi*, "Tammuz of the nether sea," or "the faithful son of the waters which came from the earth"[6]; the lover of the goddess known to the Assyrians as Ishtar. This interesting figure, the Mesopotamian counterpart of the Syrian Adonis and the Egyptian Osiris, is known chiefly as the hero of the vegetation cultus and lamentation rituals,[7] where he appears as "the child of the deep," the brother-husband or lover-son of the goddess, personifying the generative force in plants and animals. In the

[1]Gardiner, op. cit., p. 125, Wainwright, *The Sky-Religions Egypt* (Camb., 1938), pp. 20ff., 86ff.

[2]Moret, op. cit., p. 256. *Mystères Égyptiens* (Paris, 1913), p. 187ff. Frankfort, op. cit., pp. 79f., 82.

[3]Petrie, op. cit., Frazer, *Golden Bough*, Pt. IV, Vol. II, p. 151ff. Wainwright, op. cit., p. 19ff., Seligman, *Egypt and Negro Africa* (Lond., 1934), p. 56ff. Moret, op. cit., p. 190. Hornblower, *Journal of the Egyptian and Oriental Society*, XVII, 1932, p. 22.

[4]M. A. Murray, *Man*, 1914, p. 22.

[5]H. Labat, *le caractère religieux de la royauté assyro-babylonienne* (Paris, 1939), p. 55, n. 19. C. S. Gadd, *Ideas of Divine Rule in the Ancient East* (O.U.P., 1948), p. 43.

[6]Langdon, *Tammuz and Ishtar* (Oxford, 1914), p. 6.

[7]Langdon, *Semitic Mythology* (Lond., 1931), p. 342ff.

Tammuz liturgies still surviving,[1] his death at the hands of super-natural foes is described, together with his imprisonment in the underworld, the lament of Ishtar and her descent to the nether regions to secure his release, and his triumphant return celebrated with processions and feasting.

This myth is a recurrent theme in the Ancient East in the third and second millenniums B.C., and, as Professor S. H. Hooke main-tains, doubtless it is based on a ritual which was brought into Mesopotamia by the Sumerians from the highlands to the north-west.[2] When Marduk, an ancient High God with solar attributes, became the head of the pantheon as the city-god of the new capital (Babylon), he replaced Tammuz as the central figure in the Annual Festival known as *Akitu*, held at the New Year in the *Esagila*. In this capacity he became a dying and reviving year-god, though the transition is not easily explained. Frankfort thinks it was due to "an interpretation of Sumerian mythology in terms of Semitic beliefs", the functions of the Sumerian fertility deity (Tammuz) being transferred to the Accadian Sun-god (Marduk) in Sargonic times.[3] But, as Dr. C. J. Gadd has pointed out, so far from the character of Tammuz, or of the year god in general, having been "abusively foisted upon the local god of Babylon by the political ambition of his priesthood, all we know of the local gods in general suggest that this was a regular part of their character, though by no means all of it. It represents the agricultural interests and necessities upon which the cities were well aware that their whole life and prosperity depended."[4]

It was from heaven "before the throne of Anu" that the Kingship was bestowed upon the world (i.e. the ancient Sumerian cities where these divine rulers reigned in turn) before the Flood.[5] After this catastrophe "the divine shepherd", *Dumu-zi*, under the designa-tion of "the Fisherman," alone continued the antediluvian régime in the First Dynasty of Erech. The shepherd *par excellence* of Baby-lonia, however, was the old Sumerian ruler Lugal-zaggisi, who at the end of the Early Dynastic Period introduced a new title ,"King of the Land,"[6] thereby indicating his lordship over the entire country,

[1] cf. M. Witzel, *Tammuz Liturgien und Verwandtes*. Analecta Orientalia, X, 1935.
[2] *Folk-Lore*, June, 1939, p. 140.
[3] *Cylinder Seals* (Lond., 1939), pp. 95f., 105, 113.
[4] *Myth and Ritual* (Oxford, 1933), p. 59.
[5] Langdon, *Babyloniaca*, xii, p. 11.
[6] F. Thureau-Dangin, *Sumerische und Akkadische Königsinschriften* (Leipzig, 1907), p. 156f. Gadd, *Ideas of Divine Rule in the Ancient East* (Schweich Lectures, 1945), O.U.P., 1948, p. 38.

as distinct from local authority over a city-state. As this extension of his dominion was sanctioned by Enlil, it is possible that it marks a new and wider conception of divine rule involving the notion of a universal Providence as "the true shepherd of the land" reigning on earth in the person of his royal representative. But in Mesopotamia, although kings reigned by divine prerogative and selection, as each ruler aspired to hegemony his relation with the divine order became less clearly defined. It was not until Marduk was exalted over all the gods of the earth by Anu and Enlil, and at the same time declared Babylon to be the head of all the cities with Hammurabi as its ruler, that the kingship was brought into relation with a composite deity at all comparable to Re and Osiris in Egypt. But his son Nabu did not reign in the person of the earthly sovereign like the Egyptian Horus, and so while Marduk remained the supreme god and creator of mankind, instead of being relegated to the realms of the dead as in the case of Osiris, Mesopotamian kings never attained to the superhuman status assigned to Pharaoh as the pivot of society.

In the re-enactment of the creation story, or *Enuma Elish*, during the *Akitu* festival , the Babylonian king underwent a repetition of his investiture as part of the process of the renewal of nature at its dynamic centre. By delivering up his regalia to the high priest he was dethroned, and after making a negative confession and performing an act of humiliation and renunciation as a simulated death, he was re-established in his office, assured of victory over his enemies, a prosperous reign and length of days. After being conducted in triumph leading the statue of Marduk to the Festival House outside the city, the spring festival concluded, apparently with his consorting with the queen to complete the renewal of the processes of fertility at the turn of the year.[1] Thus, the "destinies of the year" were fixed.

In the ritual texts of Ras Shamra (Ugarit) in Syria, belonging to the Amarna age in the middle of the second millennium B.C., the Tammuz-Marduk cult drama reappears in a combat between the sky-god Aleyan, son of Baal, and his enemy Mot, son of El, lord of the underworld. In the heat of summer Aleyan was killed when the withering plants and parched ground proclaimed his doom. Anath his consort, the Ishtar of the episode, searched for his body and finally

[1]P. Dhorme, *La Religion assyro-babylonienne* (Paris, 1920), p. 169. Labat, *Le caractère religieux*, etc., p. 235ff. S. Smith, *J urnal f Royal Asiatic Society*, 1928, p. 849ff. In Assyria the ruler was crowned by a priest as the god's instrument and smeared with life-giving substances from a magic tree, but he was not deposed. cf. Gadd, op. cit. (1948), pp. 49, 91, note C.

went to Mot and demanded her brother. At first he feigned ignorance of the whereabouts of Aleyan and tried to persuade her to go to the underworld to secure water to revive the earth. This she refused to do and instead seized him, split his body with a ritual sickle (*harpé*), winnowed him, scorched him in the fire, ground him in a mill, scattered his flesh over the fields, like the dismembered body of Osiris, and gave him to the birds to eat. In short, she treated him as the reaped grain in a manner appropriate to harvest rites, if the texts are liturgical rituals used at the New Year Festival, as seems highly probable,[1] rather than poetic legends as Virolleaud imagined.[2]

In many of the conflicts recorded Baal is represented as being always ultimately victorious. Having conquered the powers of evil he ascends the throne as king and judge, pronounces the doom of his adversary and engages in a hierogamy to ensure the continuance of the fructifying forces in Nature. Thus, a sacred marriage between the temple priests (impersonating El) and priestesses appears to have been celebrated, and it is not improbable that the king as the incarnation of El had nuptial relations with the high priestess.[3] The text Nikal-Kotarot is another instance of divine nuptials in the Ras Shamra series referring apparently to the marriage between the Moon-god and the Moon-goddess.[4] Gaster regards it as a wedding song containing a mythological interlude describing how the Moon-god Y-r-h wooed the goddess Nikal,[5] but, even so, it would seem to lead up to a nuptial ceremony having as its precedent the sacred marriage of the divine prototypes. Therefore, it was recited at "the hour when at the sinking of the sun, the moon is to be seen," the new moon being propitious at childbirth. Similarly, in the parallel Danel text, the childless king (Danel) is represented as beseeching El to give him a son, and after fasting and lamentation he is said to repair to the nuptial couch to beget the offspring, as in a royal connubium.[6]

[1]Hooke, *Origins of Early Semitic Ritual* (Oxford, 1935), p. 32. W. C. Graham-May, *Culture and Conscience* (Chicago, 1936), p. 122ff. F. F. Hvidberg, *Grand og. Latter i det Garnle Testamente* (Kavanharn, 1938), p. 37ff. Gaster, *Folk-Lore*, 1933, p. 379ff.

[2]*Syria*, XII, 1931, p. 193ff. *Eranos-Jahrbuck*, 1939, p. 21ff.

[3]Albright, *Journal of the Palestine Oriental Society*, XIV, 1934, pp. 135n., 186. Dussaud, *Revue de l'histoire, des religions*, CVIII, 1933, p. 10f.

[4]Virolleaud, *Syria*, XVII, 1936, p. 209ff. Ginsberg, *Orientalia*, VIII, 1939, p. 317ff.

[5]*Journal of the Royal Asiatic Society*, Jan., 1938, p. 37ff.

[6]Virolleaud, *Bibliothèque archéologique et historique*, 1936, XXI, p. 126ff. cf. Is. vii, 14.

Thus, notwithstanding the confusion of the theme in the present condition of the texts, there can be little doubt that they contain a Syrian version of the Tammuz-Marduk cultus. The death of the hero, Aleyan-Baal, the lord of rain and verdure, and his descent into the underworld is the re-enactment of the seasonal drama at the Annual Festival symbolizing, as in the Tammuz liturgies, the decline in the processes of vegetation and their revival, personified in the victory of the year-god and the renewal of his earthly embodiment the king, culminating in a sacred marriage, as the union of heaven and earth, to promote the fertility of man, beast and the crops, and the proper functioning of the natural universe. By driving away or destroying the malign forces of decay, death, hunger and barrenness, and establishing right relations with divine beneficence, the streams of life were reinforced at their source through a ritual drama in which the king and queen, personifying the gods and goddesses responsible for providential bounty, played their respective roles as the dynamic centre of the community.

In Greece, Zeus seems to have been originally the sky-god worshipped on the top of mountains,[1] and since he was the giver of rain,[2] the control of nature was not entirely outside his sphere of operations. Nevertheless, when the Indo-European warrior culture was established on the plain of Thessaly about 2000 B.C., the Olympian theology was essentially anthropomorphic and reflected the behaviour of fighting chiefs rather than the ways of Providence. In the Homeric literature the agency of the gods in everything is recognized but no such thing as providential purpose is to be discerned either with regard to nature or history. Though immortal and possessed of unlimited power, the Homeric gods were subject to all the faults and frailties of human beings. They were capricious so that in the battle between the Achaeans and the Trojans, Zeus changed sides twice in one day.[3] They discussed their plans like warrior chieftains, they thwarted and conquered one another, they ate, drank, danced, married and gave in marriage—in short, they were simply glorified and none too edifying mortals.

Yet in Homer there is nothing higher than Zeus, the Father of gods and men, and he is subject to none. It was he who assigned the "portion" (Μοῖρα), and although "Moira" cannot be regarded as synonymous with "Fate," it seems to coincide with the will of the

[1] A. B. Cook, *Zeus* (Camb., 1914), Vol. I, p. 1ff.
[2] *Iliad*, xii, 25ff., 286, cf. v. 91, xi. 27ff., 493.
[3] *Iliad.*, viii.

gods, and more particularly with that of Zeus. At all events he was represented as administering the fate of men, and was the symbol of some power apportioning human destiny.[1] As the source of all things both good and evil prayer was addressed to him as the wielder of justice by his righteous and inscrutable will, a theme expressed by Theokosmos of Megara in his representation of the Fates with the Hours as subordinate adjuncts to the form of Zeus.[2] Pinder in the *Pythian Ode* declared that "God bringeth every end to pass according to his desires,[3] and Aeschylus, while never abandoning the polytheistic tradition, virtually made Zeus the embodiment of Deity as "king of kings most blessed, most perfect powers."[4] But in the fifth century B.C. thought in Greece was moving away from the cruder aspects of polytheism towards a pantheistic immanentism in which Providence, under the title of Zeus, became a supreme cosmic force permeating all things and beyond good and evil.[5]

Hellenic polytheism was a blend of northern elements derived from the Indo-European warrior folk with their Asiatic and Macedonian contacts engrafted upon the religious ideas and practices of a pre-Hellenic Mediterranean culture, influenced in no small measure by Minoan Crete. Despite the havoc wrought among the Hellenic settlers in the Aegean area by the northern invasion, the earlier culture was by no means destroyed. Thus, the beliefs and customs of the colonists from the Cyclades and Crete persisted throughout the Peloponnese, especially in Argolis at Tiryns, Mycenae and Asine; in Corinth, Boeotia and Attica. The trade with Crete that had been temporarily interrupted was resumed about 1600 B.C. when warrior princes were established at such centres as Mycenae, Tiryns and Orchomenos, so that a new composite culture arose on the mainland which justified the title Minoan-Mycenaean.

It cannot be assumed, however, that everything that is pre-Hellenic in Greece belongs to this Minoan-Mycenaean civilization since a Neolithic peasant culture had long been established when Aegean influences began to be felt on the southern coast in the second millennium B.C., and to mingle with those of the Nordic

---

[1]*Iliad.*, xxi, 291; xxiv, 210; *Od.* vii, 197, where μοῖρα is replaced by αἶσα which becomes the symbol of the mysterious unaccountable element in human experience.

[2]*Paus.*, i., 40, 4.

[3]*Pyth.* 2, 49ff.; 9, 44ff.

[4]*Suppliants.* 524f., 574; *Agam.*, i 60, cf. Euripides. *H.F.*, 1263.

[5]Aeschylus, *Frag.*, 70. Xenophon. *Frag.*, 23-46. Heraclitus. *Frag.*, 55, cf. Chap. v, pp. 97ff.

invaders of Thessaly. Nevertheless, Crete being the natural meeting place of the various cultural streams of the Eastern Mediterranean, Anatolian, Egyptian and Cycladic, a distinctive civilization developed on the island, to which Sir Arthur Evans gave the name of Minoan, after Minos the traditional king who ruled the waves. This culture had profound effects on the adjacent mainland. Within it the worship of the Mother Goddess of fertility and life appeared, often represented as grasping a snake which coiled about her arms, and clad with a tight bodice tapering to her slender waist and with a flounced skirt. Sometimes she was shown as flanked with lions and holding beasts or birds, or as a huntress pursuing the stag with a bow,[1] while at Mycenae her snake head-dress was surrounded by the double-axe with rampant lions standing at her side.[2]

On a late Minoan seal found at Knossos[3] the same type of figure with flounced skirt and holding a sceptre or lance is depicted standing on the top of a mountain with two guardian lions below on either side of the peak. To the left is a shrine with horns of consecration and sacred pillars as the abode and embodiment of her life-giving power, closely associated in iconography with the tree of life. Before her stands a male worshipper, but in some intaglio impressions a youthful male divinity occurs accompanied by lions, and sometimes represented as armed and descending from the sky.[4] Here doubtless the symbolism is that of the sacred marriage of heaven and earth, the Sky-god descending to fertilize the Earth Mother in order to make the soil produce its increase by renewing the creative processes at their source. But as Zeus reigns supreme in the Northern Indo-European tradition, so the Goddess dominates the Southern Aegean religion with the familiar figure of the divine king in the person of the Minoan ruler lurking in the background, exercising his customary role of the supernatural controller of the destinies of the community. Thus, the palace at Knossos was virtually a temple with emblems of the Double Axe carved on the walls and pillars and containing a shrine in the form of a throne guarded by griffins with a lustral basin opposite to it approached by a flight of steps. Through a door, also flanked by griffins, on the other side an inner sanctuary was secluded containing an altar.[5] In the western section of the palace were shrines with snake-entwined faience

[1]Evans, The Palace of Minos at Knossos (Lond. 1921), Vol. 1, p. 507ff
[2]Wace, Journal of Hellenic Studies, 1922, p. 264.
[3]Evans, op. cit., Vol. iv, p 596.
[4]Evans, Journal of Hellenic Studies, XXI, 1901, fig. 43, 48.
[5]Evans, Palace of Minos, Vol. I, pp. 101, 193n.

figures of the Goddess, a flat cross of polished marble, apparently originally fixed on the wall, and quantities of shells.[1]

The association of the Cretan Earth Mother,[2] with a youthful and relatively subordinate companion as her lover or son, though comparatively rare in its symbolic representation, connects her with the Asiatic death and resurrection cultus. And we are left in no doubt that she had a chthonian aspect like her counterparts elsewhere in the Ancient East; caring for the souls of the dead in the underworld as well as fostering the life of the seeds buried in the ground. Indeed, Evans maintains that the scene depicted on the "Ring of Nestor" indicates a belief in a blissful hereafter under her beneficent rule.[3] This would well accord with the later developments of the Mysteries which all centred on the Mother Goddess and her companion as the author and giver of a blessed resurrection through a process of initiation, or sacred marriage, which virtually made the neophytes "Kouretes," i.e. the prince-consorts of the Goddess (Rhea), and protectors of the holy child (Zeus) reborn each year, on whose rebirth the fertility of Nature and man depended.[4]

Although the Minoan-Mycenaean monumental evidence reveals nothing comparable to the story of Rhea and the orgiastic dances of the Kouretes, yet it was from the Great Mother of Crete and the Aegean rather than from the Indo-European cultus that the Hellenic mysteries derived their inspiration. Also it was from her that the Greek goddesses Athena, Aphrodite, and possibly Artemis, though genealogically linked to the Olympian pantheon, seem to have taken their origin. In pre-Hellenic Crete the Great Mother had her local manifestations in Rhea, Britomartis, Dictunna and Aphaia, but whatever her designation at particular local centres, she was always ultimately the source of life and fertility. To these life-giving functions were added other offices and characteristics when she was adopted by the Hellenic immigrants and incorporated into their pantheon. Thus, Athena acquired warlike attributes and became the patroness of the arts and of the city to which she lent her name. Aphrodite was closely allied to her Cypriote and Semitic

[1]IV., p. 110f.
[2]op. cit., p. 514ff. For the life-giving significance of shells, see J. W. Jackson, Shells as Evidence of the Migrations of Early Culture (Manchester, 1917), p. 138ff., G. Elliot Smith, Evolution of the Dragon (Manchester, 1919), p. 150ff.
[3]Journal of Hellenic Studies, XCV., 1925, pp. 1-75. Palace of Minos, Vol. III, p. 145.
[4]J. E. Harrison, Prolegomena to the Study of Greek Religion (Camb., 1903), p. 498ff. Cook, Zeus, Vol. I, p. 650.

counterparts, and incorporated many elements from Anatolia and Asia Minor, just as Artemis owed much to her association with Apollo and Delphi.

Demeter, the Earth-goddess of the corn, from her name appears to have been of northern descent, though her myth and ritual unquestionably were pre-Hellenic in origin. As the personification of the fertile soil she was the mother of Kore, the Corn-Maiden, who later was confused with the chthonian Persephone, queen of Hades, the wife of Pluto. If, as Nilsson has suggested, this agrarian ritual celebrated the bringing up of the threshed corn from the subterranean silos where it had been stored to ripen during the winter and early spring, it would readily lend itself to an interpretation in terms of the restoration of the Corn-Maiden to the Corn-Mother.[1] Thus, in February and March when the early flowers were in bloom, the Anthesterion, or annual commemoration of the dead, was held in Athens, coinciding with the Lesser Mysteries of Demeter and Kore at Agrai, a suburb of Athens where there was a shrine of the Earth-goddess. Attendance at these rites at Agrai became a preliminary to initiation at the Greater Mysteries at Eleusis in the autumn, and although no details are known of what took place apart from acts of purification, it is not improbable that the festival commemorated the return of Kore.

Therefore, it would seem that behind the complex Eleusinian ritual and its legend there lay an ancient vegetation rite performed in the open air to promote the growth of the crops and the fertility of the fields. This became fused with a chthonian cultus and Pluto, the lord of the dead, was confused with Plouton, a god of beneficence, the giver of the riches of the soil. Thus Kore, the Corn-Maiden, was transformed into Persephone, the queen of Hades, and made responsible for sending up the new crops from below ground by her annual return from the nether regions. This gave the Mysteries a deeper significance in terms of the death and resurrection drama, as in their Egyptian and Mesopotamian counterparts. The germinating ear of corn then became the symbol of life renewed and the celebration in the month of Boedromion at the autumn sowing, (approximately September) the assurance of a joyful hereafter in the delectable meadows of Persephone secured by means of an elaborate process of initiation at Eleusis, the cult-centre.

This interpretation of the Eleusinia is certainly as old as the seventh century B.C. when the so-called Homeric Hymn records the

[1]*Greek Popular Religion* (New York, 1941), p. 51f.

foundation of the rites.[1] In this composite legend Persephone (i.e. Kore) is said to have been carried away by Pluto to his subterranean realm to the despair of her mother Demeter, who, like Isis and Ishtar, wandered far and wide in search of her lost one. At length she came to Eleusis in the guise of an old woman and there encountered the daughters of the king, Keleos. Engaging herself as nurse to their infant brother, she endeavoured to make him immortal by anointing him with ambrosia and bathing him in fire by night. Disturbed in these operations, she revealed her identity and called upon the people of Eleusis to build a temple at the well where she had been hospitably received by the royal maidens, in which the ceremonial of her worship, to be made known to the princes, Triptolemus, Diocles, Eumolpus and Keleos, should be performed. In what this consisted can only be conjectured as the sacred drama was only disclosed to initiates, and to exhibit it in public was the height of profanity.

Such information as is available comes from relatively late sources but the cult legend gives some indication of the esoteric sacred actions witnessed by the neophytes at the solemn moments in the *telesterion* when, on the twenty-second day of Boedromion, they underwent a profound emotional experience as they sat on stools covered with sheep-skins in darkness and silence and beheld sights which could never be revealed. According to the post-Christian writer Hippolytus, these included an ear of corn reaped in silence in a blaze of light before the wondering eyes of the initiates and the birth of a divine child (Brimos) as the fruit of a sacred marriage between Demeter and Zeus. This passage however, has little evidential value since the second century writer depended upon Gnostic sources for his information, and apparently he had confused the Phrygian mysteries of Attis with those of Demeter.[2] Nevertheless, if behind the rites of Eleusis lay a vegetation ritual, a corn-token may have been one of the sacred objects shown, and the symbolism was in keeping with a harvest festival as a sign of rebirth, alike in nature and in the initiate. This is confirmed by a passage in Proclus, emended by Lobeck, in which the worshippers are alleged to have gazed up to the sky and cried aloud, "Rain (O Sky), conceive (O Earth). Be fruitful."[3] This formula, as Farnell has pointed out, "savours of a very primitive liturgy that closely resembles the famous Dodenaean

[1] Allen, Halliday, Sikes, *The Homeric Hymn* (Oxford, 1936).
[2] *Refutatio omnium haeresium*, V, 8. Farnell, *Cult of the Greek States* (Oxford, 1907), Vol. III, pp. 177, 183.
[3] Proclus ad Plato, *Timaeus*, p. 293 (Lobeck).

invocation to Zeus the Sky-god and Mother-earth; and it belongs to that part of the Eleusinian ritual *quod ad frumentum attinct.*[1]

Here again, then, there are grounds for thinking that the same theme dominant in the seasonal drama in the Ancient East recurred at Eleusis, and, in combination with the more orgiastic Thraco-Phrygian Dionysiac,[2] the birth of a divine child (known variously as Zagreus, Dionysos, Demophoon or Iacchos) appears to represent the fruit of the sacred marriage of the Sky-god (Zeus) and the Earth-goddess (Demeter) enacted by the hierophant in the capacity of the heavenly Creator, and the chief priestess impersonating Demeter. The royal character of the ritual is indicated by the representation of the torch-bearers in the official robes of the high priests, resembling the vestments of a deacon in the Eastern Orthodox Church, on a vase of the fifth century B.C. in the Museum at Eleusis. The hair is wreathed with myrtle and tied at the forehead with a broad fillet, the *tout ensemble* giving the appearance of a king. Moreover, the hierophant, the torch-bearer, the herald and the other principal officiants were members of the ancient Eleusinian families of the Eumolpidai and the Kerykes, to whom application had to be made for initiation. Therefore, while the Mysteries were open to all who could speak or understand Greek, and had not been polluted by blood-guilt or similar taboos, the rites were the hereditary possession of a priestly caste who may have been of royal descent.

Among other objects found during the excavations of the sacred precinct are reliefs depicting the mission of Triptolemos, one of the princes of Eleusis, who, having been instructed by the goddess to cultivate wheat on the Rarian plain, travelled in a chariot far and wide like Osiris to disseminate the knowledge of agriculture.[3] Thus, he is shown as a youth holding a sceptre in his raised left hand and seated on a magnificent carved throne drawn by winged dragons. In his right hand he holds the ears of corn, and he looks intently at Demeter in an attitude suggestive of listening to her instructions. Another plaque, dedicated to the gods of Eleusis by the priest Lakrateides in the first century B.C., represents him again seated on a throne transformed into a car, and holding out his left hand to take the ears of corn from Demeter, who sits in front of him with Persephone (Kore) behind holding torches. Close to her is

[1] op. cit., Vol. III, p. 184.

[2] Euripides *Bacchae*, 20ff. Farnell, op. cit., Vol. V, p. 86ff. Rhode, *Psyche*, p. 250ff.

[3] According to a later legend he was the son of Keleos who was brought up by Demeter and so intimately related to her in the role of Demophoon. cf. Allen, Sykes, Halliday, op. cit., p. 157.

Pluto with the royal sceptre, as king of the underworld, and to the right an unnamed god on a throne and a goddess with a sceptre. At the back is the upright figure of a young man carrying a torch, probably Eubonleus, one of the youthful Eleusinian king-gods, to whom the relief is dedicated. The royal character of the cultus, therefore, is clearly indicated in the iconography.

With the spread to Greece of the orgiastic Thraco-Phrygian worship of Dionysos (Zagreus) in the sixth century B.C., Demeter in the Orphic literature was identified with Rhae as the mother of Zeus by whom she conceived Kore who in her turn bore Dionysos to Zeus. Behind this Hellenic complex mythology may lay a pre-Hellenic fusion of the Thraco-Phrygian cult of Dionysos and his mother with an orgiastic ritual celebrating the birth, death and resurrection of the vegetation king-god (Dionysos), the Cretan Rhea displacing the Thraco-Phrygian earth-goddess Semele. Be this as it may, the union of heaven and earth, symbolized by the sacred marriage of the sky-god and the Earth-mother, is deeply laid in the *teletae* which became associated with the names of Dionysos and Orpheus, and eventually developed into the comprehensive movement known as Orphism.[1] As Mr. Guthrie says, the tales of Dionysos son of Zeus, and his sufferings must have been "the central point of Orphic story for the worshipper," though Orpheus was regarded as a saint and a hero rather than a god, and he was not a Bacchic figure.[2] Actually the only god mentioned in the early literature in relation to the rites of Orpheus is Persephone whose mysteries at Athens seem to have been confused with the *teletae*, possibly because eventually most sacred rites of this nature were associated with the magical musician.[3]

Once the connexion between Orpheus and Dionysos was established, the story of the dismemberment of Dionysos under the title of Zagreus and his revival became the central theme interpreted in terms of a doctrine of resurrection and rebirth, which, under Apollan influence, became allegorized.[4] Doubtless the

[1]For the latest discussion of the Orphic problem, cf. I. M. Linforth, *The Arts of Orpheus* (Berkeley, Cal., 1941). Nilsson, *Harvard Theological Review*, XXVIII, 1935, p. 185ff.

[2]*Orpheus and Greek Religion* (Lond., 1935), pp. 107, 41.

[3]Diodorus, V., 64.4. *Test.* 42. cf. Plato, *Phaedrus*, 265B. If there were no such thing as an Orphic Church with a systematized theology, at least an extensive literature collected round Orpheus as a legendary musician and prophet of Thrace, the hero of the Orphic way of life.

[4]Diodorus, iii., 62, 8ff., *Frag.* 301. Olympiodorus, *In Plat. Phaedon* (βρκή), pp. 111, 114.

myth and ritual had been transformed into an eschatology at any early period since the story of Dionysos and the Titans is very deeply laid in Hellenic mythology and closely associated with the movements comprehended in the term "Orphism." In the absence of any operative idea of a future life in the State religion and the Homeric tradition, the Dionysian-Orphic "enthusiasm" bridged the gulf between mortals and immortals, first by crude ecstatic frenzy and later by a system of purifications designed to secure by a protracted process of reincarnation the purging of the soul from its Titanic defilements and ultimate release from the hampering body in which it was incarcerated.[1]

In this form the Orphic doctrine had certain resemblances to Eastern categories of thought and doubtless paved the way for the welter of oriental mystery cults in the Graeco-Roman world that followed the conquests of Alexander. Among these the worship of the Anatolian Mother-goddess with Bacchic rites, reminiscent of the Thracian orgies, reached Rome (perhaps from Etruria) by way of Lydia and the Troad after the end of the second Punic War.[2] So great, however, were the scandals of the ritual that it was suppressed in 185 B.C. Hardly less orgiastic was the cult of the Magna Mater, Cybele and her lover Attis, at Pessinus. But when it was given a permanent home in the precincts of Victoria, and later in its own temple on the Palatine, it was Romanized and sobered. Nevertheless, no Roman citizen was permitted to become a mutilated priest (*gallus*) of the Magna Mater, or to hold any office in her service, or to take part in the procession held in her honour in the capital.[3] Moreover, it was not until the reign of Claudius, or possibly later, in the second century A.D. that the Attis cult was officially sanctioned, and the annual commemoration of the death and resurrection of the youthful lover of the Mother of the Gods recognized as a legitimate element in the religion of Rome.

In this resurrection drama Cybele preserved the traits of the many local Earth-goddesses she had assimilated, and played the role of her counterparts in Egypt, Mesopotamia, Asia Minor, Crete, and the Aegean, as a parallel cult-figure to Isis, Ishtar, Aphrodite and Demeter. Similarly, her companion Attis as the Phrygian Osiris, Tammuz or Adonis, was the vegetation hero dying in the

---

[1]Julian, *Adv. Christian*, i, pp. 167, 7, Origen. *Contra Cel.*, iv, 17, Clement *Protrept* ii, 18, 2, Pindar, *Frag.* i. 35, Bergk. 127, Bowra. Plato *Laws*, 70C. *Phaedo*, 70C.

[2]Euripides, *Bacchae*, 78ff, Livy, xxxix, 8–19.

[3]Dionysius, *Hal*, II, 19, 5. Lucretius, II, 600–43. Ovid *Fasti*, IV, 181–6.

autumn and rising again to new vigour in the spring, however much more, as a collective assurance of a personal immortality, initiation into the mysteries may have meant in the Graeco-Roman cultus. Thus, at some point in the ritual it would seem that initiates underwent a ceremonial regeneration which constituted a new birth enduring beyond the grave, symbolized by going down into the bridal chamber (παστός: presumably the cave-sanctuary) of the Goddess and emerging reborn to a new and endless life.[1]

A more drastic regeneration was effected by the baptism of blood, or Taurobolium, in the sanctuary of the Magna Mater on the Vatican hill. The high-priest of the Great Mother, with a golden crown on his head and wreathed with fillets like a victorious king, descended into a pit to stand below a grating over which a bull, adorned with garlands of flowers and bedecked with gold, was stabbed to death with a consecrated spear. Drenched in the life-giving blood, the priest emerged purged and purified either in his own person, or, as in the earlier form of the rite as practised at the beginning of the Christian era, having undergone the experience as a regenerative act performed on behalf of the community.[2] Thus, the taurobolium appears to represent a later development of a renewal ritual, comparable to the Sed-festival in Egypt or the Akitu in Babylon, in which doubtless originally the king was regenerated. His place was taken by the initiate who went down into the pit (i.e. the grave) with Attis and came forth reborn for a stated period, such as twenty years, or as one inscription affirms, *renatus in aeternum*.[3] This is confirmed by the regalia of the high-priest of the Magna Mater, and the purpose of the rite being that of the welfare of the Empire, the Emperor and the nation, before the taurobolium was transformed into the baptism of the individual and opened to all and sundry, regardless of status, rank or sex.

Notwithstanding the spiritual significance attached to the later forms of the crude ceremony, it was clearly a survival of a very primitive method of renewing life at its ultimate source, interpreted in terms of the union of heaven and earth enacted in a death and resurrection royal drama. Introduced into the West from Asia Minor at the beginning of the Christian era, it found its natural home in the cultus of the Great Mother with which it may have been associated in its cradleland.[4] Behind the Phrygian Cybele and the

[1]Clement of Alex. *Protrept*, II, 13.
[2]Dill, *Roman Society from Nero to Marcus Aurelius* (London, 1904), p. 547.
[3]*Corpus inscriptionum Latinarum*, VI, 510, VIII, 82-3.
[4]cf. Hepding, *Attis Sein Mythen und sein Kult* (Giessen, 1903), pp. 168ff, 201.

D

Cretan Rhea lie the universal figures of the Earth-goddess of fertility and her divine son or lover, in close association with the sacred tree and the deified king. The identification of Cybele with her Semitic counterpart Ishtar, or Astarte, must have existed in Asia Minor from very early times, and all over the Ancient East the marriage of the divine powers of fertility, personified as the Sky-father and the Earth-mother, was enacted in the seasonal drama to stimulate the reproductive forces of nature, while the corresponding death and resurrection of the priest-king represented the annual decay and revival of vegetation.

Victory cannot be won without suffering and so the central figure underwent a real or simulated death, as in the case of Attis who in the Pessinian tradition poured out his life's blood as well as his virility when he emasculated himself under a pine-tree.[1] This was perpetuated by his votaries who sacrificed their organs of generation to ensure the continued fruitfulness of the Earth-mother, and thereby the renewal of the crops; a privilege originally confined perhaps to the priest-king. Thus, both at Pessinus and Rome the high-priest of Cybele bore the name of Attis,[2] and doubtless played the role of his namesake at the Annual Festival[3] like the Babylonian king at the *Akitu*. In later times, for emasculation the cutting of his arm on the *Dies Sanguinis* (24th March), when the death of Attis was commemorated in his mysteries, was accepted as a substitution for the more drastic operation.[4] Two days earlier (22nd March) a pine tree, possibly in origin representing the divine hero himself,[5] was brought in solemn procession to the Palatine temple where it was accorded divine honours. To it an image of Attis was tied, the trunk was bandaged like a mummy and adorned with wreaths of violets, for violets were said to have sprung from his blood.[6]

Thus, the sacred tree would appear to have been the symbol of the year-god (either incarnate in the priest who bore his name, or in effigy) who was slain each spring and rose again as the new life like Osiris whose pillar, the *Ded*, called the "backbone," also originally seems to have been a tree. Similarly, Dionysos, who died a violent death and was revived every year, had a stake as his image,

[1]Arnobius, *Adversus Nationes*, V, 5ff.
[2]Hepding, op. cit., p. 79.
[3]Strabo, xii, 5, 3, p. 567.
[4]Tertullian, *Apol. adv. Gentes*, 25.
[5]Cumont, *Les Religions orientales dans le Paganisme romain* (Paris, 1909), p. 89.
G. Wissowa, *Religion und Kultus der Römer* (Munich, 1912), p. 322.
[6]Julian, *orat*, V, 168C, p. 215.

while in iconography the symbolic revivification of the god is associated with the figure of the king and of the sacred tree, brought into conjunction in cult-scenes.[1] In a Syrian cylinder these figures are shown doing homage to a stylized tree, or palm, which is topped by a head wearing the horned spiked crown of the gods as the emblem of divinity and heaven.[2] Thus, the tree, the god and the king are all brought into relation with the Sky-god as the ultimate source of all life whose providential bounty is mediated through his earthly embodiments immanent in the vegetation deity as the year-god, in the king as his incarnation, and in the sacred tree as the symbol of the life-giving functions of the king whose sacred marriage with the queen consummates the bond between heaven and earth upon which depends the maintenance of the natural order.

[1]Hooke, *The Labyrinth* (1935), p. 214ff, Frankfort, *Cylinder Seals* (London, 1939), p. 205f.
[2]Frankfort, op. cit., pl. XLIV.

CHAPTER III

ORIENTAL PANTHEISM

In India the conception of Deity started from very much the same presuppositions as those which found expression in the divine kingship in the Ancient East but the subsequent course of religious development took a different direction. As in Greece, before the arrival of the Indo-European immigrants from the plateau of Central Asia between 2000 and 1500 B.C., with its highly developed pantheon of nature gods, in the third millennium a prehistoric culture was established in the Indus Valley in which the Mother-goddess and the sacred tree played a prominent part. These pre-Aryan people were of a mixed race with a predominant Mediterranean strain. Culturally they were allied to the Proto-Elamites and Sumerians, with whom they shared a common ancestry; and in the light of the latest excavations at Harapp, they appear to have adopted a "citadel-rule" administered by priest-kings as at Sumer and Akkad.[1] When they entered North-west India from Baluchistan they must have been in a relatively advanced state of civilization, comparable to that which obtained in the valleys of the Nile and the Euphrates and in the Aegean, with a well-planned and highly organized city life, protected by massive defences.[2]

It was from this non-Aryan substratum that the fertility element in Hinduism seems to have been derived since images of female deities and tree and phallic emblems occur in abundance on seals, clay tablets and other objects at Mohenjo-daro, which are absent in the records of the Vedic mythology. A figure of a three-faced god sitting on a stool cross-legged in *yogi* fashion with outstretched arms and the hands resting on the knees, would seem to be a prototype of the Hindu god Shiva, who, with his consort, variously described as Kali, Uma, Parvati, Bhavani or Durga, typified the sky and earth as the sources of reproduction.[3] The representation of a bull on seal-amulets is suggestive of the widespread veneration of cattle in association with the worship of the Mother-goddess, recurring in

[1]R. E. M. Wheeler *Ancient India*, No. 3, Jan. 1947, p. 58ff.
[2]Op. cit. and J. Marshall, *Mohenjo-daro and the Indus Civilization* (London, 1931), Vol. I, p. 15ff.
[3]Marshall, op. cit., Vil. I, p. 49ff.

Phoenicia as a heifer and in Egypt as a cow (Hathor). The sanctity of the cow in Hinduism doubtless is to be traced back to this stratum in Indian civilization as no mention of the cultus occurs in the Rig Veda, the earliest Indo-European epics compiled between 1500 and 1000 B.C. in honour of the nature deities. Indeed it was not until very much later, in the Atharva-Veda, that cattle were exempted from the altar, and then only as a concession to the earlier non-Aryan taboo.

Thus, the religion of India arose out of a dual tradition, the one centring in the Mother-goddess of Asia Minor and the associated vegetation cultus of the Ancient East; the other representing a highly developed nature worship of cosmic gods. In this later Vedic tradition the wide expanse of sky and ocean was personified by Varuna, the supreme ruler and sustainer of the universe and upholder of the natural order and the moral law. Pre-eminently a royal god, kings bore the title Lord of the Law as his earthly representatives and embodiments,[1] although the king was not one god but many, being associated with Indra, Rudra, Brahman, Savitri, Agni, and with the goddess Parasvati.[2] This is in line with the movement of thought in Vedic tradition towards a monistic unification of the universal order.

When in due course the institution of sacrifice replaced Varuna and the nature gods under Brahmanic influence (800–600 B.C.), Prajapati became the Lord of Production and the personification of the creative principle, at once Creator and creation. As the ruler of the macrocosm and microcosm he pervaded all things, and through the universal cosmic and moral order (rta) he fulfilled his operations as an immanent dynamic process permeating all things. By his primal sacrifice at the hands of the gods the phenomenal universe came into being as so many parts of his body. Having produced the waters, the sun, the stars and the earth, he created animals and man, and finally the gods. The unity was reconstituted by the repetition of this sacrifice by the king and the Brahmins. As "the sacrificer is the god Prajapati at his own sacrifice"[3] so the king and the priest, upon whom the duty of carrying on the ritual of creation devolved, offered the sacrifice. Moreover, since the offering was the god, the king and priest became Prajapati, renewing the creative processes and inaugurating the social organization.

[1] *Satapatha Brahmana*, IV, i, 4, 1ff.
[2] *Sat. Br.* v, 3, 5, 8.
[3] *Sat. Br.*, v, 1, 1, 2; iii, 2.2.4.

In the Rig-Veda the king was identified with the sun and the sky through his relationship with Mitra, Agni, Indra and Varuna.[1] This association with the god *par excellence* who gives life and birth made him the bestower of all good things to mortals and to gods, though in fact in Vedic theology all divine activities were shared by a number of deities, all of whom the king and the priests comprehended in their complex personalities. As the Sun-god he (the king)was the active force and fertilizing agent, as Mitra the Lord of justice; as Indra the controller of storms and the giver of victory; as Varuna he was the regulator of the moral order and upholder of the universe; and as Agni he was equated with the sacred altar-fire and all that this involved in the sacrificial maintenance of the world, incidentally making the priest the official sacrificer no less divine than the king. Inasmuch as it was the priests who upheld all things in heaven and on earth by their sacerdotal functions, and controlled the gods, they were themselves assigned the attributes and status of the deities with whom they were identified. And in bringing together many gods in a common sacrificial ritual the pantheistic leaven was actively at work, gradually producing first the idea of a general transcendental Father-god and then an immanental conception of the All-god. Thus, Agni became Varuna and Indra, and the Sun-god as "the bird in the sky" summed up in himself all the gods so "that which is but one they call variously."[2]

Creation in the Rig-Veda was interpreted in terms of the sacrifice of the Primal Man, Purusha, with his thousand heads, eyes and feet pervading the earth. When the gods prepared the sacrifice with Purusha as their victim, from his head the sky was produced, from his feet the earth, from his eyes the sun was born, the moon was engendered from his mind, from his mouth was the Brahman (priesthood). From his arms the nobles were formed, from his thighs the yeomen, from his feet the commoners. Indra and Agni also were born from his mouth and Yayu, the wind-god, from his breath, the air from his navel and the sky from his head.[3]

The altar, known as Agni, on which the sacred fire was kindled consisted of a quantity of bricks built up in seven layers in the form of a falcon, representing the body, wings and tail of the seven "persons" composing Agni who became Prajapati, Lord of genera-tion. In the midst a fire-pan was very carefully fashioned as a repro-

[1] *Rig-Veda*, i, 164, 46.
[2] R.V. I. 164, 46. X. 114–5; III. 38,7.
[3] R.V. X. 90.

duction of the creation of the universe, for "the sacrificer who makes the fire-pan thereby makes the world." And as it was also the "self" of Agni, "he who makes the fire-pan thereby makes Agni."[1] Moreover, since Agni was "yonder sun" supporting all things on earth, when he was born anew every morning the sacred flame kindled by the fire-sticks of the priests recreated the life that pervaded the universe and sustained it. Therefore, since Agni as the personification of fire (which in its turn was connected with the sun as the ultimate source of life and heat and regenerative power) became identified with the cosmic figure Prajapati, Lord of generation, the building of the fire-altar was a repetition of creation, and the fire deposited upon it derived its vitalizing essence from him (Prajapati).[2]

Now behind this exceedingly complex development of the conception of Deity, which appears to have emerged originally within much the same sequence of ritual and belief as that which obtained in the Ancient East,[3] there was a pantheistic strain. In the Rig-Veda the priests, as we have seen, assumed the offices and functions of a great variety of gods representing different aspects of the sun and heavens—Indra, Mitra, Varuna, Agni, etc. . . . One god, in fact, was the same as another and was the same as all the deities, so that in the Brahmanas it is declared, "Agni said, 'In me they shall sacrifice for all of you and thus I give you a share in me'." For this reason in sacrificing to Agni oblation was made to all the gods. Similarly, Soma said, "me they shall offer up to all of you, and thus I give you a share in me," Further, "since all the gods were abiding in Indra, they said that Indra is all the deities, that the gods have Indra for their chief."[4]

This merging of one divinity into another is the inevitable result of the cosmic principle expressed in the term *rta* and given expression in Varuna as the unifying element in nature and man and different aspects of the universal order. When the institution of sacrifice became predominant under Brahmanic influence, Prajapati was regarded as at once creator and creation. "May I be more (than one) may I be many (reproduced)."[5] He created the waters out of

[1] *Sat. Br.*, vi, 5, 1f, cf. i, 9.2.29.
[2] *Sat. Br.*, vi, 1.I.7.
[3] The Fire-Altar ritual is virtually the equivalent of the royal renewal rites (cf. Chap. II, p. 35ff), the priests as gods playing the same role as the king in the cosmic drama of regeneration and for the same purpose, viz., to ensure the prosperity of the community.
[4] *Sat. Br.*, i, 6.3.20–2.
[5] Op. cit., vi. 1.I.8.

speech and from the all-pervading waters he reproduced himself by means of a golden egg. Out of this came the neuter Brahman as the first-born of All, while the earth was generated from a combination of water, foam, clay, mud, sand and gravel, and its other constituent elements or contents. In the form of Agni he entered into union with the earth (i.e. the familiar marriage of the Sky-father and the Earth-mother) to produce an egg from which an embryo emerged, the wind, as the parent of the air and the sun, with the shell of the egg becoming the sky.[1]

So the process continued until the entire phenomenal order was established with Prajapati as the ruler of the macrocosm and microcosm pervading all things. Through *rta* he fulfilled his operations as an immanent dynamic process, and by his primal sacrifice at the hands of the gods the universe was represented as parts of his body, reconstituted by the continual repetition of this offering by the Brahmans, very much as the several parts of the universe were summed up in the victim. Thus, the head of the cosmic sacrificial horse was the dawn, its eye was the sun, its breath the wind, its back the sky, its belly the air and the earth, its limbs were the seasons, its feet the days and nights and its bones the stars.[2] By means of this symbolism the sacrificer in becoming the sacrifice was united with the universe in all its parts resolved into a unity and sustained by a cosmic offering in which the body of the Creator (Prajapati) was broken anew and restored for the conservation of the world.

Furthermore, in the Brahmana texts the universe was also equated with Brahman, a neuter term signifying spell, or the sacred utterance, comparable to the Melanesian conception of *mana*, operative in the spoken word. Therefore, the priest who exercised the supernatural force was Brahman (masculine), the one who prays, the wielder of spells, setting in motion cosmic activity even greater than the gods, generated by the sacrificial ritual.[3] From this it was but a step to the deification of Brahman as a personal god, called also Varuna, Rudra, Indra and Prajapati,[4] or however the Father-god might be designated. But since it was the cultus that vitalized all things, the correct knowledge of the texts (Brahmanas) and their prescribed actions as handed on by tradition was of supreme importance, so that the rites became the real deities obscuring the divine

---

[1] Op. cit.
[2] *Sat. Br.*, x, 6.4.1.
[3] *Rig-Veda*, x, 141.3.
[4] *Sat. Br.*, v, 4.4.9ff.

personalities in the background. The efficacy lay in the things done by the priests with absolute precision, and the gods were merely names for certain powers and principles liberated and made efficacious by the ritual duly performed. Therefore, they ceased to play a vital part in the religious life, and with the rise of a new mysticism, philosophic conceptions readily took the place of deities who had already passed into oblivion behind the veil of a ritualistic Brahmanism.

Thus, in the voluminous Sanskrit literature known as the Upanishads, which in its earlier sections dates from 700 to 500 B.C., Brahman became the divine principle identified at once with the entire universe and the transcendent self, or *Atman*, of man. The old gods were retained as aspects and attributes of the Absolute and Eternal in the same way as man was regarded as a form of the One Reality, or Universal Being, described philosophically as "That is that" rather than "He who is" of Western ontological thought. Brahman had now ceased to be either the Hindu equivalent of *mana* or a personal deity. In line with Varuna and Rta, the power originally applied to spell and prayer was transformed into a pantheistic principle which was brought into conjunction with the breath-soul, ego or self (*atman*) of the human species. In this way the Brahmanic dualism of a microcosm within and its co-ordinate macrocosm without was resolved into a monism. The self and the not-self were manifestations of the same Reality. "That thou art, I am Brahman"—the Upanishadic equation declaring the sole reality of Brahman as the absolute being of man.[1] To know the atman only is the goal of all true living and the bridge to immortality.[2]

Although the worship of the Vedic gods went on little changed among the masses, and the Brahmanic sacrificial system retained its prominence and significance in popular practice, for the more intelligent section of the community a definitely pantheistic tradition began to take shape centring in the unchanging, unknowable, actionless Absolute set over against the unreal phenomenal world in a perpetual state of flux. Thus, Prajapati was gradually displaced by Brahman as the essence of all that is "unmoved, yet moving swifter than the mind," "himself at rest transcending the fleetest flight of other beings, Who, like the air, supports all vital action. He moves, yet moves not; He is far, yet near; He is within this universe" as the

[1] *Chandogya-Upanishad*, VI, 8, 7f. *Brihadatanyaka*, i, 4.10.
[2] *Brih.*, II, 4, 5; II, 5, 3ff.

one impersonal Reality apart from which nothing really exists.[1] Consequently, the human spirit is the world-spirit and as such is unknowable and indefinable. All that can be said is that "there is One Being no second,"[2] and of "Him" or "It" everything is a part. As the sun reflected on mirrors is one but apparently many, so is the Brahman one and many. As the potter makes a pot with clay, so the Atman causes various births until emancipation from the law of karma ends the weary round of reincarnation and transmigration.

With the rise of the doctrine of metempsychosis karma became the inevitable working out of the action and reaction in everyday existence through a series of lives. As an actor plays many roles so the atman assumes the bodies caused by its deeds, bringing all things to their appointed ends.[3] Thus, as the atman-belief became more and more personified it took over the guise of a kind of Providence guiding the self to its goal of complete emancipation. But Upanishadic thought was too deeply rooted in pantheistic monism to admit of a providential interpretation in a genuinely theistic sense, the control of the universe being ascribed to an eternal impersonal principle absolutely One yet composed of a plurality of essences.

In the Sankhya system, which was established not later than the sixth century B.C., two ultimate realities were postulated. From all eternity an immaterial indestructible individual self, *Purusha*, was thought to have existed and to have entered into relation with an eternal primordial simple material matrix, *Prakriti*, to become conscious of its own essentially spiritual character by the realization of itself as an onlooker at the drama of existence. Its function was that of contemplating these manifestations as a passive spectator, and its highest quest was that of emancipation from all that is not self in order to become the immutable and supreme Self—the sovereign principle encompassing and permeating the entire universe. In such a system there was no room for Deity since all souls were equal as modifications of *prakriti* with which they could unite, and all were finite, in so far as they were capable of reciprocal actions. Similarly, the phenomenal world as an objective reality was ascribed to forces inherent in the primary substance underlying the universe, including human thought and desire. In process of time the idea of God was introduced into Hindu mysticism but Deity always remained essentially the whole of which nature and man are parts.

[1] *Isa Upanishad*, iff.
[2] *Chand. Upan.*, iii, 14ff.
[3] *S'vetasvatara-Upanishad*, vi, 11.

Starting from an animating principle permeating the natural order and manifest in man either as the breath-soul (*atman*) or as a homunculus (*purusha*) in the heart, as the cause of all life, change and action, a complex mysticism was developed in which all finite existences were held to proceed from and return to their ultimate source in the Absolute as the supreme unity. By meditation and the elimination of everything external and mundane the atman was thought to discover its real essential being—the individual self or soul—and become identified with Brahman. To equate this idealistic conception with the realistic requirements of empirical consciousness, finite beings had to be given some measure of individual existence, however much this might be confined to the phenomenal order, regarded as fundamentally illusory (*maya*). In the Vedanta in due course the notion of a personal God, or *isvara*, emerged distinct both from the Absolute and the world over which He ruled and closely related to the atman as "the inner guide" of man.[1] This "Lord of the universe" and "Governor of living beings" was "the bridge that holds asunder these worlds," and it only required the concept to be transferred from the atman within man to an *isvara*, or "lord," external to and independent of the inner self, to give it a theistic significance.

In the Upanishads thought began to move in this direction when the atman was contrasted with the universe and the soul.[2] But the non-dualistic Advaita doctrine, which reduced the phenomenal order to *maya*, reacted against Brahman being interpreted in terms of personal Deity, for if the universe was merely an illusion caused by the supreme God, only atman survived as Reality.[3] The one universal essence was said to be related to the external world as yarn to cloth, or milk to curds, being both creator and creation, actor and act. It was only in Sectarian Hinduism, in the Bhagavad-gita and in the Vedanta Sava, that the worship of a personal deity under the form of Vishnu "the Preserver" (or saviour), and Shiva "the Propitious" was established. Even so, neither god was regarded as a single personality of one universal Being. Since both were subject to reincarnation they stood within the cosmic process so that Vishnu was held to have been born not only in human form as Krishna, but as a tortoise, a fish, a boar, a man-lion and a dwarf. Originally a personification of the sun, he was equated with the sky and the atmosphere surpassing

[1]*Brih.*, iii, 7, 3–22, iv, 4, 22.
[2]*Kathaka Upanishad*, iii, 1, ii, 20. *Svetasvatara Upan.*, iv, 6, 7.
[3]*Svet.*, iv, 10, cf. i, 6.

the shining orb by his splendour.[1] But for the benefit of the gods he assumed a "monstrous form" and with three steps gained the possession of the worlds. "With one step he occupied the whole earth, with the second the eternal atmosphere, with the third the sky. He made that demon Bali a dweller in the underworld and gave the empire of the three worlds to Indra after removing his enemy."[2]

Shiva ᵣas the god of many names who it would seem was worshipped five thousand years ago in the Indus valley, since, as we have seen, his prototype was portrayed at Mohenjo-daro in a three-faced figure seated on a low throne with arms outstretched in the typical attitude of *yoga*. In this tripartite form he may have combined the nature and function of three gods in a single personality, and so prepared the way for his later pantheistic syncretisms. Thus, he was identified with the ancient Vedic god of the storm, Rudra, and with Agni, especially in his more distinctive aspects, while on his orgiastic fertility side he was Bhairava, a Bacchic figure and centre of a licentious cultus revealing traces of the Mother-goddess as exemplified at Mohenjo-daro.

The veneration of the female principle (*Sakti*) unquestionably was of great antiquity in India, and although it was not peculiar to Saivaism it was very prominent in the worship of Shiva. Hence the recurrence of the *linga* and *yoni* symbols at Saivite shrines, typifying the union of male and female. At a higher level *sakti* was interpreted as the eternal reproductive principle (*prakriti*) united with the eternal male principle (*purusha*) in the generation of the gods and the universe, and Shiva became pure spirit assuming a body "not of matter but of force" to render himself perceptible. As the absolute and efficient cause he determined everything without himself being determined by anything. Thus, the way was opened for an idealistic Saivaism in which he is the only substance. Objects are his ideas, and as he is identical with man and the phenomenal world, what is perceived by the ego (*atman*) is merely a reflection of ultimate reality (i.e. the transcendental Self). Consequently *linga* from being a phallic symbol stands for a Supreme Being as the cause of the evolution and involution of the universe like the motion of the wheels and hands of a watch that has been wound.[3]

Vishnu similarly assumed the functions and pantheistic attributes that formerly belonged to Brahman. But his association with

[1] *Vanaparva*, 486, J. Muir, *Sanskrit Texts* (London, 1873), IV, p. 136.
[2] Muir, op. cit., p. 130f.
[3] Cf. S. Shivapadasundaram, *The Saiva School of Hinduism* (London, 1934), p. 15.

Krishna and his other avatars, or "descents," brought him into intimate relation with the world and gave him a status not far removed from that of a personal god. Indeed, "every time that religion is in danger and that iniquity triumphs I issue forth," he declared in the Bhagavad-gita. From age to age he manifested himself for the defence of the good, the suppression of the wicked and the establishment of justice.[1] But these avatars for the regeneration and preservation of the world at times of crisis were nearer to the renewal of the divine kingship in ancient society than to the idea of incarnation underlying the Christian doctrine of the Word made flesh.

As Vishnu himself was an *isvara* occupying an intermediate position between the Absolute and the avatar in whom he projected a part of his divine essence, the fulness of the Godhead could not dwell bodily in Krishna or Rama, except in so far as in Advaita thought the One Reality permeates all things. Nevertheless, the two principal descents of Vishnu—Krishna the son of Vasudeva and Rama the son of Dasaratha—came to be given divine worship, and for the purposes of religion to be regarded as the earthly and visible form of God, as Deity is understood in the Bhakti sects.

At the beginning of the fifth century B.C., Krishna and Rama were both heroes around whom the two great Indian epics, the Mahabharata and the Ramayana, developed respectively, and by the opening of the second century B.C. they had been assigned the position of avatars. Eventually Krishna was raised to the status of a man-god, and Rama represented as an incarnation, or descent, of half of the essence of Vishnu. During the succeeding centuries as "the way of devotion" (*Bhakti-marga*) gained strength it incorporated the mystical philosophy of the Upanishads and Sankhya, and Krishna, the popular divinity, collected a cultus as the supreme Vishnu incarnate as an earthly prince, allegorized to embrace the earlier pantheistic philosophies.

Thus, in the Bhagavad-gita, "the Song of the Blessed One," the earliest sections of which probably date from 300 to 250 B.C., as the product of this eclectic syncretistic movement, is an eternal gospel having a message for every age, being virtually the Hindu story of "Everyman". In it are to be found some of the most sublime thoughts of the Upanishads united with the doctrines of Sankya and Yoga superimposed on those of the Vedanta, and unified in a common devotion to Krishna as a personal saviour and *isvara*. With

[1] *Bhagavad-gita*, iv, 7, 8.

considerable skill the various threads have been woven into a system to form a many-coloured woof shot across with a Bhakti warp. The pattern, however, is too composite to be harmonious. Standing out most conspicuously are the threads of Sankhya which do not blend happily with Vedantic monism; and the weakness of the avatara doctrine has always been that its pluralism is limitless. The new path of salvation sought by the universal self at war with sensual experience is represented as the surrender of the heart to a living personal saviour-god, Krishna, the human embodiment of Vishnu. The highest good is to abide for ever in a god-like existence in the divine presence, "free from attachment to earthly things and without hate to any being." Works, faith and knowledge, in fact, each and all are given their place in the Gita, together with the doctrine of Bhakti. But although the Supreme God is both Creator and Saviour, the conception of the universe is pluralistic and the theology syncretistic.

In the Mahabharata and the cultus of the five sons of Pandu, Krishna would appear to have been a divinity of the king-god type with solar affinities, who, under the influence of Vishnaism, was brought into relation with the Brahmanic pantheon and their avatars. His worship was allegorized until in the Bhagavad-gita he became the Absolute Being in human form, immutable and the sole Reality, giving peace and safety to those who enter into conscious union with him. The various ways in which "God-realization" was achieved were recognized and given their respective places in this scripture in the belief that the endeavour of the human spirit to reach the Supreme was like the zig-zag courses of rivers pursuing their several channels to the sea.

Under the form of Brahma, Vishnu and Shiva the concept of the Divine has been brought within the grasp of the finite mind as the supreme knower, the great lover and the perfect will,[1] as three aspects of one complex "personality," if such a term can be used in connexion with a fundamentally pantheistic concept. In the Bhakti system, however, the anthropomorphism of the principal avatars was so complete that it became virtually a polytheism under a Supreme God, very much as in the Vedic pantheon Agni, Vayu and Surya were grouped together as a triad. So the Absolute was manifested as creator (Brahma), preserver (Vishnu) and destroyer (Shiva), united symbolically by the letters A.U.M. in the sacred syllable OM. But the "persons" of the "trinity" were not co-equal and it was either

[1] Cf. S. Radhakrishnan, *The Hindu Way of Life* (London, 1912), p. 27.

Vishnu or Shiva who was the principal object of devotion in the sects that derived their names from one or the other divinity, while Brahman fell into the background as a Supreme Being without cultus, so that to-day only one temple, that of Puskara, is sacred to him.

For practical purposes it was Krishna who called forth the most popular response and next to him Rama. Both in theory and practice the religion of the Gita is a way of salvation by divine grace, just as in the later books of the Ramayana Rama is represented as voluntarily undergoing suffering and privation in order to give strength and grace to struggling humanity. But the real philosophy of India is the Vedanta in which the only reality is Brahman, the Absolute, and the world is maya, illusion. Sankara (c.800 A.D.), its most profound exponent, admitted *isvara* as a personal god, it is true, but only as a Demiurge who through maya produces the world in his own mind. Behind the world Brahman alone exists as the pantheistic All. In the eleventh century Ramanuja endeavoured to establish a monistic realism in which a place could be found for a Deity who is loving and personal. But while he maintained that love is the highest divine attribute, matter and individual souls though real are the body of God, so that finite selves only have an actual existence as integral parts of the supreme Atman, the soul of the world.

In all these systems the emphasis was placed on spiritual consciousness as the means by which the Mystery that lies at the heart of the universe might be known, rather than on an external transcendental personal Being as the ground of all things. Therefore, in the Sankhya scheme and its derivatives—the Jaina and Buddhism—Deity could be eliminated altogether without materially affecting the way of life and of salvation. For the followers of Vardhamana (c. 540 B.C.), the founder of the Jain movement (deriving its name from "Jina," "the victorious") the bliss of Nirvana was secured by right faith, right knowledge and right living according to a rule of rigorous asceticism and scrupulous care to avoid taking life in any form. The only objects worthy of veneration were perfected souls (Jiva) as a sort of collective "Deity." Similarly, the end and aim of the Buddhist Eightfold Path, as revealed by Gotama, (c. 560 B.C.) was enlightenment (*sambodha*) such as he experienced when, seated in the mystic posture at the foot of a pipal-tree at Buddh Gaya, where the Mahabodhi temple now stands, he discovered the Four Noble Truths leading to "peace, to insight, to higher wisdom, to Nibbana."

Having satisfied himself that neither the metaphysical mysticism of the Upanishads or the Sankhya nor the Jain method of self-discipline could afford a practical solution of the ultimate problem of existence in a world of suffering, the Buddha evolved his "Middle Way" of securing release from the principle of becoming. Starting from a characteristically Indian world-outlook, he reduced the human ego to an organic aggregate of five skandhas, or causally-conditioned elements of the life-impulse. So regarded, human and divine personality, Absolute and Atman, were equally excluded, and in a phenomenal order governed by a rigid law of mutability, karma was the latent power which produces life without reference to any other creative source. Like Rta, Varuna or Purusha, it was an immanent impersonal principle revealed in every phase of terrestrial existence and determining the course of reincarnation as part of the cosmic order. But the Hindu doctrine of *personal* karma was rejected and in its place the eradication of all selfish desires by the Eightfold Path was substituted as the way to the attainment of the passionless peace of Nirvana.[1]

It is significant, however, that his "noble silence" on the ultimate metaphysical problem led the Buddha to the adoption of a creed of negation. Even if Mrs. Rhys Davids is correct in her contention that in his original teaching, before it was perverted by monastic pessimism, it was only release from impermanence and the extirpation of the lower nature that was sought,[2] this involved escape from individual existence. The wheel revolves regardless of all personal considerations, as rigid in its operations as any other aspect of the fundamental law of mutability in the physical world, ending in a waning out which at best is "an existence that is beyond reason and conception."[3] The denial of Deity finds its natural conclusion in a doctrine of the unreality of the self (*non-atta*) and the cessation of conscious existence in a state of "not-being". In that ultimate condition "no candle gives light, no sun beams, no moon shines, no darkness is. And when the enlightened has attained to stillness, to insight, then he is free from form and formlessness, from pleasure and pain."[4] And to the all-important question whether this amounts to annihilation, Gotama was as inconclusive as he was about the existence of Deity.[5]

[1] J. E. Jennings, *The Vedantic Buddhism of the Buddha* (Oxford, 1947), p. xxiiif.
[2] *Manual of Buddhism* (London, 1933), p. 129ff.
[3] *Samyutta*, III, 109.
[4] *Udana*, I, 10.
[5] *Majjhima*, I, 139, 489.

In the light of the available evidence it is impossible to determine whether he had any clear conception of the implications of his attempt to solve the problem of emancipation from suffering, but his shrinking from all metaphysical and ultimate issues pre-disposed him to adopt an agnostic position in matters which for him did not appear to have any practical bearing on his main concern. He had found passionless peace himself at the time of his enlightenment (*bodhi*) without reference to the concept of Deity, or to the final state of consciousness, and so he failed to see that for the guidance of his followers anything need be or could be added to his own experience of beatitude. But, in fact, his own *Dhamma*, or universal law, did not suffice when the movement he initiated became a missionary religion.

Thus, when Buddhism divided into two systems, the Northern, or Mahayana, section developed a doctrine of the Buddha as the supreme Reality of the universe, beyond knowledge and eternal but capable of appearing as man (*nirmanakaya*), as a spiritual being (*sambhogakaya*), or in an abstract form as truth (*dharmakaya*). Having been a historic personality he was not a mythical hero, or avatar, of the Supreme God, but he was thought to have lived in the world in every age as the personification of wisdom, strength and compassion —as the Elder Brother and Saviour of mankind. Moreover, the Buddha-spirit was incarnate in all *bodhisattvas* who through a series of lives attained at length to quasi-divine status and became objects of worship.

These later developments in a measure were latent in early Buddhism inasmuch as the disciples were thought to receive spiritual aid as they gained a clearer inward vision (*jnana*) of the nature of existence and the way of escape from its misery by the practice of the *Dhamma* revealed by Gotama. Indeed the Buddha is alleged to have declared that the *Dhamma* and the *Vinaya*, the Truth and the Rule, should be their Teacher after he had left the world and entered Nibbana,[1] very much as Christ promised to his followers the gift of the Holy Spirit to be their guide and sustainer for all time. *Dhamma*, in fact, constituted a new order of unseen reality corresponding to Brahman in Hinduism, the "Sons of the Blessed One" (i.e. the disciples of Buddha) being "*Dhamma*-born, *Dhamma*-formed and *Dhamma*-heirs."[2] Moreover, *Dhamma* was independent of any particular Buddha manifestation, and it only

[1] *Dialogues*, ii, 171.
[2] *Digha-Nikaya*, iii, 84.

E

required the revealer of the way of self-salvation to be represented as the compassionate saviour of mankind to transform him into an embodiment of Providence, and *Dhamma* into his mystical body after his bodily presence had been withdrawn. So regarded, the Buddha became he who "brings the roots of the good to maturity that all beings may attain the unending happiness, undreamt of happiness, the happiness of omniscience, with me as driver, with me as guide, with me as torch-bearer, with me as guide to salvation, with me, who know the means, with me, who know the advantages . . . with me as guide to the farther strand," the goal can be reached.[1]

Nevertheless, in early Buddhism the Buddha was always represented as showing men how they could save themselves, and never was in any sense a redemptive saviour or vicarious mediatorial sacrifice. This, however, did not suffice in the Far East where human effort was felt to be insufficient without divine aid as a gift of grace. Thus, in Tibet, China and Japan, a benevolent deity, Amida, or Amitabha, possibly of Iranian origin and unknown in the oldest Buddhist literature, early in the Christian era was venerated as a Bodhisattva. His merits were such that he was able to save all who trusted in him solely for salvation and gained merit through the continual repetition of his sacred name. Under the influence of Honen in the twelfth century, and his successor Shinran, a great religious movement known as Jodo was initiated in Japan in which the principal religious exercise was this cult of the name Amida in order to attain to the Pure Land, or Paradise, where he reigned and gathered together his followers in glory. Although in practice Amidism was open to the charge of the formalism condemned in no uncertain terms in the Christian gospels (St. Matt. vi. 5), it provided, as Honen claimed, an easy and intelligible religion which brought comfort and assurance to simple souls for whom the negations of true Buddhism were as futile as were the metaphysical speculations of Hinduism for Gotama and his disciples.[2]

It is only a very specialized type of mind that can readily accept a conception of endless change which denies the reality of personality in man and God. While such a strain was not wholly absent in Chinese mentality, as is revealed in Taoism, the great majority of the population both in China and Japan have always been practical, optimistic and world-affirming, rather than passive and contemplative in their outlook. In ancient times a divine kingship in which the

---

[1]Cf. M. Winternitz, *Der Mahayana-Buddismus* (Tübingen, 1930), p. 35.
[2]*Honen, the Buddhist Saint*, p. 138, E.T. by Coates and Ishizuka.

Emperor as the son of Heaven was the earthly embodiment of Providence, formed the background of the theocratic State which later characterized both civilizations. In Japan this found expression in the worship of the Mikado as the son of the Sun-goddess who was herself the product of a crude and complex polytheistic system (*kami*) in which gods and goddesses intermingled freely. A similar pantheon of inferior deities and spirits constituted the matrix of Chinese religion out of which in due course emerged a quasi-personal Being, Shung-ti, who governed all creation and upheld the moral order, while in the ancient documents T'ien is also represented as "the man-in-the-sky" and "the vault of heaven" (sky). These theistic ideas, however, were modified by the introduction of two interacting self-existent principles, the *Yang* and the *Yin*, as the source of all creative activity, together with the conception of *Tao* as "the way of heaven," eventually regarded as the originator of all things. Amid all these conflicting notions of Deity, polytheistic, pantheistic and monotheistic, the only unifying element in Chinese religion was the State cult, centring in the veneration of the Emperor as the divine vice-regent who biannually was worshipped at the Altar of Heaven and the Altar of Earth respectively to secure the blessing of Providence (i.e. Shang-ti as the sovereign Ruler of the universe with his subordinate divine powers) on nature and the nation.

But neither in China nor Japan did the divine kingship meet the entire spiritual and material needs of the community. For practical purposes public worship was confined to the cult of the Emperor as the pontifex maximus who alone had the ear of heaven, and, therefore, when Buddhism, as interpreted in the Mahayana, reached the Far East it was able to supply what was lacking in the indigenous religions. The local lesser gods, ancestors and spirits, who were the only supernatural beings with whom the masses had any point of contact, were absorbed as bodhisattvas and so brought into relation with the universal Buddha-spirit. Sharing his gracious compassion for struggling humanity, they were represented as loving gods to whom man could turn for help and consolation in a manner unknown in the official State cult, as this was practised in Confucianism in China and in Shinto in Japan. Having denied themselves the privilege of entering Pari-Nibbana in order to devote themselves to the saving of mankind from the misery of continued existence in this world of woe, the Buddhist bodhisattvas offered a way of escape on the principle of justification by faith, carrying with it the hope of everlasting bliss in a Western Paradise, or Pure Land, leading at the last to Nibbana.

Nevertheless, underlying all these oriental quasi-theistic systems there has always been a fundamental pantheistic trend. The roots of Buddhism are deeply laid in Hinduism, and despite its later developments, Mahayana has never completely emancipated itself from the source from which it sprang. The final goal was and is deliverance from all striving and the attainment of a state of passionless peace—"the end of sorrow, unborn, unoriginated, uncreated, uncompounded"—beyond the temporary radiance of Paradise. Thus, for the Mahayanist Nibbana means much the same in the last analysis as it does for the Hinayanist. Virtually it is merely the Pali equivalent of the Sanskrit Nirvana, which is hardly distinguishable from Brahman as the ultimate goal of all existence, final emancipation, supreme bliss. What differentiates Mahayana from Hinayana is the conception of the bodhisattvas intent on the salvation of others, as against that of the Arhant primarily and solely concerned with his own release from the suffering of the realized self and the law of karma. But in neither Vehicle is a personal Deity an integral concept since all personalities, human and divine, are impermanent, changing, compound and dependent on various causes.

Similarly, in China, the notion of *Tao* is not very far removed from that of the universal cosmic law (*Dhamma*) in Buddhism and the idea of *Rta* and Brahman in Hinduism—"just being without a second." In the philosophy known as Taoism, attributed to the elusive Lao-tze, a quietist mysticism—"acting without action" in solitude and humility of spirit—arose out of an impersonal conception of the course of nature interpreted in terms of a universal supreme reason pervading all things. As such it did not follow any law higher than itself, and being creative without purpose and effort it never strove. As the unconditioned ways of Heaven it resembled a pantheistic principle revealed in an impersonal law to which man and nature conformed. "All existence in the universe sprang from Being (Tao) as the active principle; Being itself sprang from Non-being (Tao) as absolute." Ultimately all things return to the source of their origin, and while they pursue their course they can only function correctly through Tao in which subjective knowledge and the objective world are harmonized. Between the ruler (i.e. the Emperor) and Tao a connexion exists anacrocosmically in that by passing on and on through successive stages of his own consciousness back to the initial Unity, he can arrive at the Way which controls the multiform apparent universe.[1] This, however, is achieved not through a process of reincarnation and transmigration as in Hinduism and Buddhism, but by living in accordance with Tao, and since Tao works calmly without effort, the good life lies in mystical quietude.[2]

Confucius (581–478 B.C.), on the other hand, like Gotama, repudiated all metaphysical and mystical speculation, and interpreted the concept of Heaven as the Way in which all things are made and in which man ought to live. As a practical teacher and administrator his concern was right conduct in human relationships —e.g. filial piety and the principle of reciprocal propriety within the family, the state and the home. If he did not actually deny the existence of Deity, he limited the term to the ground of the moral order and the power that controlled human destiny and the course of history. He may have looked to Heaven in an impersonalized sense as the source of his own power,[3] but his attitude was essentially fatalistic.[4] Death and life, wealth and status were predetermined by a "providence" that does not speak or enter into conscious relations with the world.[5]

Within the movement that derived its name from this great Chinese sage, a philosophy has struggled to find expression in a cosmology that was pantheistic rather than theistic in its general trend. Thus, in the Neo-Confucianism that arose under the influence of Chu Hsi (1130–1200 A.D.) an ultimate eternal principle (Li) was sought in the universe determining the form of everything, causing it to be and interacting with Ch'i, the "plenum of the universe." By the ultimate action and inaction of Li as the sphere of Ch'i, the positive and negative Yang and Yin principles were produced. These held together the five elements in embryo in each of which a Yang and Yin quality was present and were all pervaded by Li. Out of the ceaseless revolution of the two forms came first the earth and then the world of existences, the succession of the seasons and the rotation of day and night. At the last all things will return to the original state of undifferentiated Ch'i indwelt by Li, and a new heaven and earth will be called into being.[6]

[1]A. Waley, The Way and its Power (London, 1934), pp. 74, 175.
[2]J. Legge, The Religions of China (London, 1882), p. 90.
[3]Analects, VII, 22.
[4]XI, 87.
[5]XVII, 19.
[6]F. J. Maclagany, Chinese Religious Ideas (London, 1926), p. 101ff.

While, as Dr. Bruce maintains,[1] there may be a theistic element
in the teaching of Chu Hsi, he substituted for a personal Ruler an
impersonal law, and by identifying Heaven with *Li* he made God
less than personal. The ultimate Power in the universe for him was
an abstraction and unknowable, identified with the creative process
but outside all directive control and human relationships. Such a
conception of the Divine inevitably leads to a pantheistic fatalism
ending in either a world-denying self-abnegation or an effortless
quietism.

To cease to struggle is to cease to live in any creative sense, and
the quest of perpetual calm and unruffled peace is the abrogation of
life. But if God and man are equally part and parcel of all that is,
subsisting side by side in time and space—the expressive symbols
of a hidden vital principle within the cosmic order—there can be
no independent personal existence. All things pass from their
origin to their decay, never continuing in one stay because the finite
is as groundless as it is devoid of individuality. A single paramount
principle pervades the universe, and the highest aspiration of the
mystic is to attain absorption into the Absolute so conceived, or, as
in Buddhism, to attain an unconditioned state. But inasmuch as for
pantheism God is the All, divine union implies loss of human
self-consciousness and independent existence since the Absolute is
equally manifested in nature, in mind and in spirit, as the reality
of everything that is. This is a heavy price to pay for the establishment of a unifying principle behind the variety of phenomena and
the elimination of the age-long problem how to ascribe personality
to God without limiting infinite Being. Moreover, as we have
seen, pantheism must be fatalistic in its attitude to a universe in
which neither contingency nor human initiative and freedom of
action are possible, and all endeavour is devoted to contraction out
of the ceaseless process of becoming. To make God all that is, is to
involve ultimate reality in the limitations, evil and errors of finite
existence, for the parts are contained within the whole. It would
seem, therefore, that this cannot be the final solution of the problem
of Deity.

[1]*Chu Hsi and His Masters* (London, 1923), pp. 316, 294.

CHAPTER IV

ANTHROPOMORPHISM

WHILE Pantheism constitutes a recurrent feature in the history of religious thought inasmuch as it meets the need for unity and completeness in the philosophic conception of the universe and satisfies the mystical experience of oneness with the Divine, in the West the tendency has been to adopt an anthropomorphic rather than a cosmic view, making "man the measure of all things." From time immemorial the human mind has transferred to the objects of its veneration the qualities it recognizes in itself, so that, as we have seen, among the most rudimentary representations of Deity has been the idea of a "magnified non-natural man" having his abode in the sky and sharing the attributes and limitations of earthly chiefs and medicine-men. Similarly, natural phenomena—the sun, sky, wind, the oceans, clouds and rivers—have been assigned human qualities and endowed with personality, while men of renown have been raised to divine rank after their death as deified heroes and ancestors. Conversely, gods have been supposed to have their earthly embodiments in kings and rulers, begotten by a deity, born of a woman, and in possession of divine powers.

Moreover, in the higher religions, the principle of analogy has been employed to give positive expression to the conception of Deity based on the observation of certain qualities belonging to finite persons, very much as in pantheism divine activity has been interpreted in terms of finite substance and its constituents. That some resemblance exists between the spiritual and material orders is a basic assumption of religion though the extent to which the divine nature can be inferred from its human counterpart, and the invisible things seen and understood by the things that are made, has been and still is a matter of controversy among philosophers and theologians. Both in Judaism and Christianity, the analogical principle was freely admitted[1] and subjected to careful inquiry by the scholastics in an attempt to estimate the significance of the anthropomorphic language used in Holy Writ in relation to the nature and attributes

---

[1]Wisdom, xiii, 5. Ps. xix, Rom., i, 20.

of God.[1] Having justified the ascription of perfect being to Deity, St. Thomas proceeded to argue that the perfections manifested by creatures exist in God supremely (*eminenter*) as their source and cause. But they can be expressed only by an analogy of proportionality because in Him alone are they present infinitely, in an absolutely perfect form, manner and content. What is partial and incomplete in man is perfect in God.

When our knowledge of Him is acquired by an inference from, or a modification of, human qualities, it is anthropomorphic in the sense that the attributes of man (goodness, power, wrath, wisdom) are attributed to God in an infinitely higher degree; yet even so this is not necessarily to conceive of Him as "a magnified non-natural man" since all limitations and imperfections are eliminated in respect of Deity. To rest the goodness, wisdom and power of God on the idea of goodness and wisdom and power as inherent in and valid for the universal order of being of which He is the ultimate ground, is doubtless philosophically more convincing than to apply the human analogy to the divine nature in the knowledge that the difference between the two natures is so great that real identity is excluded. Nevertheless, if man is in fact the crown of creation and reflects in any sense the divine image and likeness, some measure of anthropomorphism is implied.

In primitive society this is taken for granted and the spirit world becomes largely the projection of the human world, reproducing its hopes, fears, struggles and conquests, its triumphs and its failures. Nowhere is this more apparent than in the Olympian theology of Ancient Greece where the mountain gods of the invaders from the north were represented as behaving exactly like their earthly counterparts—the conquering chieftains, princes and royal buccaneers who fought, feasted and caroused, thwarted one another and misgoverned the land they subjected to their rule in the same manner as did Zeus and his companions on Olympus.[2]

Moreover, it was in the anthropomorphic form in which the gods were conceived and described with all the literary skill of Homer, that they were given permanent expression in statues and vase-paintings. But Homer was neither a theologian nor a philosopher, and he had little or no historical sense or interest. As a storyteller he is unrivalled, and it was in this capacity that he extracted from the current mythological material all the best tales he could

[1]Aquinas, *Summa Theol.*, I, Q, iii, xiii, a, 2, 3, 5, 10, 12.
[2]Gilbert Murray, *Five Stages of Greek Religion* (Oxford, 1925), p. 66ff.

find, and wove them into immortal poems concerning the Trojan War and the adventures of its heroes, human and divine. Therefore, when Xenophanes tried to prove that man created his gods in his own image by asserting that "Homer and Hesiod have ascribed to the gods all things that among men are a shame and a reproach—theft and adultery and deceiving one another"[1]—he, like many after him, failed to recognize the nature of the literature he criticized. The *Odyssey* and the *Iliad* are not theological treatises or historical records of past events. They are just excellent tales giving doubtless a more or less correct picture of the life and manners that prevailed in Greece at the transition from the Bronze Age to the Iron Age, but composed to provide entertainment for princes and nobles in Ionian banqueting halls.

Nevertheless, there is very profound truth in the assertion of Herodotus that "Homer and Hesiod created the generations of the gods for the Greeks; they gave the divinities their names, assigned to them their prerogatives and functions, and made their forms known."[2] And within the limits of their interest in and understanding of the situation, no doubt they believed in the anthropomorphisms they so vividly described. The gods they thought resembled man and, therefore, they were subject to the faults, failings and limitations of human beings, while at the same time were capable of exercising superhuman powers. They discussed their plans like warrior chieftains and crossed each other in a shameless manner. They were capricious like mortals so that Zeus changed sides twice in one day in the battle between the Achaeans and the Trojans.[3] Yet there is nothing higher than Zeus and he is represented as subject to none, apportioning to man his destiny (Μοῖρα).[4] But the Homeric gods never move in a realm of ends as part of a teleological process. Zeus has a will of his own but he has to take account of his wilful and refractory vassals in the council of the gods on Olympus, each having his own whims and local allegiances.

All these anthropomorphisms imposed on the Olympians of the Homeric tradition serious limitations in respect of divine omnipotence, omniscience and omnipresence, and eventually they led to their becoming so much like men that they failed to fulfil their divine functions altogether. From them those whose gaze was fixed

[1]*Frag.*, II, 15, 16 (Diels).
[2]Herod, II, 53.
[3]*Iliad*, VIII.
[4]*Iliad*, XXI, 291, XXIV, 210. *Od.*, VII, 197.

on the eternal world turned to the Mystery divinities for supra-mundane sustenance and guidance, while the epic poets identified the world and its processes with a pantheistic divine unity, and Euhemerus eventually reduced the gods to the heroes of a former age. Where the Homeric anthropomorphism failed to hold the spiritual allegiance of Greece was in its being essentially and primarily a literary and artistic creation. Transcendentally the gods had little or nothing to offer to mortals since they differed from man only in having greater power and knowledge, and this in degree rather than in kind. In other respects they were subject to all the ethical weaknesses to which flesh is heir and too much involved in their own political intrigues to be concerned with human affairs. At its best Homeric Olympianism was a mystical idealism of artistic imagination, a symbol of idealized qualities belonging to an age of chivalry which such thinkers as Socrates and Plato could retain and re-evaluate. But the Olympian anthropomorphism proved to be inadequate as a guide to the deeper understanding of the things of the spirit and the mind for the great majority who turned elsewhere for the satisfaction of these needs.

Yet the old gods retained a romantic significance as the chief actors in a heroic age of chivalry and adventure. Sometimes they were allegorized or made the symbols of virtue and justice, if they were not given a fanciful naturalistic interpretation in terms of physical phenomena, such as the contests between the elements, and so were dismissed by the Sophists as the creation of the human imagination. But even as such they were at least glorified and idealized men rather than snakes or bulls or monstrous centaurs and giants. The Homeric anthropomorphization had eliminated or modified the crude representations of the pre-Hellenic period and given a clear definition and a new significance to the literary and artistic types it produced. That is what Herodotus meant when he attributed to Homer and Hesiod the creation of the gods and the making known of their forms. The *Iliad* and the *Odyssey* made the impression of a consistent unity on the popular mind and gave a distinct shape to the Olympian religion which was rendered permanent and of exquisite beauty in stone and paint as well as in a literature that has become a classic and a text-book for all generations. The heroic anthropomorphic figures became a universal possession in Greece and transcended all the local and tribal divinities limited to particular places and traditions. And they have gained an immortal heritage which will redound to their glory in all lands.

Notwithstanding these triumphs, the Olympian theology failed at the crucial point. It was unable to secure and maintain the religious allegiance of either the individual or the nation. In this respect it fell far below the Mysteries which offered and gave their initiates a transcendental way of life. The Homeric gods were so completely anthropomorphized that they ceased to play any significant part in the phenomenal order, or in human society. Their morals like their powers being more human than divine, the attempt to set up an ethical boundary between the gods and men, as Nilsson says, "was diverted by anthropomorphism into the idea of the jealousy of the gods." The belief in 'power' was transformed into the belief in Fate to compensate for that which was lacking in the gods, and this consistently developed was calculated to remove the Olympians from their thrones.[1] But as they lost any religious significance they ever had through excessive humanization and the failure of the generalized cult of the State to gain the allegiance of the smaller unit represented by the city and the secret society, they became enthroned in the imagination—in mythology and allegory—as material for literature and art.[2] Translated as symbols of something beyond themselves, they were given lip-service by doubtful philosophers, and so survived when the stream of religious thought in Greece pursued its course in two concurrent channels, the one of poetry and the other of philosophy. But they were gods in whom no one believed seriously, and the humanizing of the myths constitutes the first step towards a rationalistic criticism of religion in which man became the measure and master of things, and this world the scene of action. The myths had ceased to be representations of reality, and their heroic figures, however impressive, were hardly more than mortals.

In striking contrast to Hellenic anthropomorphism, the Hebrew conception of Yahweh as a tribal god in the similitude of man was primarily and essentially religious and ethical. In the earlier tradition in the Old Testament he is described in terms as naïvely anthropomorphic as are the Olympians in the Homeric poems, but for very different purposes and reasons. Throughout the Hebrew literature Yahweh is the Holy One of Israel who by his mighty hand and stretched out arm manifested his power on behalf of his people in a series of miraculous interventions directed to certain specific ends. Instead of being the conqueror of the world like

[1]M. P. Nilsson, *A History of Greek Religion* (Oxford, 1925), p. 178.
[2]G. Murray, op. cit., p. 97f.

Zeus and his companions, he was the Creator of the universe. His attributes might be conceived on the basis of human qualities, but as the Maker and sovereign Ruler and Sustainer of all things, and the Father of mankind in general and of Israel in particular, he was brought into a unique relationship with the world and its inhabitants. It was he who wrested the power from the primeval monsters of the "deep" (*Tehom*),[1] brought order out of chaos, and as a result of his victory, gained possession of heaven and earth. Hencefoth he alone held sway, setting on the mountain pillars the solid vault of the "firmament," causing life to emerge out of the "waste", and giving his enemies as meat to the "howling things" of the desert. When the "fountains" had been established, the succession of day and night was determined, the sun and the moon and the stars were set in their courses and the "bounds of the earth fixed". The waters brought forth abundantly living species of every kind by the commanding word of the Creator, and finally man was fashioned in his own image and likeness.

In this very ancient mythology the whole ordered scheme of things is represented as the result of the divine fiat concentrated in a single creative Deity upon whose vitalizing spirit all creatures depend, so that when it is withdrawn they expire.[2] Every phase and aspect of nature, in fact, wait upon God as the upholder of the universe in its entirety, and all its processes and operations are dependent upon Him. Although this conception of creation arose out of a crude polytheistic mythology that flourished in Babylonia (and probably in Palestine and Syria) until after the period of the Exile in the sixth century B.C., and was expressed in anthropomorphic terms, it maintained that Yahweh was Lord of nature in its entirety as well as the helper and deliverer of the people over whom he reigned as a tribal god. Before he was given universal jurisdiction as the sovereign ruler and judge of all the earth, in post-exilic Judaism, it would seem that he had acquired this wider significance. Thus, in the pre-exilic Yahwistic creation story[3] he is represented as having "made heaven and earth," however narrow may have been its bounds between the four rivers where he walked in the cool of the evening and talked with the man he had fashioned

---

[1] In the post-exilic Priestly creation narrative (Gen. i) these mythological monsters have been eliminated, but reference to them occurs elsewhere in the Old Testament under the names of Rahab and Leviathan, cf. Ps. lxxiv, 13ff.,lxxxix, 10ff, Job, ix, Is. li, 9ff.

[2] Ps. civ., 27–30, Gen. ii, 7.

[3] Gen. ii, 4b–25.

to be his friend. The divine horticulturist of Eden is less transcendent
and more anthropomorphic than the impressive Creator of order
out of chaos of the later priestly tradition,[1] but in both narratives the
phenomenal order—be it regarded as a rainless fertile plot of land,
or a three-storied house constructed out of chaos—owed its origin
to the free initiative of a personal god. In both he may have been
supposed to have worked on a pre-existent earth or watery deep,
rather than having called all things into being *ex nihilo*, but once his
task was accomplished his sovereignty was unchallenged, and as
he became Lord of history as well as Lord of nature, his rule inevitably was made all-embracing[2] and his presence inescapable.[3]

This followed naturally from the association of the Hebrew
doctrine of creation with that of the control of human events. By
adopting the bold anthropomorphism in the Genesis story, respecting the fashioning of man by Yahweh in his own image as a potter
shapes his clay, breathing into the nostrils of the manikin the breath
of life,[4] the human race was brought into a special relationship with
the Creator. According to Hebrew psychology only a body animated
by a breath-soul constituted a personality. Therefore, the kinship of
Adam with his Maker was expressed in terms of a particular divine
inflatus of his physical integument which gave him and his descendants the spiritual understanding essential to his status in creation.
He was equipped with a spiritual consciousness so that he could
commune and converse with his Creator as with his wife, who was
bone of his bone and flesh of his flesh.[5] Indeed, so intimate was the
union between God and Adam that there was no means of escaping
from the omniscient presence of Yahweh.[6] The anthropomorphism,
therefore, was not just a crude conception of God having the form
and fashion of man. On the contrary, it was the Hebrew manner of
giving expression to the conviction that man stands in a unique
relationship with the sovereign Lord of the universe Who made and
sustains all things.

This fundamental element in the religion of Israel characterized
the doctrine of revelation in the Old Testament as will be seen later,[7]
the vicissitudes of nature being in the hands of Yahweh who worked

[1] Gen. i-ii, 4a.
[2] Is. xl, 12-15, 26; xlv, 1-7, 18.
[3] Ps. cxxxix, 1-12.
[4] Gen. ii, 7.
[5] Gen. ii, 23, iii, 8f.
[6] Gen. iii, 10, Ps. cxxxix, 1-12.
[7] Cf. Chap. ix, pp. 172ff.

out his purposes for his people, and through them for mankind as a whole, by a series of divine interventions and controlling activities. Unlike the Olympians, he was always operative in human affairs and especially in those of the nation over which he presided, and with which he was in a peculiar relationship by virtue of his covenant with Abraham and his seed. Having created man in his image he made his presence known to him in stirring signs and wonders, employing the clouds as his chariot, walking on the wings of the wind and having angels at his command as his ministers. To him supreme power belonged and upon him all things depended, so that when he hid his face they were troubled and when he took away their breath they died and returned to the dust.[1]

Although all this was conceived and expressed anthropomorphically it, nevertheless, was understood as part of a moral order of the universe. Yahweh might be represented as acting arbitrarily and sometimes vindictively, but before the prophetic movement had placed its imprimatur on ethical monotheism, the god of Israel in his most primitive aspects and attributes was never thought of as behaving like Zeus and his companions on Olympus. Nathan speaking in his name to David rebuked moral evil,[2] Elijah as his spokesman condemned without reservation Ahab's appropriation of Naboth's vineyard,[3] and in the very early Book of the Covenant embedded in the later narratives of Exodus (xx. 22–xxiii. 10), a high standard of conduct is set forth as required by him for Israel. While it is true that in its present form the literature dates at the earliest from the tenth century B.C., yet the ancient documents reflect the thought and outlook that were established long before the influence of the great Hebrew prophets from the days of Amos and onwards was felt. The first requirements of Yahweh of his people, to do justly, to love mercy and to walk humbly with their god,[4] was recognized before the reformers of the eighth century began their campaign to restore the former ethical standards, as they themselves maintained. And these precepts were based on the nature and character of Yahweh himself.

According to the Old Testament, the moral order is the order of the Holy One of Israel in whose nature man partakes because he has been made in his image. Therefore, he fulfils his vocation and destiny

[1]Ps. civ., 3ff.
[2]II, Sam. xii, 1ff.
[3]I. Kgs xxi, 17f.
[4]Micah. vi, 8.

only in so far as he conforms to this ethical standard. Even as the tribal war-god Yahweh was thought to be working towards these ends, controlling the fortunes of nations and the course of history in accordance with his ultimate providential purposes which were fundamentally good. Sometimes he was represented as acting in an unethical manner, as when he was said to have moved David to order a census in order to bring destruction on the nation,[1] a story that has parallels in the behaviour of gods in this manner in other ancient traditions. But despite these lapses, for the mono-Yahwists he was primarily the Lord of morality moved by ethical motives in the exercise of his sovereign power although conditioned by an arbitrary favouritism arising out of the predominant nationalism in which the tradition took shape.

Thus, in the event *par excellence* in which he was thought to have demonstrated his supreme might, the Exodus, although it was a deliverance of oppressed slaves from a grievous bondage, the story is told in a series of anthropomorphic incidents which reflect the outlook of a tribal morality. On the other hand, regarded from this standpoint, it revealed the good hand of its god upon the captive nation and for ever has remained the outstanding proof of his divine power and goodness towards Israel. The incident, in fact, occupies in Jewish tradition a position hardly less important and significant than that of Christmas Day and Easter in Christian theology, though with a vastly different content. Yahweh had visited and rescued his people with a strong hand and with a stretched out arm. Therefore, the Exodus was for them the supreme redemptive act of which the return from the Exile in Babylonia in 538, and the subsequent Messianic eschatology, were the sequel.[2] From the great day "when Israel came out of Egypt" Yahweh had been the rock of its salvation, and, therefore, he is God of gods and Lord of lords and "his mercy endureth for ever." He who had divided the Red Sea in sunder and made Israel to pass through the midst of it, and had overthrown Pharaoh and his host, would not fail or forsake his inheritance.

This conviction received confirmation in the events alleged to have occurred at Sinai, or Horeb, after the fugitives had made good their escape. There a new relationship was established with the tribal god set forth in anthropomorphic terms. Yahweh may have

[1] II Sam. xxiv, 1ff.
[2] Amos ii, 10, Hos. xii, 9, Jer. ii, 2ff, 5ff, Ezek. xx, 5f, Is. xliii, 16–20, lxiii, 7–14, Ps. lxxiv, 12–17, Ps. cxxxv, 1ff.

been originally a Kenite deity whom Moses encountered during his sojourn in Midian, but he also had a wider significance if the words *Yau, Ya, Yami* and *Yahveh*, found in Babylonian, Aramaean and Cannaanite inscriptions and documents, represent divine titles having reference to a Western Semitic High God.[1] It is not improbable, therefore, that he was known to some of the Hebrew tribes as the god of their fathers[2] before a particular and more intimate link was established with him by Moses after the theophany in Midian. If this were so it would explain how a powerful desert deity became a consolidating force and unifying centre in a confederation of pastoral people brought into a covenant relationship with him at the holy mount.[3] The existence of other tribal and national gods was, of course, taken for granted, but so far as Israel was concerned, henceforth it was wedded to Yahweh and forbidden to worship any other deity. The transaction was conceived anthropomorphically and ratified amid the numinous signs of volcanic eruption and earth tremors [4] which made a lasting impression on the mind of the nation. The event placed a supernatural seal on a relationship which was destined to develop into a new realization of ethical monotheism when eventually the localized jealous god of Sinai became transformed into the sovereign Ruler of the universe and its moral order, moulding history in a process of absolute selectivity purposed from the creation of the world.

From his primitive anthropomorphic beginnings as a tribal All-Father speaking in the thunder, writing his laws with his own finger on stone tablets, conversing in secret with his earthly friend and spokesman in the seclusion of a mountain sanctuary, and leading his people in a pillar of cloud by day and pillar of fire by night, he was always regarded in Israel as a personal god; a divine ruler, deliverer and judge. Standing over against man and creation in this relationship, he remained throughout more than a cosmic process or life-force striving to attain its goal. As sovereign Lord of history he inevitably assumed universal control over nature when he shed his purely tribal content. But even in his more primitive and anthropomorphic guise he was intimately concerned with human

[3]Albright, *Journal of Biblical Literature*, LIV, 1935, p. 173ff. R. Dussaud, *Revue d'histoire et de Philosophie religieuses*, 1932, p. 247. *Les Découvertes de Ras Shamra*, 1937, p. 107.

[4]Ex. iii, 16.

[1]Ex. xx, 3, xxxiv, 14.

[2]Ex. xix, 18, Dt. iv, 11f, Ps. lxviii, 7f, Jud. c, 4f, I Kgs. xix, 8–14, cf. W. J. Phythiam-Adams, *The Call of Israel* (Oxford, 1934), p. 123ff.

needs and the destiny of his people. In this way he was brought into such a close relationship with the course of events in time and space that his jurisdiction could not be confined solely within the limits of a given territory, be it the desert or Palestine. He had to be all-embracing, holding the waters in the hollow of his hand, meting out the heavens with a span, containing the earth in a measure and weighing the mountains in a balance.[1] In unique historical events and miraculous divine interventions he manifested his will and determined the course of the world accordingly.

In contrast to oriental pantheism with its Ultimate Reality conceived as impersonal necessity expressing itself through natural processes, Hebrew transcendentalism regarded Deity anthropomorphically as the consciously intelligent Creator from Whose will the phenomenal order takes its origin, and in Whose will all things are sustained and guided to their appointed ends. He is self-conscious Being, and if this involves human attributes being assigned to Him, the anger, love, goodness, knowledge and power of Yahweh were interpreted theocentrically and ethically. Anthropomorphism, in fact, is inseparable from any conception of personal theism ascribing will and self-consciousness to the Deity. The human mind cannot comprehend, leave alone give expression to, the infinite perfection and goodness of God except in terms borrowed from human consciousness and the region of the infinite interpreted analogically and symbolically. The limitations of conceptual capacity compel man to represent God to himself in ideas and forms drawn from his own being and that of the objective world of his experience. When the Old Testament writers spoke of Yahweh walking in Eden, talking with Moses on Sinai, or sitting on his throne in heaven with the Earth as his footstool, they were thinking along these lines and endeavouring to put into concrete language and thought-forms abstract concepts which defied any other mode of expression for them.

In post-exilic Judaism, however, efforts were made by the scribes to remove some of the more crude anthropomorphisms, or to paraphrase and spiritualize them. Thus, in the Targums the finger of God of Exodus viii. 19 was rendered "this is a plague from before Yahweh," and when He was said to abide in, come to, or depart from a place, the phrase was made to read "God caused his presence (*shekinta*) to abide there, and the like,[2] just as seeing God, or God

[1] Is. xl, 12f.
[2] e.g. Ex. xxv, 8, xxxiv, 6; Dt. xii, 5, 11, 21; xxxii, 20; Hos. v., 6.

F

manifesting himself to man, was interpreted as "the glory (*yekara*) of God".[1] Where the earlier anthropomorphisms were retained (e.g. in references to God having eyes, ears, hands and feet) the terms *memra*, meaning "the divine in self-manifestation," was introduced as a reverend circumlocution for God as active in the affairs of men.[2]

Against these subtle attempts to render innocuous naïve expressions in the Pentateuch respecting the nature, function and operations of Yahweh in Israel, a reaction set in the third century A.D. By removing the anthropomorphisms the Holy One of Israel was in danger of becoming an abstract Platonic Deity—a mere idea—under the influence of current speculative philosophic thought. At least, so it seemed to the Jewish Rabbis who restored the human and physical qualities and imagery attributed to God in the Hebrew Bible, the Talmud and the Midrashim. As in the apocalyptic literature, He was represented enthroned in glory in the highest heaven and surrounded with the angelic host as a consultative body assisting in the divine government of the world. Before it Satan accused Israel, and Michael successfully defended the chosen nation. On the altar of the heavenly Jerusalem the archangel offered the souls of the righteous, while the celestial Rabbis discussed the Halakha, promulgated afresh by God every day.[3]

In Christian apocalyptic thought much the same imagery recurred[4] but the doctrine of the Incarnation gave a new direction to anthropomorphism. By making the Godhead fully manifest in time and space in perfect manhood, instead of the Deity being fashioned in human likeness and assigned human attributes and qualities, the situation was reversed. The action proceeds from the side of God and not from that of man. If a knowledge of God as personal is derived from a knowledge of personality in man, it is never assumed in Christian theology that God is merely another creature like ourselves. Divine personality is rather a potentiality of personal relationship,[5] and the doctrine of the incarnation is not that a particular man is God, as in the case of the divine kingship in the religions of the Ancient East, nor that *a* man (i.e. a hero or

[1]Ex. xxiv, 10; Is. vi, 1; Gen. xvii, 22.
[2]Cf. Etheridge, *The Targums on the Pentateuch* (London, 1862), p. 14ff. Moore, *Judaism* (Camb., 1927), vol. I, p. 418f.
[3]*Targ. Jon.* Gen. xxviii, 12. *Jerus Ber.* ix, 5, Bab. *Meg*, 86.
[4]Especially in the Johannine Apocalypse.
[5]C. C. J. Webb, *Divine Personality and Human Life* (London, 1920), p. 18ff; *God and Personality* (London, 1918), p. 61ff.

ancestor) has become God, nor that the Creator of the universe appeared in human type. It is rather the affirmation that "in the fulness of time" the Godhead was clothed in human flesh in a specific individual Person Who is truly representative of all mankind, and so establishes a new relationship between God and man. As Professor C. C. J. Webb says, "man was, it teaches, from the first in the image of God, and the Son is eternally an element in the Godhead. That is, the union of God and man belongs to the very essence of both the one and the other."[1]

It would seem, therefore, that the Christian doctrine of the Incarnation is based more on a theomorphic conception of man made in the likeness of God than on an anthropomorphic conception of God made in the image of man. The former Jewish imagery and symbolism were retained but the new personal relationship between the human and the divine was conceived in terms of redeemed humanity, in which the love of God for man and man's response in love of his fellow men are self-expressed. In this "higher anthropomorphism"[2] Deity is no longer regarded simply as a human person, or "magnified non-natural man." If qualities and attributes such as love and fatherhood are still assigned to Him, and the anthropomorphic tendency in Judaism was carried over into the New Testament by writers who had been nurtured in this mode of theistic thought and expression, the Hellenic philosophic tradition exercised a powerful corrective influence in the formative period of Christian theology.

Thus, the Early Fathers with their Neoplatonic background inclined to the view that the nature and attributes of God could only be expressed in negative propositions. While it was impossible to reconcile this doctrine of the Incarnation with a Neoplatonic conception of the Absolute as "beyond existence" and unknown to us, the patristic thinkers adopted an agnostic attitude towards all affirmations about God in His essential being. That He had a human body, as the Anthropomorphics and Audians held, was condemned as definitely heretical,[3] and although the analogical method was employed in the Early Church, it was not until a systematic investigation of the validity of analogy was undertaken by the Schoolmen that a serious attempt was made to find a philosophic justification

[1] The Relations of God and Man (London, 1915), p. 240.
[2] Streeter, Reality (London, 1926), p. 134ff; Matthews, God in Christian Thought and Experience (1930), p. 33ff.
[3] Cf. St. Jerome, Epist. VI, Ad Pammadium.

for the anthropomorphic language of Scripture. This involved an examination of the problem of the finite and infinite and the relation of beings to each other.[1]

While the limitations of the human mind to know God as He is in actuality were fully recognized, given the existence of two beings having a common relationship, the same terminology, it was held, could be applied to them, though one be contingent upon the other. Thus, St. Thomas maintained that we "do not know what God is, but only what He is not, and the relation of all things to Him. The axiom that in God essence and existence are the same is to be understood of the existence whereby God subsists in Himself, the manner of which is unknown to us, as also is His essence; not of the existence which signifies an affirmative judgement of the understanding."[2] Therefore, as being is analogically applied to Deity, so the attributes of being as they are known in human experience can be employed to render the concept intelligible. If, in fact, God is the highest evaluation of conscious intelligence, rational and moral qualities are ascribed to Him on the ground that these are essential to the perfection of personality. Distinguishing between the univocal and the equivocal, the term "wisdom," it was claimed, could not be applied in the same sense to God and man. With reference to man the word describes the reality it signifies; but in speaking of God it cannot be used in a univocal sense since He is the plenitude of divine wisdom —a perfection not distinct from His essence and His being. But between divine and human wisdom there is an analogy inasmuch as that which is imperfect, incomplete and selective in man has its fulness in Him.[3]

In making analogy the *via media* between agnosticism and anthropomorphism St. Thomas and the Scholastics went a considerable way in justifying Biblical terminology respecting the nature and attributes of God, if in the process they introduced technicalities and subtilties of reasoning which confused rather than illuminated the issue. The question, however, is not whether the method is justifiable but how far the attributes assigned to Deity in this symbolical manner have any basis in fact. Is God really as He is represented to be analogically? Since the Middle Ages, when the problem was ceaselessly debated by the Scholastic theologians, the

[1]Cf. A. Farrar, *Finite and Infinite* (London, 1943), 23ff, 88ff.
[2]Aquinas, *Contra Gentiles*, I, 12, c, xxx.
[3]*Summa Theol.* I, xiii, 5, 6, ad Resp. *Contra Gentiles*, I, 32.

philosophic and scientific approach to and interpretation of the universe has fundamentally changed.

In the eighteenth century Berkeley and Butler could take for granted the general principle of anthropomorphic analogy. As God is infinitely above man, so, it seemed to Berkeley, "the knowledge of God is infinitely above the knowledge of man, and this is *analogia proprie facta*. And after the same analogy we must understand all those attributes to belong to Deity which in themselves simply and as such denote perfection."[1] Similarly, Butler in his memorable volume *The Analogy of Religion*, assumed that the universe was created and its laws ordered by a reasonable, all-wise, and all-powerful God, though he devoted two sections to meeting objections to the analogical mode of reasoning. It can hardly be said, however, that he supplied the vigorous and demonstrative proof of the being and attributes of Deity that the age required. For him "the ways of God are too vast, of too large extent for our capacities."[2] He is "not a creature but Almighty God, of infinite power and wisdom and goodness," and as such "the natural object of those affections which He hath endued us with, and which correspond to those attributes."[3]

In the light of our deepening and widened understanding of nature and its processes Butler's plea against over-estimating the range of our knowledge or our faculties, and raising up new difficulties by an injudicious use of anthropomorphic and analogical language and thought, to-day has even greater force. Nevertheless, if it be granted that man is a divine creation, when every allowance has been made for "the limits of the human understanding" concerning "things in themselves," stressed by post-Kantian philosophers in the last two centuries, his very origin and dependence upon his Creator gives an innate disposition towards feeling after and finding the source and ground of his being. This is accomplished within the range of his own vision and as part of a process of self-realization continued through many ages and stages of mental and spiritual development.

Ideas about God, as about other aspects of reality, have been conditioned by the thought, knowledge and understanding of the age in which they occur, and have been adapted to its needs. But it by no means follows that the germ of truth is not to be found in these rudimentary modes of expression. On the contrary, the history

[1]Berkeley, *Alciphron, or the Minute Philosopher* (1732), i, p. 257.
[2]*Sermon*, XV, 5.
[3]*Sermon*, XIII, 11.

of theism is a demonstration of the unravelling of the mystery of Ultimate Reality, and an ever-deepening perception of all that is involved in the concept of Deity. From a clearer apprehension of his own nature and attributes man has arrived at a transcendental evaluation of infinite being, power, wisdom, truth, goodness and love, comprehended with the Ground of reality (i.e. God) as absolute perfection or worth in all its completeness. But perfect being has to be made intelligible to finite minds, and this involves a re-interpretation of the qualities alone found in their fulness in Deity in terms of their human reflections, with all the inevitable limitations and imperfections at the human level of experience and understanding.

That there is a fundamental distinction between the phenomenal order and the real order of existence is beyond dispute, but this does not prevent the scientist or the philosopher from interpreting the inward processes of nature by their manifestations in the external world through analogy and what is virtually anthropomorphic reasoning. The thunder is said to roll, the wind to howl, the sun to rise or set, and if this merely is figurative language, the fact remains that it is through human personality that all knowledge functions, and only through human experience are phenomena—matter, energy, cause, time and space—apprehended realities. Nature is said to behave as a "mechanism" or as an "organism," and society to have a "structure," because all reality is regarded after the analogy of human experience and knowledge of things and their behaviour. So the First and Final Cause of all existence is assigned the highest human attributes—fatherhood, power, wisdom, love and creativity —because they are the dim reflections of the one and only perfect Being in Whom alone all that is divine exists in the completeness of Ultimate Reality and Absolute Value. By looking into himself man has seen and found as it were an image of the Infinite and Eternal, and while he may have inferred that God must possess these same qualities only in a higher degree, beyond this anthropomorphic reasoning lies the further consideration that the highest human attributes are also valid for the right ordering and existence of the world as a cosmos. If this in fact is a divine creation, they must be of the very nature and essence of the Reality in which all things are grounded.

CHAPTER V

MONOLATRY AND MONOTHEISM

In most religions of antiquity the multiplicity of minor divinities was coupled with a movement towards unification which found expression in the practice of making different gods the names of one abstract Deity. Thus, pluralism and monism, polytheism and monotheism, represent recurring phenomena, appearing and re-appearing first in one form and then in another. Nevertheless, despite the fact that existence is reducible to a plurality of distinct and independent beings or elements, there is an underlying fundamental unity which leads to the conviction that in the last analysis the universe is grounded in a single Ultimate Reality, conceived either as a pantheistic Principle or a universal personal God.

In primitive society, as we have seen, while a genuine monotheism never occurs, Supreme Beings occupy a unique position as the highest evaluation of the transcendental order of which the human mind is capable at that stage of its development. To them is attached a value superior to that of all other gods or spirits, but since they tend to be remote they are invariably eclipsed by the more popular and accessible divinities with a localized cultus. Moreover, tribal All Fathers are neither the ground and support of the universe in a philosophic sense, nor are their minds and wills revealed in its final purpose. They are, in fact, part of a pluralistic cosmological order in which a variety of beings and causes are held to have been responsible for creation in the beginning, and for the present ordering of the world and its institutions. For the primitive observer it is multiplicity rather than unity that is the most insistent fact. Thus, even in the case of a High God like Ruhanga in the relatively advanced culture of Uganda, although he is regarded as "the Maker of all", other gods and spirits have their own personalities and attributes, however much he may be thought to contain their qualities in himself.

In the highly organized pantheons in the great polytheistic communities of the Ancient East a tendency arose to group gods and grade them in hierarchies with one of the number raised to a superior status above the rest. In Mesopotamia, for example, three principal deities were associated respectively with the heavens, the earth and the waters—Anu, Enlil, and Ea. This triad became the divine type of everything in these three aspects of the universe, as in the celestial sphere the triad represented by Shamash (the sun), Sin (the moon) and Ishtar (the planet Venus) reigned supreme. Around these six great gods a host of lesser beings were grouped, and as each city had its own god, whose power and influence was always liable to wax and wane with the course of political events, the pantheon was in a constant state of flux. Anu and Enlil, indeed, were originally local gods—the one the patron of Uruk and the other the chief deity of Nippur, while Ea presided over Eridu on the shores of the Persian Gulf.

When Enlil from being a storm God was raised to his exalted position at the head of the pantheon, his city, Nippur, acquired the status of an ecclesiastical capital, or spiritual centre, to which Sumerians and Semites resorted to pay their respects to the Lord of the earth. Even when, with the transference of political jurisdiction to Babylon its divine patron, Marduk, replaced him, Enlil still remained theoretically the principal deity though his attributes were absorbed by his successor, and Ninlil, "the lady of the mountain," became the common consort of both gods. Henceforth Marduk was the director of the Triad, and as the practical oversight of the universe had been assigned to him by the gods at his victory over Tiamat, he naturally assumed the powers hitherto exercised by his predecessor and the other great gods. As Bel he became "Lord of the lands," the personification of sovereignty and strength, "the sole god" and "lord of lords," with only one serious rival, and he was Ashur, the chief deity of the rising power of Assyria.

Here lay the weakness of this monolatrous form of polytheism. Anu, Enlil and Marduk might, each in his turn, become abstractions, summing up the principal aspects and manifestations of divine power in the universe. But they were one and all personifications of natural phenomena and subject to the vicissitudes of the various political centres where they were worshipped. The myth associated with one god was transferred to another with impunity, as when the story of the conquest of chaos as a great monster was referred first to Enlil, then to his son Ninurta (Ninib), and finally to Marduk. In each of the chief centres the patron deity was represented as the Creator, and the mighty deeds of the respective gods were combined by the priesthood of Babylon in a composite cosmological legend, re-enacted at the Annual Festival, in which Marduk played the leading role.

Here we have a notable instance of sacerdotal manipulation and formulation constituting the determining element in the elevation of a local god to the headship of the pantheon. The creation story was re-told as the central theme of a death and resurrection drama redounding to the praise, and establishing the sovereign rule, of the deity whose cultus they maintained, and who was represented as holding the destiny of the human race in his hands. Around him were grouped all the other gods, and even the once mighty Enlil of Nippur was made to hail him as "lord of lands," thereby assigning to Marduk his own office, function and designation. Ea then completed the transformation by conferring his name upon the hero of Babylon—"He shall be even as I am; Ea is his name."[1] Henceforth he (Marduk) became the ruler of the universe, the principal deity of the rituals of expiation; and eventually he was identified with Tammuz as the dying and reviving king-god.

This monolatrous tendency, however, being the result of political circumstances and priestly enterprise, was never recognized in the ancient Sumerian cities of the south (e.g. Nippur Erech, Ur and Kish). Thus, any move towards monotheism that may be discerned in this syncretism was confined to the priesthood of Babylon. Outside the capital Marduk had no temples or shrines, and there is no reason to suppose that in popular belief and estimation he was accorded either the status, function or veneration of a universal God of all the earth. The assembling of the gods in the Esgalia at the Akitu in Babylon was a formal ecclesiastical "gathering of the clans" rather than a general proclamation of the Lordship of Marduk comparable to the celebration of the kingship of Yahweh at the Feast of Tabernacles (Sukkôth) in post-exilic Israel, when apparently he was worshipped as Lord of creation.[2] In the available evidence there is nothing to suggest that at any time in Babylonia and Assyria the conception of a transcendent Deity obtained. Marduk unquestionably was "a great king above all gods" but not to the exclusion of Enlil, Ninurta, Nabu, Shamash, Sin, Ishtar, Ashur and the rest of the pantheon.

Similarly, in Ancient Egypt, while, as we have seen, the all-enveloping Sun-god in his various manifestations tended more and more to dominate the cultus,[3] except one very temporary interlude,

[1] S. Langdon, *The Babylonian Epic of Creation* (Oxford, 1923), Tablet vii, p. 207. Cf. A. Heidel, *The Babylonian Genesis* (Chicago, 1942), IV, 49–64.
[2] Ps. xciii, xcv, 3, xcvi, 10, xcviii, 1. Cf. Hooke, *Myth and Ritual* (Oxford, 1933), pp. 122ff.
[3] Chap. II, pp. 32f.

a genuine monotheism was never established. Nevertheless, the solar theology moved more definitely in the direction of divine unity than did the worship of the localized city-gods in Mesopotamia. Indeed, the Heliopolitan influence brought Re within an ace of becoming a universal Deity, the supreme Lord of heaven and earth. When this priesthood equated their god with the life-giving sun in its various aspects, they gave expression to a very deeply laid trend in the religious thought of Egypt towards the unification of all divine activity in the central luminary which, as Breasted has pointed out, is "the most insistent fact in the Nile valley."[1] Out of primeval chaos, regarded as a vast ocean, "the one Lord of heaven" (i.e. the Sun-god) emerged in the form of Atum, the self-existent, and became the begetter of the Heliopolitan Ennead. As the State developed, his rule extended over the entire hierarchy of gods inasmuch as he was the heavenly father of the one Pharaoh who reigned over Upper and Lower Egypt.[2]

To affirm, however, that "when the Egyptian called his god 'One,' or the 'only One' he meant exactly what the Muslim means to-day when he says, 'There is no god but God',"[3] undervalues the independent existence of the rest of the pantheon. That local priesthoods and "religious formulators" from time to time gave a quasi-monotheistic significance to the "Only One" as to a Supreme Being exercising sovereign rule over all that is, cannot be denied. But this, we have maintained, is a recurrent phenomenon everywhere, and no more proves that monotheism prevailed in the Nile valley than in any other country where the All-Father belief occurs.

Popular religion unquestionably was predominantly polytheistic, each of the original nomes having its ancient myth and ritual which was only very superficially brought within the syncretistic solar theology of the Dynastic period. The great gods of the temples were essentially the gods of Pharaoh their priest, and those to whom he delegated his sacerdotal functions. While they were the recipients of prayers and votive offerings from the people, the masses usually sought the patronage of the lesser divinities with whom they were in more intimate relations. It was not until the royal Heliopolitan solar cultus was popularized and Osirianized that it was brought within the reach of the nation as a whole, and then for practical

[1] *Religion and Thought in Ancient Egypt* (London, 1912), p. 9.
[2] Chap. II, pp.
[3] E. A. W. Budge, *From Fetish to God in Ancient Egypt* (Oxford, 1934), p. 4f.

purposes the gods were regarded as normal polytheistic divinities with anthropomorphic qualities and attributes, having the feelings, needs and habits of men, and themselves under human control. Even the obelisks and embodiments of the Sun-god were given offerings of bread and beer in a manner that implied that within them resided a supernatural power independent of their solar symbolization.

In Egypt the conception of a quasi-magical potency called *Hiké*, as a kind of *mana*, was originally interpreted in terms of a mysterious creative activity predicated of certain individual acts and transferable from one person to another. Thus, in the Pyramid Texts of the fifth Dynasty (*c.* 2600 B.C.) in a passage that doubtless went back to predynastic times, a description occurs of a Pharaoh (Unas) who on arriving in the sky after his death proceeded to slaughter the gods in order to assimilate their *hike*,[1] and so to imbibe their power and wisdom. This divine essence became personified as a god, also called *Hiké*,[2] created by Re-Atum "when as yet no two things existed." From him sprang all living things, he being the incarnation or embodiment of life-giving potency. For this reason he was represented as escorting Re in his perilous nightly journey through the underworld, and at Luxor he appeared assisting at the birth of the divinely conceived son of the reigning Pharaoh.

This breaking up of a single force or influence into different personifications with a variety of powers and aspects, gave rise to a polytheism in which a unifying element was very deeply laid. Behind the multiplicity of gods and spirits there was this generalized conception of divine life-giving potency—a providential order of reality—on which the gods as well as the world and its inhabitants and processes ultimately were dependent since they only existed and performed their functions by the help of *hiké*. This term, therefore, seems to be virtually the equivalent of Deity in the abstract sense, and as such it may be regarded as a unifying principle in Egyptian religion. It regulated the relations of the human and divine orders inasmuch as those who were able to manipulate the mysterious power were the real masters of the situation, like the Brahmins in India, having within their control the very essence of existence—the source of all life and being in heaven and on earth. Apart from it the gods could not be born, the Creator remaining "One by myself"

[1] Sethe, *Die Altaegyptischen Pyramidentexte,* 393ff.
[2] Very much as in India Brahman was regarded both as supernatural power and a god.

until he brought his own name (*Hiké*) into being.[1] In other words, it was the creative force by which he made himself out of the primeval waters, so that, by virtue of this mysterious power, water was known as "the father of the gods."

When the Heliopolitan priesthood raised Re to his exalted position as the self-created Creator of all things, and were instrumental in bringing the entire pantheon into relation with him, they developed this monotheistic trend in the official religion. In popular belief and practice polytheism remained unchallenged, but in most of the temples the cultus was based on the Heliopolitan solar liturgy. Other gods, however, were regarded in much the same way by their respective priesthoods, as, for example, Ptah, the master craftsman or divine artificer, who by his worshippers at Memphis was represented as the Creator of the universe and the product of self-conceived thought.[2] Having brought himself into being by an effort of the mind, he became the "Overlord of the Two Lands" and the source of all the gods, giving them their "seats of worship," their bodies and cult-images.[3] He too had his Ennead composed of himself as a quasi-philosophical self-created Cause, and eight manifestations of his essential nature.

But this remarkable attempt at abstract theistic thought on the part of the Memphite theologians in their endeavour to counteract the growing influence of Heliopolis, made little or no impression on the concrete mind of Egypt, where the more materialistic solar theology and anthropomorphic cosmology held the field. If the Sun-god was in the sky, at least he was visible in the solar disk, and he had his embodiment on earth in the person of the reigning Pharaoh. Thus, he was something tangible and understandable, however much a priestly fiction and political motive might lie behind the cultus. So the future lay with the practical solar "formulators" rather than with the abstract Memphite thinkers.

Therefore, in the New Kingdom, when the princes of Thebes in Upper Egypt succeeded in throwing off the yoke of the usurping Hyksos about 1580 B.C., they attributed their victory to their hitherto obscure god Amon. The extension of Egyptian influence in Nubia and Asia in the eighteenth Dynasty stimulated the conception of a

[1]B. M. Papyrus, No. 10188, Budge, *Hieratic Papyri in the British Museum* (London, 1910).

[2]B. M. Stela, No. 498, M. S. Holmsberg, *The God Ptah* (London, 1946), for a detailed study of the significance of the god and the relevant literature.

[3]Budge, op. cit., p. 15f. K. Sethe, *Dramatische Texte zu altaegyptischen Mysterienspielen* (Leipzig, 1928), pp. 1–80.

world-state and fostered the tendency towards universalism. It only remained for the divine patron of the reigning family to be completely solarized to give him sovereign rule in the new imperial age. Thutmose III (c. 1500 B.C.) appears to have merged the priesthoods of all the temples into a single organization under the High Priest of Amon as pontifex maximus, thereby making the old cosmic god of Thebes the symbol of the new unified State and "more exalted of nature than any other god, at whose beauty the gods rejoice." His unity was absolute, and like his predecessors, he was represented as self-created, without father or mother, existing before any other being had emerged. "He shaped his own egg, he mingled his seed with his body to make his egg to come into being within himself." Yet, despite his oneness, he was worshipped in conjunction with two other deities—his consort Mut and his son Khensu—who with him composed the divine triad of Thebes. Nevertheless, there is a quite unmistakable monotheistic strain in the "Cairo hymn to Amon," which was composed probably in the reign of Amenhotep II (1447–1420):

"He who made herbage for the cattle,
    And the fruit tree for men.
He who made that whereon live the fish in the river,
    And the birds which inhabit the firmament.
He who giveth bread to him that is in the egg, and sustaineth
    the son of the worm,
He who made whereon the giants live,
    The worms and the flies likewise.
He who maketh that which the mice in their holes need,
    And sustaineth the birds (?) on every tree."[1]

Amon-Re, however, remained a composite deity with a complex polytheistic heritage, and it was not until Amenhotep IV came to the throne about 1375 B.C. that a genuinely monotheistic movement was vigorously launched. The new king was a devotee of Aton, an ancient designation of the Sun-god Re-Herakhty, associated particularly with the luminous disk in which he shone on the world. The son of a Syrian mother, Tii, who himself married a Mitanni princess, Nefertiti, the new Pharaoh was of a different stock and outlook from his predecessors. Having ascended the throne as the incarnation of Amon-Re, aided and abetted by Tii and Nefertiti, he deposed his

[1] Erman, *Literature of the Ancient Egyptians* (London, 1927), p. 286.

divine patron in favour of Aton and set up a new priesthood and ecclesiastical organization at Tell-el-Amarna, where he established his capital under the name of Akhetaton (the Horizon of Aton) as the centre of the reformed faith.

With all the iconoclastic zeal of a Somerset or Cromwell, he endeavoured to suppress every vestige of the old religion. Not content with closing the temples of Amon-Re and confiscating their property, the ardent youthful reformer erased the names of all the gods from the monuments, changed his own name to Ikhnaton (Profitable to Aton), and re-stated the Heliopolitan theology in terms of an all-embracing monotheism appropriate to the imperial State, which at this time extended from Nubia to Syria and Mesopotamia, with tentacles spreading towards Crete and the Aegean. Aton as "the sole god whose powers no other possesseth," the Creator and Sustainer of all things, ruling over the entire earth, the sky-world and the nether regions, was no longer essentially a Theban or Heliopolitan god of a local prisethood. His dominion knew no limits, and as the solar disk was one alone, without counterpart or equal, so Aton reigned alone.[1]

For the former anthropomorphic and theriomorphic symbols, the disk with emanating rays was substituted, and apart from this no cult-image was permitted in the new cultus. The singing of remarkable monotheistic hymns constituted the principal act of worship, together with the presentation of food and drink offerings, of perfumes and flowers, censings and libations taking the place of the earlier Toilet Ceremonies in the House of the Morning. A male and female choir was in attendance during the rites in which the queen equally with the king had her part. Pharaoh was still the earthly embodiment of the Sun-god (Aton), and as the dispenser of good fortune he was the giver of life and of good days. But the monotheistic simplicity of the new faith is revealed in the following exaltation of the universal splendour and power of Aton, inscribed in one of the tomb-chapels at El-Amarna:

> Beautiful in thine appearing in the horizon of heaven, thou living sun, the first who lived!
> Thou riseth in the eastern horizon, and
> Thou fillest every land with thy beauty.

[1] Budge, *Tutankhamen, Amenism, Atenism and Egyptian Monotheism* (London, 1923), pp. 21, 79, 113.

Thou art beautiful and great and glisteneth, and art high above
every land;
Thy rays, they compass the lands, so far as all that thou hast
created.
Thou art Re, and thou reachest unto their end and subduest
them for thy dear Son.
Though thou art far away, yet are thy rays upon earth;
Thou art before their face—thy going.[1]

Notwithstanding the fact that it was still the physical sun that
was extolled in language which would not be difficult to reconcile
with the Theban solar theology, Atonism lacked a cultus and so
made little or no general appeal. It was almost exclusively the work
of Ikhnaton and his retinue, and had behind it no powerful priesthood
comparable to that which had raised Amon-Re to his exalted
position in the New Kingdom. As a ruler the king was weak and
disinterested in imperial affairs; the dispossessed Amonite priesthood
has been antagonized, and Egypt was full of dissatisfied soldiers.
Therefore, in the confusion that followed his death in 1350, the
movement came to an inglorious end. With the accession of his
son-in-law Tutankhaton the nation speedily returned to its former
gods. The new Pharaoh took up his abode in Thebes and changed
his name to Tutankhamon as the faithful son and devotee of Amon-
Re. The *status quo* was maintained by all the subsequent priesthoods until paganism was finally suppressed in Egypt by an edict
promulgated in 390 A.D.; a year after the temple of Serapis at
Alexandria had been captured by a Christian mob and turned into a
church. Then the Sun-god of many names, powers, forms and
attributes was finally abandoned in favour of the One God in Three
Persons, though not to the total exclusion of the traditional polytheism which lived on in a Coptic guise.

In India, as we have seen, the tendency to assimilation and
interchange of the attributes of the Vedic gods moved in the
direction of pantheism rather than of monotheism. The deified
heavens, the earth, the waters and the air never stood over against
man and the world in the relation of Creator to creation, as in the
Egyptian solar theology. As they fell into the background an all-
pervading spiritual essence alone remained as the expression of the
divine life permeating the universe, with a considerable residuum

[1]Davies, *Rock-Tombs of El-Amarna* (London, 1903–8), VI, pl. xxvii, xxix. Erman,
Literature of the Ancient Egyptians (1927), p. 289.

of animistic popular cultus in which the multiple aspects of Deity found expression. Thus, the theism that emerged out of Vedic mythology, Brahmanic ritual and mystical philosophy consisted of a great variety of gods grouped round the Trimurti, Brahman, Vishnu and Shiva. In his turn each member of this Triad was regarded as infinite, eternal, self-existent and absolute, having his proper place and function in the universe. The offices of all three, however, were so interchangeable that each was thought to be capable of maintaining the cosmic order independently of the others. If for purposes of thought and mystical experience they were collectively resolved into a single pantheistic Unity—the Absolute[1] —the existence of the Vedic gods (e.g. Agni, Indra and Varuna) was not denied in the Upanishads any more than were their Olympian counterparts in the Homeric and Epic literature in Greece, or the solar pantheon in the Egyptian Book of the Dead.

In Greece from the last decade of the seventh century B.C. to the end of the following century, the Milesian thinkers, Phales, Anaximander and Anaximenes, broke away from the polytheistic tradition in search for "the divine" in a first principle, such as water or air, as the underlying unity of the universe and its processes. As for Aeschylus and Pindar, Zeus was the supreme ruler of gods and men, the other gods existing merely to do his bidding, so for Anaximenes air as the originative source of all becoming and change, was the divine ground of the cosmos, including both life and consciousness. It only remained for Xenophanes (c. 570-480 B.C.) to dismiss the Homeric gods as "thieves, adulterers and deceivers" and erect in their place the One God who "sees as a whole, thinks as a whole, hears as a whole," comparable to mortals neither in form nor thought.[2] The world of change then became a manifestation of this changeless, imperishable, timeless Being conceived as a unity endowed with intelligence, ruling all things by the power of His mind alone, as in Aeschylus's conception of Zeus in the Suppliants,[3] where divine swaying of the world is shifted from the cosmic to the ethical sphere. A god worthy of worship must be transcendent and free from any moral weakness or human limitations. Moreover, he must be the world-ground, and, therefore, the unity of the highest and most sublime principle.[4]

[1]Brihadaranyaka, I, 4, 6, ii, 13; 4, 3, 33; 4, 4, 22.
[2]Frag, ii, 23.
[3]Suppl. 96-103 (Murray), cf. W. Jaeger, The Theology of the Early Greek Philosophers (Oxford, 1947), p. 45.
[4]Xenoph, Frag, 30, cf. Aristotle, Metaph, A, 5, 986B, 18ff.

That a pantheistic strain ran through the Ionian and Eleatic theology was inevitable in a system that reduced all things to a single substance immanent in the natural order and in its relation to change and generation. The quest of "the One that remains" was in great measure lost in the confusion and complexity of the Many. When the cosmos was regarded as eternal, sentient and intelligent it it was difficult to set it over against a Creator in the monotheistic sense of Deity. Thus, for Parmenides the concept of Being was that of the eternal One as an Absolute, which ruled out altogether the sensible world of motion, change and becoming an illusory appearance—the process of coming-to-be and passing away—as in Indian mysticism. From the primal-ground all things proceeded and to it they returned; and for Parmenides True-Being could have no place in Not-Being.[1] The force of law alone was unchangeable and held the existent together in the world of appearances, but absolute Being was never identified with Deity in any intelligible sense of the term, however much it might be interpreted as intelligent, timeless and indestructible. Thus, for practical purposes this interpretation was nearer to a static pantheism than to monotheism.

Heraclitus, on the other hand, in making change and becoming the essence of reality, introduced the idea of divine "law" as the all-controlling cosmic process acting rationally, reconciling all opposites.[2] It is this *Logos* which gives the process its significance and worth and guides the universe through all its transformations, so that the fundamental fire-principle acts rationally according to law and measure. "All things are exchanged for Fire, and Fire for all things, as wares are exchanged for gold, and gold for wares." Like Fire, God changes Himself, "which, when mingled with various kinds of incense, is named from the fragrance of each."[3] Thus, for Heraclitus Deity was the principle underlying all harmony in tension and the rhythm of opposing forces—day and night, summer and winter, peace and war, plenty and hunger. That is to say, it was the unity of opposites and movement, or incessant change, that was the Lord of the universe; a concept which fell short of that of a personal God, despite the fact that the cosmos was represented as the revelation of one all-supreme divine law to which all things are subject.

Anaxagoras, an elder contemporary of Socrates, moved further in the direction of a teleological interpretation of the universe in

[1]Parm. *Frag.* B, 8.
[2]*Frag.* 20, 28, 65, 72–4.
[3]*Frag.* 67.

G

trying to find a place for Mind (*Nous*) in the ordering of the world and its processes. Infinite and self-ruling, mixed with nothing, it is alone, itself by itself, and controls all things that have soul.[1] Thus, it rules over the entire natural order of living species of which it is independent, even though it be the same in kind as the human mind. If nowhere is Mind referred to as divine, nevertheless, divinity is attributed to its epithets. It was, however, Diogenes (who equated Mind with air) who sharply distinguished Mind from everything else in the material world, and made it the basis of a new teleological interpretation of the universe,[2] standing both behind and within it.

Unlike Empedocles, who in his *Sphairos* brought together the manifold revelation of the divine in nature in complete harmony as the function of God in multiplicity,[3] Anaxagoras and Diogenes felt the need of a single basic principle as the conscious Creator, analogous to Mind, to account for the rational purposefulness underlying creation. But they never emancipated themselves from the materialistic interpretation of the cause of phenomena, and so were driven to a dualistic distinction between mind and matter, with far-reaching effects on subsequent thought and speculation. In the Platonic differentiation of the phenomenal order visible to us and the invisible, permanent, real world of ideas, if the cosmology was dualistic[4] the doctrine of God was monotheistic inasmuch as it rests on a single personal ground Who is Good. While the Olympian pantheon was not wholly excluded,[5] the polytheistic tradition was completely foreign to the Platonic philosophic approach to the problem of reality.

This applies equally to the Aristotelian re-statement of Platonic theism based on the current scientific conception of motion. Starting from the initial assumption that every body has an essence ($\varphi\acute{\upsilon}\sigma\iota\varsigma$) which governs its behaviour and impels it to realize its inherent purpose ($\tau\acute{\epsilon}\lambda o\varsigma$), Aristotle saw in motion the means by which a condition of potency ($\delta\acute{\upsilon}\nu\alpha\mu\iota\varsigma$) was reduced to a condition of act ($\grave{\epsilon}\nu\acute{\epsilon}\rho\gamma\epsilon\iota\alpha$). The essence, he contended, can never be separated from that of which it is the essence, and, therefore, ideas cannot have an existence apart from things, as Plato imagined. "Ideas," "forms" and the phenomenal world could not, he thought, exist apart. "Prime matter ($\pi\rho\acute{\omega}\tau\eta$ $\H{\upsilon}\lambda\eta$) was endowed with the potentiality

[1]*Frag.* B. 12.
[2]*Frag,* B, 5, 12.
[3]B, 27.
[4]*Timaeus,* 30A.
[5]*Tim.* 41A.

of becoming a substance when it received a "form" (ἐιδος) which made it what it is (i.e. an individual concrete object) as an indissoluble union of matter and form related to each other as potency and act.[1] In them, however, he could find no principle of movement or change, and so he was led to seek a Prime Mover Who is Himself unmoved, as at once the first and final cause of all things. From this original divine source all potentiality received the essence of its being, and, therefore, all nature was potentially divine as the realization of the thought of God Who is Himself supreme Mind.[2]

But so regarded, Deity is just pure actuality so wrapped up in the process of contemplation—"thinking of thinking"—that He is not even aware of the existence of the universe with all its imperfections. The eternal Thinker can be but One, and so monotheism is the logical result of Aristotle's reasoning. But He is so "wholly other," so completely transcendent, that mundane affairs are not His concern. While "all that exists or happens exists or happens for an end," the course of events is not determined by a personal Deity. The God of the Stagirite never leaves the eternal repose in which His blessedness consists, and will and intellect have no place in His unchangeableness. Consequently, for the purposes of religion Aristotelian theism was of little avail until in the Middle Ages it was re-interpreted in terms of Scholastic theology.

It is hardly surprising, therefore, that in the political and social conditions that prevailed after the death of Alexander in 323 B.C., there was a reaction in favour of earlier ideas. The influence of philosophy on popular religious belief and practice in Greece had been relatively slight, and, unlike the Hebrew prophets, neither Plato (or Socrates) nor Aristotle had taken a determined stand against the traditional polytheism, or made any effort to establish a religious monotheism in its place. Their respect for the old gods may have been slight, but their worship was taken for granted and given a place in the ideal social order which they visualized. With the break-up of the old city States and the rise of the new Empire extending to the banks of the Indus, eclectic philosophies fitted into the cosmopolitan society better than the restricted system of a single school. Thus, while the mystery cults provided a vent of religious emotion and a means of genuine spiritual experience, the monism expounded by Zeno in the *Stoa Poikile* at Athens became the guide of life for the more sophisticated.

[1] *Metaphysics*, I, 9, 990, 996ff, VI, 1, 8, XIII, 5.
[2] *Physics*, VIII, 6, 2586, 10ff. *Met.* XI.

Reducing the world to a single eternal substance manifesting itself in spirit and matter, he followed Heraclitus in interpreting the universe in terms of a materialistic monism in which the Aristotelian theory of an active and passive principle existing in all things was introduced, in combination with the λόγος, or reason, of Heraclitus and νοῦς of Anaxagoras.[1] God being the universal-reason (λόγος σπερματικός), or rational principle, permeating the entire universe and overruling its processes to beneficent ends as a divine law or destiny (ἑιμαρμένη), the Stoic philosophy was pantheistic in its trend. Yet fundamentally it was monistic inasmuch as behind the quasi-materialistic conception of ultimate substance (ὕλη) there was that of the divine breath (πνευμα), "the spirit" manifesting itself as "reason." This, taken in conjunction with the doctrine of Providence (πρόνοια)[2]—that all things are governed for the best—made it possible for the Stoics to adapt their theology to the growing tendency in Greece and Rome to exalt Zeus and Jupiter into a position of supremacy above all the other gods. Thus, Cleanthes, who succeeded Zeno, employed monotheistic language in his famous *Hymn to Zeus*:

> "O King of Kings,
> Through ceaseless ages, God, whose purpose brings
> To birth, whate'er on land or in the sea
> Is wrought, or in high heaven's immensity;
> Save what the sinner works infatuate.
> Nay, but thou knowest to make crooked straight;
> Chaos to thee is order: in thine eyes
> The unloved is lovely, who didst harmonize
> Things evil with things good, that there should be
> One Word through 'all things everlastingly'."[3]

But although "Zeus of many names" was represented as "the Ruler of nature" governing all things by law, and Jupiter as "the Ruler and Guardian of the universe," the Lord and Maker of creation,[4] neither of these ancient deities really lost his original significance, and in the rest of the poem traditional beliefs and philosophic ideas are skilfully blended in an abstract Stoic syncretistic

---

[1]Cicero, *De Natura Deorum*, II, 20ff, 45ff.

[2]*Aetius*, I, 27, 5.

[3]James Adam's translation of *Stob.* i, i, 12, in *The Vitality of Platonism*, essay IV (Camb., 1911), p. 105f.

[4]Seneca, *Nat. Quaest.* ii, 45, Virgil, *Aen*, x, 112, iii, 375.

theology. The ancient Sky-gods with their thunderbolts and lightning weapons could be given universal sovereignty without materially altering their earlier character, just as the Roman divinity Fortuna could be equated with the doctrine of Providence.[1] The rest of the pantheon had been allegorized by the earlier Stoics,[2] and it remained for their successors to maintain either that all the gods actually were but different names of one Supreme Being,[3] or that they were lesser supernatural powers (*daemones*) in a divine hierarchy acting as intermediaries between God and man.[4] Thus, the monotheistic tendency in the later period of the Republic was not without its influence on Stoic monism, but it was from a tradition with a very different origin and significance that eventually the movement towards the idea of one sole Deity reached its goal.

While the religions and philosophies so far considered arrived at an absolute or relative conception of divine unity by syncretistic or speculative processes, Judaism, Christianity and Islam followed another road to their respective convictions that God is One and that there is no other. The Hebrew monotheists, unlike the Egyptian, Greek or Roman innovators and philosophers, did not derive their distinctive faith from observation and reflection upon nature, or establish it through the agency of powerful priesthoods or scholarly academies. On the contrary, they were anti-sacerdotal and made no pretence of learning. Completely devoid of metaphysical, scientific or ecclesiastical interests, they were essentially deeply religious men who saw behind all phenomenal existence the one, creative, sustaining, omniscient and omnipotent Will of Yahweh, the righteous Ruler of the universe, Who spake in the thunder, controlled the earthquake and smote His enemies.[5] In one respect only did they claim pre-eminence—viz., that their religious experience was deeper and their spiritual insight clearer than that of the rest of the community.[6] They spake that they did know and testified that they had seen and heard. In short, they were just the type to whom the monotheistic evaluation of the numinous always has made an overwhelming appeal, as against the more intellectualistic animistic and polytheistic tradition, or the mysticism of pantheism.

If it were Moses who rescued from oblivion an ancient High

[1] Warde Fowler, *Roman Ideas of Deity* (London, 1914), p. 61ff.
[2] Cicero, *Nat. Deo.*, ii, 23, 60.
[3] Servius, *ad Georg*, i, 5.
[4] Apuleius, *de Deo Socrates*, 11, 15.
[5] Is. lxv, 17, xli, 4; Ps. v, 25, x, 3ff, cxlvii, 16f.
[6] Amos. vii, 14.

God of the desert peoples and consolidated in and around him the
Hebrew tribes, welding them into the semblance of a nation, the
unique achievement of his successors lay in the ability of a small
minority to maintain the tradition until at length it became the
accepted belief of the entire community. In pre-exilic Israel, as we
have seen, the existence of other local gods among the surrounding
nations and tribes, Moab, Ammon, Edom, Egypt and Syria, was
freely recognized, but in his own domain Yahweh reigned as
the sole Elohim of his people. The struggle between the Canaanite
Baals as the tenants on the Palestinian high-places in the indigenous
vegetation cultus, and the jealous god of the desert tradition, continued until the time of the Exile, and in practice the religion of
Israel was almost as syncretistic as elsewhere in the Ancient East.
Yahweh himself was assigned consorts, and the worship of the
Mother-goddess persisted at Mizpah. Winged serpents (seraphim)
had their recognized place in the temple at Jerusalem, and the
animal names of the officials at the time of the Josiah reformation in
620 B.C.[1] suggest that theriomorphism was by no means unknown
and perhaps officially recognized even in the central sanctuary,[2]
where women weeping for Tammuz and men worshipping the sun
were included in the "abominations" described by Ezekiel in the
first of his series of visions.[3]

The Deuteronomic writer condemns the cult of Baal and Asherah,
and of the heavenly bodies, as well as male and female prostitutes, in
the fertility rites practised in the temple. At the entry were the horses
and chariots of the Sun-god, and to the south of the city children
were passed through the fire to the god Molech.[4] After the death of
Josiah things went from bad to worse,[5] and this is confirmed by the
evidence of the Elephantine papyri in the fifth century B.C. Thus,
in this Jewish colony on the banks of the Nile, three goddesses were
brought into much the same relation with Yahweh as was Ishtar
with Tammuz.

Notwithstanding this stark polytheism and the less blatant
syncretism, the fact remains that in spite of these sporadic relapses
and persistent deflections, the monolatrous minority ultimately
triumphed. Deeply laid in Hebrew religion there was a creative

---

[1] Cf. Huldah meaning a weasel or mole; Achbor and Shaphan, a mouse and
coney resepectively.
[2] Cf. Robertson Smith, Religion of the Semites, p. 625; Is. lxv, lxvi; Ezek. viii, 10ff.
[3] Ezek. viii, 14ff.
[4] II Kgs. xxi, 6, xxiii, 10f.
[5] II Kgs. xxiii, 32, 37, xxiv, 9, 19; Jer. xliv, 17ff.

concept which prevented it from becoming merely a mixture of
two or more elements, and this enabled it to absorb influences from
various sources without being itself absorbed. Long before the
eighth century B.C., when the prophetic movement assumed a new
vigour with the rise of such outstanding personalities as Amos,
Hosea and Isaiah, Yahweh must have secured an assured position in
Israel in accordance with the monolatrous principles laid down by
Moses and consolidated by Elijah. He was recognized as the true
divine Head of the nation which by his mighty acts he had delivered
from slavery in Egypt, and to which he had given victory over its
enemies, guiding and leading his people from the desert to the
Promised Land.

The crisis came, however, when the fortunes of the nation were
reversed, first in the Northern Kingdom and later in Judah. Could
it be that Yahweh had suffered defeat at the hands of the worshippers
of other gods? Here the prophetic movement had provided the
answer in advance of the events. The catastrophes were acts of
divine judgment meted out, it was alleged, to a gainsaying people
who had brought all their troubles upon themselves by their failure
in their allegiance to their jealous god. But even so, if Yahweh was
in any sense the Creator of the universe and the controller of history,
his sovereign rule could not be thwarted or his righteous will frustrated.
Gradually it came to be realized that actually there was only one
God of the whole world, and that this Deity was none other than
the Holy One of Israel. This raised the paradox, how a universal
Deity could also be the god of a particular people and nation.

When the post-exilic priesthood applied itself to this problem
it evolved the theory that while the God Who revealed Himself to
Moses under the name of Yahweh was in fact the omnipotent
Creator of the universe,[1] by a process of absolute divine selection
from the foundation of the world He had deliberately chosen Israel
out of the rest of the nations to be the instrument and agent of His
omniscient Will.[2] Moreover, this paradoxical conclusion had some
justification in the course of events in the Fertile Crescent where
Palestine occupied a central and crucial position geographically,
midway between Mesopotamia and Persia and Egypt and the
Aegean, maintaining itself always on the circumference of the
surrounding great powers.

This made for a measure of independence and for the development

[1] Gen. l, 1–31.
[2] Gen. xvii.

of a distinct tradition animated by the conviction that the vicissitudes of Hebrew history were divinely ordered and controlled. Therefore, they were the chief medium of the revelation of God's will and purpose for and through Israel disclosed to a continuous series of men of outstanding spiritual genius and leadership—Moses, Elijah, Amos, Isaiah, Jeremiah, Ezekiel and the Deutero-Isaiah. This minority movement was carried on in the post-exilic community by a complex priestly and legalistic organization, and under its influence the faith of the entire nation was transformed into an ethical monotheism, interpreted in terms of a theocracy in which the prophetic and priestly traditions reacted on each other under the powerful stimulus of the temple worship. Since this central sanctuary acted as a consolidating force symbolizing all for which the new Judaism stood, once again belief found expression in rite, and Sion became the point on which all the hopes of the nation and the world were concentrated. There the divine purpose would find its fulfilment when all the nations of the world had been forgathered within its sacred precincts to worship in the beauty of holiness the one and only God of the entire earth.[1]

If there is but one God,[2] there can be but one religion, and as Israel alone knows and worships the true universal Deity it must be a light to the nations that salvation may be as wide as the world.[3] It was along this line of approach that Jewish monotheism acquired an eschatalogical outlook and in due course produced within itself a "New Israel" claiming to be the fulfilment of the implications of the prophetic, priestly and apocalyptic movement, embracing the whole of mankind in a universal faith. The unity of God was maintained as a basic doctrine in Christianity so that the relation of the incarnate Christ to the Godhead was conditioned by and remained within the limit of Jewish monotheism, with which Judaic apocalyptic thought was assumed to be in harmony. Jesus in His Messianic role was represented as the embodiment of the divine will and purpose in such a manner as not to conflict with the absolute claims of Yahweh as the sole and supreme living God of prophetic revelation. Having disclosed Himself in His mighty acts in Israel, now, "at the end of these days," He "has spoken in His Son whom He appointed heir of all things, through whom also He made the worlds."[4] This

[1] I Chron. xvi, 29; Is. lx.
[2] Is. xlv, 5.
[3] Is. xlii, 1ff, xlix, 1ff.
[4] Heb. i, 1f.

was the Christian claim which it was maintained fell within the concept of monotheism.

Already in Judaism the conception of Wisdom had been semi-hypostatized,[1] assigned creative functions and brought into close relation with life-giving pneumatic influences.[2] This paved the way for the Philonic interpretation of the Logos as the "first-born" or "elder" Son of God—the thought of God objectified in the universe ($\varkappa \acute{o} \sigma \mu o \varsigma$ $\nu o \eta \tau \acute{o} \varsigma$)[3]—and its Johannine counterpart,[4] where "the Word made flesh" was distinguished from God the Father without any lack of complete union between them. He was in the beginning with God and in God, and having wrought in creation He had become human flesh and was tabernacled with men. Thus, the Logos was no longer regarded as the companion of God, as in Judaism, or as reason or thought, as in Hellenic philosophy. He was with God in a personal loving relationship which transcended all human distinctions.[5] "I and my Father are one." This was the Johannine interpretation of the Logos doctrine in its Christian form, and became the basic assumption of the doctrine of the Trinity when this was formulated in Christian theology.

The conception of Deity in Christianity will be considered in greater detail later.[6] Suffice it to say here that the recognition of distinct hypostases in the Godhead united in a personal relationship one with the other, does not conflict with an absolute monotheism as taught and maintained in Judaism. Nowhere is the single sovereign rule of the one Creator and Sustainer of the universe and Redeemer of mankind more explicitly asserted than in the New Testament and the writings of the Christian Apologists. Even when a polytheistic trend re-appeared with the cultus of the saints in post-apostolic times, special care was taken to distinguish between the worship (*latria*) that may be addressed legitimately alone to God, and the honour and veneration (*dulia*) that may be given to the saints, martyrs and heroes of the faith, or to holy objects. In practice the differentiation often has been very difficult, if not impossible, to maintain, but as the wearisome Christological controversies in the formative period show, every effort was made to safeguard the

[1]Prov. viii, 22–30; Wisd. vii, 24–7; Ecclus. i, 1.
[2]Gen. i, 2; Ex. xxxi, 2.
[3]Phils. *De Opif*, 24–5.
[4]Jn. i, 1.
[5]C. C. J. Webb, *God and Personality* (London, 1918), p. 67.
[6]Cf. p. 155ff.

unity of the Godhead in the official definitions of the Trinitarian faith.

Nevertheless, to such a rigid monotheist as Mohammed, to say that "God is a third of three" appeared to be polytheism, which is hardly surprising since he was under the impression that the Christian Trinity consisted of God, Mary and Jesus, with the archangel Gabriel as the Holy Spirit.[1] Although his central affirmation—"there is no God but Allah"—was derived from Jewish sources (mostly Talmudic), his knowledge of the Hebrew scriptures was as vague and erroneous as was his understanding of Christian theology. This was the result of his having been acquainted with a late form of Judaism in which Mazdaean and Maccabaean eschatology and Rabbinic Midrash featured prominently, together with debased versions of Christianity strongly influenced by Coptic, Gnostic and other heretical accretions. The name Allah probably was derived from *Al Ilah*, "the Deity," related to the Semitic *El, Eloah, Elohim*, as a generic designation of divinity. In breaking away from the highly developed animism and polytheism current in Arabia in the seventh century A.D., the Prophet of Islam took his stand on the absolute unity of the all-wise, eternal, beneficent God, "Allah the Rahman the merciful," omnipotent, omniscient, and compassionate in mercy.[2]

Being neither a philosopher nor a logical thinker, Mohammed was incapable of abstract reflection on, or of giving a clear exposition of, the nature of Deity and the implications of divine sovereignty. Since the attributes of God are beyond comprehension, it was idle to inquire, he maintained, why the omnipotent Allah "leads astray Whom He will and Whom He will He guides aright."[3] "Nothing can befall us", it was said, "but what God hath destined for us."[4] "God will cause Whom He pleaseth to enter into His mercy," and make the wicked more wicked, even as Yahweh hardened the heart of Pharaoh.[5] The essence of Islam, as the name reveals, is submission to the will of God,[6] and the Muslim is he who surrenders himself wholly to Allah as the supreme Cause of all things, which are created after a fixed decree.[7] This leaves little room for human initiative or resistance.

[1]Qur'an, Sura III.
[2]Sura, II, 19, III, 25f.
[3]XIV, 4, LXXVI, 30.
[4]IX, 51.
[5]XXV, 9-12.
[6]III, 17, 11, 106, 125, LXVIII, 35.
[7]LIV, 49.

The outstanding achievement of Mohammed lay in his making of a Meccan High God, Al Ilah, the unifying centre of a movement which was destined to conquer the Persian Empire, spread eastwards to India, westwards along the North African littoral, thence to Spain and France, until the tide was stemmed by the Frankish army at Tours, in A.D. 732. These successful campaigns fostered the belief in the absolute rule of Allah Who waged war like an oriental despot, and before Whom His enemies were powerless. Therefore, when the nature and being of God became questions of theological speculation in later ages, absolute power, will and knowledge were the divine attributes stressed, producing from all eternity an irresistible decree (qada). The Qadarites, however, as against the rigidly predestinarian Jabarites, maintained that man was not subject to divine compulsion, while their scholastic successors, the Mutazalites, urged that the unity and justice of God demanded fair dealing towards his creatures, working out His purpose to beneficent ends. Since all that comes from God is necessarily good, evil must have its source in the human will. But as this seemed to lay a necessity upon God to act in justice, it was rejected by the orthodox in favour of an absolute divine omnipotence and sovereignty which made Allah ultimately responsible for all human actions; man being merely the channel through which the divine will is expressed for good or ill. Al-Ghazali (A.D. 1058-1111) affirmed that nothing happens except by His will in the material world where He reigns supreme, though in the realm of the sensuous and psychical a relative freedom, he allowed, must be recognized. There in mystical union with the divine, the soul as distinct from the body, returns to its source in the supreme Essence, but is neither annihilated nor absorbed.

Al-Ghazali sought a foundation of religious assurance in spiritual experience, and against the Aristotelianism of the theologians (e.g. Aricenna and Averroes) he turned to mysticism to secure union with the God Who had created all things *ex nihilo*, and yet Who was the inner light which illuminated the soul and perfected the character. His influence, however, was not sufficient to check, on the one hand, the tendency in Suffiism towards pantheism in thought and antinomianism in conduct, or, on the other hand, the absolute transcendence so deeply laid in the orthodox tradition of Islam, which made the relation of man to God virtually that of a menial subject to an oriental despot. To Allah the omnipotent and omniscient everyone in heaven and on earth must resign himself willy-nilly,[1]

[1]Sura III, 77.

and demonstrate his faith by explicit obedience to divine commands revealed in the Qur'an and supplemented in the Sunna (orthodox tradition), which is thought to amplify the teaching of the Prophet.

As Otto has pointed out, "in Allah the numinous is absolutely preponderant over everything else" so that the rational and specifically moral aspect of the idea of God never has been able to secure a firm basis.[1] In the presence of the "Mighty One" the overpowering sense of majesty and sovereignty transcend all intellectual and ethical considerations—a feature which incidentally Barthian Christianity shares with Islam. The prophetic movement in Judaism escaped the more extreme implications of divine transcendence by placing the emphasis chiefly on divine righteousness, although in the Tannaitic period thought began to move in the Islamic direction when the absolute supremacy of Yahweh was established.

In Christianity the conception of divine love seeking and saving that which was lost,[2] while it retained personal sovereignty, introduced a paternal and redemptive element in the relationship between the Creator and the creature. By bringing together the justice and mercy of God in a doctrine of salvation, a new attitude towards divine Fatherhood was established. The one and only Ground, Ruler, and Sustainer of the universe stood revealed as "the God and Father of our Lord Jesus Christ" giving Himself to restore a fallen creation and to raise redeemed humanity to a new status of sonship by the spirit of adoption in willing obedience to an all-loving Father.[3] The crux of the problem of ethical monotheism, however, to which attention must now be given, lies in the reconciliation of the benevolence of a loving and all-righteous Creator with the persistence of evil in every phase of the development of the universe.

[1] *The Idea of the Holy*, p. 94, cf. 77.
[2] St. Lk. xv, 4–7, 11–32, Jn. iii, 16; Rom. viii, 32.
[3] Rom. viii, 15; I Jn. iii, 2.

CHAPTER VI

DUALISM

So long as the universe was thought to be under the control of a multiplicity of supernatural agencies, benevolent and malevolent, blessings and misfortunes were attributed to divine favour or hostility according to the nature, will or whim of the beings concerned. Consequently, in the ancient civilizations when the gods were organized into pantheons they tended to be resolved into two clearly defined opposed groups, each struggling against the other. This dualism found expression in the mythology of Ancient Egypt in the enmity between Horus and Seth, reflecting possibly the earlier dynastic struggles between Upper and Lower Egypt.[1] Be this as it may, when the falcon-headed solar Horus, the old rival of Seth, was equated with Horus the son of Osiris, the hostility between the two gods, and all that they represented in the history of the nation, became absolute. Moreover, at a later period the feud was intensified by the conquering Hyksos adopting Seth as the traditional foe of Horus and Osiris, and so increasing his sinister character for the Egyptians. If the Hyksos were of Semitic origin, the stage was now set for the perennial contest of the forces of the beneficent Nile, personified as Osiris, against those of the hostile desert, represented by Seth, to assume the form of a perpetual dualistic battle, interpreted in terms of good and evil.

Therefore, after the restoration of the Egyptian dynasty about 1580 B.C., Seth was allied with Apepi, depicted as a huge serpent, the embodiment of evil and chief of the fiends of darkness, who attacked the Sun-god in his nightly passage through the twelve divisions of the Am-Tuat (underworld), to prevent his rising in the sky at dawn. In the grim subterranean realms the perpetual struggle between light and darkness went on, just as the conflict between abundance and want, life and death, was re-enacted in the seasonal drama in terms of the Horus-Seth myth in its Osirian setting. The protagonists and their respective allies had various names and entered into mortal combat in different frays, but always the ultimate purpose was the same; viz. the victory of benevolence over malevolence. As the

[1] Cf. Breasted, *Ancient Records of Egypt* (London, 1907), Vol. I, p. 66.

victor was the embodiment of Providence (Re-Horus symbolizing the life-giving rays of the sun and the fructifying waters of the Nile) so the enemy was the malign principle as the personification of evil —Seth-Apepi representing the desolation of the desert and the darkness of the nether regions.

In an environment like that of the valley of the Nile or of the Euphrates, characterized by successive seasons of flood and drought, natural conditions readily became anthropomorphized as two antagonistic principles struggling for the mastery and bestowing their respective gifts, good and evil, upon humanity. Thus, in Mesopotamia, as in Egypt, the duality of water and the sun reappeared under the mythopoeic forms of Ea, Marduk and Nabu, and their adversaries, the storm-gods (Enlil and Adad). Even Ishtar, the symbol of the fructified earth, had a more sinister side as she was also represented as the destroyer of life, decreeing the annual death of her lover-son, Tammuz, and causing the consequential decline in vegetation. When Tammuz was identified with Marduk, the solar spring-god and son of Ea, the cosmogonic struggle between good and evil was re-enacted, as we have seen, in the sacred combat at the New Year Festival (Akitu), Marduk playing the role of Tammuz (i.e. Horus) in the defeat of Tiamat (Seth). The king as the incarnation of the divine forces of benevolence was the principal actor in the drama because, as has been explained, it rested with him to conquer the malign powers of death and decay in order that the earth might bring forth her increase, and his kingdom be established in peace and prosperity.

Notwithstanding, however, the prominence in Egypt and Babylonia of the belief in personified evil in opposition to the good, it never assumed the form of a gigantic dualistic struggle in the same proportions as in Iranian Mazdeism. Persian kings ruled by the grace of the Creator of heaven and earth, represented by the *hvareno*, or nimbus of glory, which they shared with the gods as a reward of their perpetual victory over their spiritual enemies. Thus, they became *Sol Invictus*.[1] In India the Vedic king was identified with Indra in a solar capacity and so defeated demons, representing darkness, in order to secure abundance in the land. In the Brahmanas, Mitra was equated with the light of day, especially that of the sun, and subsequently in the Atharvaveda he was said to uncover what Varuna, "the thousand eyes" of right, had concealed. In the Indo-Iranian period Mitra, in the Persian literature, became the omniscient

[1]Cumont, *Mystères de Mithra* (Paris, 1913), p. 93ff.

Guarantor of good faith between man and man, while the place of Varuna was taken by Ahura Mazdah, the Wise Lord, whom Zarathushtra raised to the level of a monolatrous Deity.

In the reforms initiated by the remarkable founder of Zoroastrianism (probably about the seventh century B.C., and therefore contemporary with the prophetic movement in Israel), Mitra dropped out and Ahura Mazdah alone was worshipped to the exclusion of the rest of the Indo-Iranian pantheon. In the earliest Gathas of the Avesta, which may contain the teaching of Zarathushtra, the Prophet appears as the servant of Ahura Mazdah commissioned to struggle on behalf of the pacific Iranian agricultural tribes against the more aggressive pastoral nomads, and to establish the supremacy of the Wise Lord against all rival spiritual beings. In opposition to Ahura Mazdah were arrayed the *daevas*, or demonic spirits, of the wandering tribes, and in due course this dualism found expression in an age-long struggle between good and evil personified as opposed forces, issuing finally in an apocalyptic triumph of light over darkness.

Exactly, how, if at all, the Prophet himself laid the foundations of the subsequent developments of Mazdeism it is difficult to determine in the absence of reliable literary evidence concerning his actual teaching. If the earliest Gathas go back to his time, it would seem that he taught that while Ahura Mazdah was the Supreme God, conceived as essentially good and the author of all beneficence, there existed also two primeval twin-spirits—Spenta Mainyu (Good Thought) and Angra Mainyu (the Lie, also described as the Druj)—with their respective angelic and demonic followers in continual conflict with each other. These became two opposing deities in the later literature, so that, according to the priestly *Vendidah*, Ahura Mazdah created all that was good and Angra Mainyu all that was evil. But when the Druj (Angra Mainyu) became the author of evil is not explained. He appears to have been regarded as coeval with Ahura although not co-eternal with him. Unlike the devil of Christian and Moslem tradition, he was the actual creator of the *daevas* under his control, together with the noxious creatures and serpents, wolves, ants, locusts, and men of diabolical character, disease, magic, witchcraft, extremes of temperature, and all the evils in the world.

This conception of a double creation readily developed into an absolute dualism in the post-Avestan period, when Ahriman was made a rival deity to Ahura Mazdah with a hostile army and supernatural equipment equal to that of his beneficent adversary. Ultimately, however, he was destined to be destroyed at the consummation of all things. Meanwhile, as the Lord of the kingdom of evil and prince of the powers of darkness, he had dominion over all that is vicious and calamitous, from evil spirits and constellations to insects and loathsome pests. Only in omniscience, and ability to destroy the followers of Good Thought, were his powers limited and brought into subjection to those of the Wise Lord. Mazdeism, nevertheless, retained the fundamental doctrine of Zoroastrianism, that at the last evil would be conquered and the good ultimately established.

In the Gathic Avesta the precise relation of the twin-spirits, Spenta Mainyu and Angra Mainyu, to Ahura Mazdah is not very clearly defined, but whether they were regarded as having sprung originally from a shadowy High God hovering somewhere in the background of Iranian religion, as the Zervanists affirmed, or from the unity and indivisibility of the All-wise Lord of the universe who called into being his independent spirits, the one beneficent and the other destructive, the approach was fundamentally dualistic. Even in the Gathic Avesta the Lie is represented as the essence of evil, with some degree of personification, and this is further emphasized in the Mazdaean literature.[1] Consequently, it only remained for the Magi to divide the world into two diametrically opposed and balanced creations—the one the work of Ormazd and the other that of Ahriman —to complete the process.

Exactly how far this Iranian dualism affected post-exilic Judaism is difficult to decide. Prior to the Exile, Yahweh's jurisdiction over his chosen people and their land was unquestioned by the upholders of the desert tradition. While, as we have seen, in the popular cultus the god of Israel in practice tended to become indistinguishable from a local baal, there was no suggestion of two rival Causes at the base of the universe, bisecting creation into two halves, good and evil. Belief in evil spirits, such as the *seraphim*, or winged serpents, *se'irim* (satyrs), *lilith* (a dreaded monster of the night), and the *'aluqah* (ghoul), was widespread among Semitic tribes including the Hebrews. But there is no indication in the pre-exilic literature, or the archæological evidence, that any of these demons was a serious rival in power to Yahweh, challenging his sovereign rule in Israel or endeavouring to pervert his moral government. Their domain was confined for the most part to the desert, or the waste places

---

[1] *Vendidah*, i, 1ff; *Yasht*, x, 97, xiii, 77; *Yasna*, ix, 8, x, 15; *Bândahisû*, i, 1-28.

they haunted, although the serpent, who was regarded as a "demon of the waste" before he was transformed into an angelic being, was venerated in the temple, and apparently in the cultus of the wilderness.[1] In the creation story he was assigned superior knowledge, but there is nothing in the narrative[2] to suggest that he was equated with the Satan of later tradition, still less with the devil as the embodiment of the principle of evil.[3] This association did not occur until the post-Biblical period when speculation about the origin of sin and the Fall of man became a conspicuous feature in the Jewish and Christian apocalyptic literature. It is here, if anywhere, that the influence of dualism may have been felt.

The absolute transcendence of Yahweh in post-exilic Judaism mitigated against attributing to any independent supernatural being the origin of evil.[4] He may have implanted the *yetser-ha-ra*, or evil imagination, in the heart of man,[5] but in the Rabbinical literature it was God Who created two mutually antagonistic powers, the evil within the soul, and the Law without it, man being free to make his choice between them.[6] Ben-Sirach maintained that the grain of evil seed was sown in the heart of Eve and brought death in its trail.[7] This reference back to the Eden catastrophe was an innovation, but it is only in the later book of II Esdras that the transmission of sin to all her descendants is clearly stated.[8] The author of the Wisdom of Solomon goes a step farther declaring that this evil seed was sown by the Devil,[9] thereby unconsciously creating a dualism. Up to. this point the *yetser* had been represented as part of the divine constitution of man.[10] This is more definitely stated in the Midrash *Bereshith Rabba*,[11] but it is never attributed to any external supernatural cause, however much it may assume the form of a malevolent second personality within man seeking his destruction.[12]

In the canonical literature the Satan is a subordinate figure acting under the control of God[13] as a member of the heavenly court

[1]II Kgs. xviii, 4; Num. xxi, 4-9; Is. xiv, 29, xxx, 6, cf. vi.
[2]Gen. iii.
[3]Wisd. ii, 24; Rev. xii, 9.
[4]Amos iii, 6.
[5]Gen. vi, 5.
[6]Ecclus. xv, 11-17.
[7]xxv, 24.
[8]iii, 21f, miv, 30-2, vii, 118.
[9]ii, 23f.
[10]Ecclus. xv, 14f. mxxxiii, 14f, xxxvii, 3.
[11]xxvii, *Kiddushim*, 30b.
[12]Ps. lxxxi, 10; *Shabbat*, 105b.
[13]Job i, 6ff; Lech. iii, 1, 2.

H

permitted to act as "the adversary" to test the integrity of Job. In this role he was a divine agent. Nevertheless, he was the accuser of Israel and responsible for leading David astray.[1] Therefore, once a dualistic conception of good and evil was established, he readily became the Jewish counterpart of the Iranian Ahriman with a host of demons under his command. In the book of Enoch the demonic creation was portrayed as an organized host led by the Prince of Darkness intent on seducing mankind and filling the world with corruption.[2] Thus, from being the Adversary of Israel Satan became the arch-enemy of Yahweh from whom he wrested the control of the whole earth, which henceforth was his domain. His reign was destined to be destroyed ultimately when God became all in all, but in the meantime Satan was virtually the lord of creation.

It is difficult to believe that this reversal of divine omnipotence was a natural development of the prophetic movement and of post-exilic monotheism. A latent dualism, it is true, occurs in the Hebrew doctrine of Yahweh's choice of Israel, but so far from "the world lying in the Evil One," in the Biblical tradition[3] creation had been pronounced "very good." The Jews were merely the divine instrument for the establishment of the divine purpose for mankind and the gathering together of all things to their Creator. With the rise of a new secular tyranny in the days of Antiochus Epiphanes prior to the Maccabaean revolt, doubtless it seemed that demonic supramundane powers were at work in the world attempting to frustrate the teleological designs of Yahweh, however much such efforts ultimately might be doomed to failure. In the book of Daniel each nation (Greece, Persia and Israel) was represented as having a "prince," or guardian angel, as its supernatural protector,[4] very much as in Babylonia cities were associated with particular tutelary gods. Therefore, the stage was set for a gigantic struggle between members of two spiritual hierarchies, with Michael, "one of the chief of the princes," contending on behalf of Israel as a divine agent.[5] If this Danielic dualistic judgment had been influenced by Babylonian and Iranian precedents, the Jewish writer was careful to lay all the emphasis on divine transcendence,[6] and the position

---

[1]I Chron. xxi, 1.
[2]I Enoch. xix, 1f, cf. vi, 5, 7; *Jubilees*, x, 10–13, xi, 4ff, xii, 20; *Testament of the Twelve Patriarchs*; Reuben, iii, 3–6; Simeon iv, 8, 9.
[3]Gen. i, 31.
[4]Dan. viii, 16, ix, 21, 23, x, 13, 21, xii, 1.
[5]x, 5ff, 20f.
[6]ii, 18f, 44, iv, 26, ix, 4.

assigned to the angelic beings was that of subordinate intermediaries between God and man;[1] not rival protagonists in an equally matched struggle between the forces of good and evil.

Despite all that had happened in the vicissitudes of Jewish history, the fact remained that the nation had been preserved and restored, while its powerful neighbours—Assyria, Chaldea and Persia—had risen and fallen one after another. This encouraged the hope of divine intervention on a grand scale in the future to fulfil the promises made to Abraham and his seed in a Messianic reign and angelic mediation in the control of natural events and the government of the world.[2] The despondency, however, that descended upon the Jews in their sorry plight during "the abomination of desolation spoken of by Daniel," and the disillusionment in the Hasmonaean degradation that followed the temporary recovery under the Maccabaean rule, gave rise to misgivings about God's providential care for His chosen people. Yet the deeply laid conviction remained that in some mysterious way the sufferings endured must be redemptive, and through all the misfortunes and ignominy that befell the much-tried nation, the power of Yahweh must be vindicated. Because "the Most High ruleth in the kingdom of men,"[3] at the final consummation His reign will be accomplished and His kingdom of righteousness established.[4]

The Roman domination and the destruction of Jerusalem and the temple in A.D. 70, which brought the Jewish state to an end, shattered, at any rate theoretically, the basis on which the providential omnipotence of Yahweh had been built in the past. In fact, however, Judaism survived the disaster and remained an entity, and its faith in its mission in the world enabled it to stand in the evil day. The basic belief in the sovereignty and justice of God never wavered, although the dualism of the apocalypses became more firmly established as the power of evil intensified the spirit of pessimism in a perverse world. God and Satan, the angelic hosts and the demonic hordes, heaven and hell, the upper and lower worlds, children of light and children of darkness, were contrasted, together with a corresponding duality in human nature of spirit and flesh, soul and body.[5] But in the very worst periods in Jewish history the

---

[1] vii, 16, viii, 16, ix, 22.
[2] *Jubilees*, iii, 15, iv, 15, x, 12, xviii, 9, xix, 3, xxxii, 21, xxxv, 17, xli, 24, cf. *Ber.* 51; *Sanh.* 38; *Yeb.* 16b; *Yom.* 36; *Bab-bathra*, 74; *Pes.* 118.
[3] Dan. iv, 17, 25.
[4] ii, 31–4, xii, 12f.
[5] Enoch xlviii, 7, cviii, 7–11; Apoc. Abraham xxiff; Wisd. ix, 12.

powers of evil were never accredited with an authority and status equivalent to those of Yahweh, Whose sovereignty over the universe was steadfastly maintained.

In the Rabbinical literature the assertion of the fundamental dogma of the unity of God left no room for dualism, and in the Haggada of the Talmud and Midrash, in the more fantastic legends of good and bad angels Satan remained a fallen creature of God.[1] Even in the esoteric mystical doctrines of the Kabbala all existences were represented as divine emanations from the Supreme Being (En-Sof, the Boundless), although the multiplication of angels and demiurges led to Satan being elevated virtually to the position of Ahriman in Mazdeism as the leader of the forces of evil. The universe was divided into a 'right side' associated with light, and a 'left side' identified with darkness. But evil was essentially finite, an appearance, the goal of all existence being reabsorption in God, very much as the Talmudic Aristotelian Maimonides denied the positive reality of evil, regarding it merely as the absence of good, the condition in which the world was created, as described in Genesis i.31.

Behind these medieval Jewish speculations lay the age-long philosophic problem of reconciling two radically different kinds of being, or substance, in a universe grounded in a single ethical and beneficent divine unity. This question had exercised the mind and imagination of such pre-Socratic thinkers in Greece as Parmenides and his followers of the Eleatic school, who, in maintaining a monistic universal unity of being as the only eternal and unchangeable Reality, reduced all becoming to illusory appearance, as against the pluralistic dualism of Empedocles, Anaxagoras and Democritus. By making the world to consist of materialistic elements—fire, water, air and earth—these empiricists distinguished between mind and matter, perception and the thing perceived, the void and the plenum, while the Pythagoreans made a similar distinction between the principles of good and evil, corresponding to the contrast of soul and body. Plato recognized the existence of two or more souls responsible for cosmic movements and so explained the disorder and irregularity in a universe which was fundamentally orderly and good. The "best soul" could not be the only source of motion though it was the supreme cause.[2] But an absolute dualism was ruled out inasmuch as nowhere was it suggested that a bad "world-soul" existed, any more than in his doctrine of Forms were two

[1]*Bereshith Rabba*, iii; *Yalk. Shim*, 68; *Pirke d. Rabbi Eliezer*, 13.
[2]*Laws*, 896E–898D.

disconnected worlds postulated; a realm of ideas ultimately real absolutely distinct from an unreal realm of sensible appearances, as in oriental dealistic dualisms.

Nevertheless, in the thought of Plato the problem remained unsolved. The eternal pattern was the supreme reality, the sum total of all Forms which, conceived as a whole, was the ideal model of what ought to be. But the idea of the Good and the doctrine of God as the highest ethical ideal developed independently in his mind so that the conception of providential beneficence was never completely reconciled with the existence of evil. Although God was the transcendent sanction of morality, He was not *the* Good, having its own being as the source of the pattern which He followed in His creation of the world. A demiurgic principle of order and harmony contended with recalcitrant "necessity" from which evil was derived by the soul identifying itself with disorderly motion.[1] Thus, matter became the source of evil but God was exonerated from any complicity because he was only responsible for the good motions.[2] Evil was pure negation (μὴ ὀύ), being that by which the world fell short of good,[3] but, unlike Aristotle, Plato never attempted to get behind the idea of God as the Supreme Soul to that of an Unmoved Mover as the ultimate Source of all movement.

In substituting a metaphysical dualism of Form and Matter, of Actuality and Potentiality, for the Platonic conception of a world of sense distinguished from a world of intellect, Aristotle still drew a fundamental distinction between soul and body (i.e. the active and the passive νους), even though he regarded the body as the instrument rather than the prison-house of the soul, each being an integral part of the individual. Since God was pure actuality, the Prime Mover wholly unaware of the universe He initiated, He stood completely outside and apart from the phenomenal order. Therefore, although evil was regarded as a necessary element in continual change to which matter was subject, its real existence was denied, as was its place in the eternal, immutable Cause.[4] But precisely why it exists was not explained, and an Unmoved Mover knowing nothing of human aspirations in an imperfect world, could hardly be an ethical Creator. Indeed, in maintaining a difference in kind between the two worlds he postulated, Aristotle arrived at a dualism

[1] *Theset*, 176A.
[2] *Tim.* 42.
[3] *Repub.* V, 477A.
[4] *Met.* XII, ix, 1074b.

far more absolute than any such trend that can be attributed to
Plato. Similarly, the Stoic endeavour to overcome this difficulty
inherent in the Platonic-Aristotelian philosophy, was no more
successful since, starting from a materialistic monism in which matter
alone existed, a dualistic active and passive element in all things was
as unresolved as in Aristole's efficient and material causes.

In all these systems which directly or indirectly influenced
Judæo-Alexandrianism in the centuries immediately preceding and
following the beginning of the Christian era, and its subsequent
developments in medieval Judaism, the sharp distinction between
matter and spirit, the dual nature of man and the two opposing
cosmic principles of good and evil, were as fundamental as they were
in Orphism, Mazdeism and Pythagoreanism. In Alexandria a large
and influential Jewish colony had sprung up in which oriental and
Hellenic thought mingled. In his attempt to harmonize Plato and
Moses, Philo, in the opening years of the Christian era, represented
God as a wholly transcendent metaphysical Absolute standing apart
from the world like an oriental monarch, and brought into relation
with inert formless matter through a series of intermediary divine
emanations (lógoi) regarded sometimes as Platonic Ideas or Stoic
Forces (δυνάμεις), sometimes as angelic beings. In this dualism
the body was mortal, evil and obstructive, from which the divine
spirit must endeavour to escape by disciplining the fleshly integument and making it subservient to its immortal tenant,[1] in order to
attain the beatific vision.

Plotinus in the next century (204-269 A.D.) went a step farther
in the direction of complete transcendence by making the Absolute
not only ineffable perfection but beyond all knowledge and reason.
He interpreted the moral struggle within metaphysically as a
division of the world into a good principle and a principle of evil
corresponding to the conflict between Ormazd and Ahriman,
light and darkness. To bridge the gap between metaphysical
monism and ethical dualism Plotinus postulated a graded series of
emanations progressively falling away from an original perfection,
to take the place of the Philonic logoi and the apocalyptic angelogy
and demonology.

In the lowest scale of existence (i.e. in the material world),
which was thought to be devoid of all reality, as the image and
shadow of a shadow, the moral standard was essentially dualistic,
although it was transcended by a monistic existential standard in

[1]De Somn. ii, 353; De Alleg. leg. iii, 29ff.

which all things were measured in relation to an inner harmony striving to attain likeness to God.[1] As this was neutral rather than actually malevolent, it did not equate matter with the evil principle, as among the Pythagoreans or in the case of Philo. It was a necessary condition of all good, being acted upon either for good or bad ends, and was "potentially all things."[2] In so far as it is real, all reality is good, it was contended, and matter, at the bottom of the scale of imperfection, is the principle of evil which infects to greater or less extent the lower stage of material existence. But it is a necessary stage in the two hierarchies of value and existence which ultimately meet in the Absolute. As the phenomenal world has its being through a falling away from the One, so the soul longs to return to the Source of its origin—"a flight of the alone to the Alone"—freeing itself from the dead weight of matter. Thus, the Neoplatonic solution of the problem of evil lay in a process of self-salvation in which the immortal element (i.e. mind and soul) in man seeks to purify and elevate itself through the ascending scale of values until it loses all thought, desire and activity, all individual life, in an ecstasy of immediate union with God where evil ceases to operate.[3]

It was in this atmosphere of Hellenistic dualism that the Christian Apologists endeavoured to re-state and interpret their own doctrine of redemption. For the original followers of Jesus and their converts during the opening years of the era, the philosophical problem did not arise. They were content to accept without question the Jewish conception of creation, and the apocalyptic theory of the fall of man, on which they superimposed their own interpretation of the Messianic hope. The Kingdom had come with power by a fresh act of divine intervention, and although its final consummation was yet to be realized—and this might occur at any moment—"the life of the age to come" was an experienced reality here and now because the omnipotent Deity had already established the reign of God on earth.[4] Consequently, the Kingdom of Satan had been attacked, and it was only a question of time before it would be subdued.[5] So far from God having abdicated and left the world to its own devices, He was more active than ever in His control of history since eternity had broken into the time-process through the Incarnation, so that the

---

[1] *Enneads*, V, 9, 1; 1, 2, 1.
[2] VI, 5, 5.
[3] En. VI, 9, II, 9, 4, III, 6, 6, V, 3, 17.
[4] St. Mk. i, 15, 24, iii, 11, v, 7.
[5] St. Mk. iii, 22, 30, v, 1–20, Mt. xii, 22–37, xi, 14–23.

temporal order had acquired an eternal significance it did not formerly possess.

This optimistic faith in a fresh outpouring of divine power and grace in a mighty redemptive act was an assurance of divine sovereignty which carried with it as a corollary the belief in a moral order—a distinction between good and evil eternally valid lying at the heart of all things, carrying with it the conviction of a final triumph of good in a new order yet to be established. The God Who "rides upon the storm," "sits upon the flood" and "remains a King for ever," had vindicated His power by the latest and only complete act of redemption. The Incarnate Christ as a cosmic Figure by His resurrection had wrought a mighty deliverance, it was declared, incomparably greater than anything that had been accomplished by divine intervention in the course of history in the past.[1] His lordship was established for ever so that the glory of God was seen for all time in the face of Jesus Christ.[2]

The fall of Jerusalem in A.D. 70, which shattered the temporal hopes of the Jews, confirmed the Christians in their apocalyptic faith, putting a divine imprimatur on the Messiahship of Jesus. The end of the Old Dispensation was symbolized by the tradition of the rending of the veil of the temple at the crucifixion.[3] The delay of the Parousia, however, led to a new vision of the Kingdom as a visible divine organization commissioned to carry on the sovereign rule of God on earth until the return of Christ in power and glory. This involved intensified missionary activity and the spread of the Church in the Roman world. But to vindicate its faith and claims in the Empire it must needs adapt its message to the current modes of thought. Men like Tertullian might regard the encroachments of philosophy with suspicion, but others—e.g. Justin Martyr, Clement of Alexandria and Origen—had been philosophers before they were Christians. They had sought for truth as Stoics, Peripatetics or Pythagoreans; but without success. Now in the religion of Christ they had found the goal of their seeking. To justify their newly found faith to their own day and generation they must present it as the true philosophy of the true life, but in the absence of a Christian metaphysic this involved a reinterpretation of the existing systems.

Already, it would seem, Gnosticism had attempted to capture

[1]Rom. x, 9.

[2]II Cor. iv, 6, cf. W. K. L. Clarke, *New Testament Problems* (London, 1929) p. 145f, Bousset, *Kyrios Christos* (Göttingen, 1013), p. 5.

[3]St. Mk. xv, 38, Mt. xxvii, 51, Lk. xi, 47, 51, xix, 41-4, xxiii, 45; Rev. xxi, 1f, 22.

the new religion in the interests of Graeco-Oriental dualism in which Christ was represented as the Divine Being who had descended into an alien sphere to save the imprisoned divine element in man, and bring it back to the higher world which was its proper abode. Postulating two creations, the Christian Gnostics (as against the pro-Jewish section of the movement) maintained that the inferior god responsible for the material universe with all its imperfections was the god of the old Israel, who had under his dominion one of the divine powers who had fallen into the lower world by a sinful aberration. It was this fallen power which constituted the divine element in man, or in a section of mankind. To rescue this divine element and restore it to the heavenly sphere, "the Saviour" descended and took up his abode in Jesus. But 'the Saviour' was always distinct from the historical Christ, whether he was regarded as quitting the body of his protégé before the crucifixion, or in some other way reducing the sufferings of the passion to an illusion.

The central idea of Gnosticism, as of all mystery religions, was that of redemption, and behind all the various systems and sects lay the dualistic conception of deliverance from the material world, regarded as intrinsically evil. The different forms which the series of aeons and demiurges took were merely attempts to bridge the gulf between the evil world and the impassible Deity, and whether Gnosticism be regarded as a syncretism which arose out of the breaking up of the pagan religions, or a movement within Christianity, as Burkitt suggests,[1] it represented an attempt to grapple with the problem of dualism, and to make the Church think out its position in relation to a wider metaphysic and cosmology. Although its affinities were with religion rather than with philosophy, it raised philosophical questions , and the Church never went back to the earlier unphilosophical Judaeo-Christianity, which would have rendered it incapable of making any lasting impression on the Gentile world.

Thus, with the rise of the catechetical school at Alexandria under Clement (150-215) and his pupil Origen (185-254), a Christian Platonism took shape which endeavoured to re-state the Faith in a manner which appealed to the common sense of all serious thinkers and intelligent men of the age. Moreover, as Harnack says, the Alexandrians "contrived to use the positive material of tradition, including the life and worship of Christ, in such a way as to furnish this reasonable religion with a confirmation and proof that had

[1] *Church and Gnosis* (Camb., 1932), p. 25ff.

hitherto been eagerly sought but sought in vain."[1] In refuting
Gnostic dualism they fell back on the Hebrew creation stories and
the Logos idea, as against the Demiurge doctrines, but they failed
to bring into conjuction Platonic transcendence and the Christian
conception of creative love. They insisted, however, that the universe
was a divine creation ruled providentially towards the establishment
of ultimate good and that man was a free moral agent, despite the
prominence of opposing Satanic powers. In the end the Devil and
all his works would be destroyed, and God would be all in all.[2]

The Church inherited from apocalyptic Judaism a developed
belief in demonology in which physical disease and death, as well as
moral transgression, were ascribed to personal demoniacal sources
presided over by Satan as the enemy and perverter of mankind.[3]
The underlying dualism in the thought of St. Paul is revealed in his
doctrine of the Two Adams,[4] and his sharp distinction between "the
flesh" and "the spirit",[5] though it was in a measure resolved by his
firm conviction that the forces of evil eventually must be destroyed,
and the victory of God in Christ become complete.[6] Then the
absolute divine sovereignty would be vindicated. The Pauline
dualism, therefore, was only relative and temporary. But at the end
of the first century, in the Johannine cosmology, the evil world was
set against the world of life and light in a manner suggestive of a
more fundamental cleavage,[7] which, under Alexandrian influences,
readily became two opposed realms with their respective spiritual
forces in perpetual conflict.

The reign of Antichrist with his hierarchy of demons henceforth
became an established doctrine in the Early Church as an elaborate
mythology, largely of Oriental origin, was formulated around the
picturesque figure of the fallen Lucifer and his host as a foil to the
Redeemer. In Babylonia about the middle of the third century a
semi-Christian movement with Gnostic and Mazdaean affinities arose
based on the eternal conflict between good and evil, light and darkness. Man was represented as "a particle of light enclosed in an alien
irredeemable envelope," created by the Devil to imprison the

---

[1] *History of Dogma* (London, 1894), Vol. II, p. 170.

[2] Clem. of Alex. *Str.*, VI, 16, *Origen de Princip. Praef.*, i, ii, 11, i, iii, ix, 111, v;
Contra Cel. VI, 49–61.

[3] Ephes, ii, 2, vi, 12; I Cor. x, 19f; Mk. iii, 22, iv, 24, xvii, 15; Mt. ix, 34, xii, 24;
Lk. xi, 15, vi, 18; viii, 2; Rev. xii, 7ff.

[4] I Cor. xv, 45ff; Rom. v, 14f.

[5] Rom. xii, 1; I Cor. v. 19; II Cor. iv, 16.

[6] I Cor. xv, 28.

[7] I Jn. ii, 15ff, v, 19.

luminous particles more closely in the material world.[1] To effect escape from this earthly entanglement a life of rigorous asceticism was required, and when this developed into a dualistic sect it became a serious rival to orthodox Christianity, numbering among its adherents the youthful Augustine, before he discovered a more excellent way under the tutelage of Ambrose at Milan.

The twelve years which the future bishop of Hippo spent as an *auditor* (catechumen) of Manichaeism were not without their influence on his approach to the problem of evil. His own violent intellectual and ethical struggles set against his Manichæan-Neoplatonic background, led him to the conviction that evil is a tremendous power in the world requiring explanation in terms of an ultimate metaphysic and redemptive theology. Against the Manichees he maintained that existence is good fundamentally because, as Plotinus had affirmed, there is no substance which has not proceeded from God Who is the unchangeable Good.[2] Therefore, if to be is good, goodness is a positive quality and evil is a negative state, a loss of good. But since evil has not substance it was not created by God, still less is it a divine quality or attribute. The phenomenal world being a divine creation *ex nihilo*, it cannot be inherently evil. But since created things are mutable they are capable of falling away from the supreme and immutable Creator, and by relapsing into not-being, as the converse of being, they partake of evil as a *corruptio*, or defect of good, as darkness is a defect of light.[3] Only good really exists since evil is a negative quality, and where its relationship with good ceases it comes to an end.[4] While nature and the world are good fundamentally,[5] only in so far as all things conform to the will of their Creator do they partake of His unchangeable goodness. Inasmuch as evil also is inherent in mutability, there is a tendency to corruption in the phenomenal order—to return to the nothingness out of which it was created. By wrong choice natural processes originally good are liable to become perverted, and to save the principle of free will, at this point in his reasoning Augustine turned to theology to complete his metaphysical argument.

Nevertheless, in Augustine the philosopher and Augustine the

[1]F. C. Burkitt, *The Religion of the Manichees* (Camb., 1925), p. 39.
[2]*De Natura Boni*, 1; *Confessions* VII, 9–12.
[3]*De Gen. contra Manich.* i, 4; *In Psalm*, VII; *Confess.*, VII, 12–13; *Contra Ep. Fund*, 35; *Contra Julianum*, I, 8; cf. Plotinus, *Ennead*, I, 8, I, III, 2, 5,
[4]*Enchiridion*, 4, 10; *Confess.*, III, 7, VII, 12.
[5]*De Trinitate*, VIII, 3.

theologian and ecclesiastic, two strains of thought opposed one another. The new theological standpoint involved more or less a collision with the old metaphysical approach. On philosophical grounds he had arrived at the nature of the self as active will. This he now proceeded to interpret in Pauline terms in relation to the "Two Adams" as "two wills," in the light of his own "twice born" religious experience. The first man, he argued, was free to adopt what course he chose, but by deliberately turning away from righteousness, the entire human race, by virtue of its seminal identity with Adam, became corrupted. Henceforth man was determined to sin and doomed to eternal death.[1] The will now became so completely under the dominion of lust that it was incapable of doing the good it would except by the supernatural aid of divine grace mediated through the Church at Baptism. Consequently, the heathen and unbaptized infants were automatically damned as a result of their corrupt inheritance.[2]

It is unfortunate that in postulating "two wills," and resting his theological speculations on a mythological foundation, the Bishop of Hippo was led astray, since in recognizing that moral evil is rooted in human volition he made a new departure in the ethical and psychological approach to the problem. Moreover, he had a deeper understanding of human nature than his opponent Pelagius, on the one hand, and of the Gnostic-Manichaean dualists, on the other hand. Man equipped with a new sense of personality and moral agency grounded in the will, and regarded as a being created in the image of God, could not be part of an independent evil creation, or a divine emanation destined to be absorbed into a monistic Absolute as a vague abstraction beyond all comprehension. His acceptance of the doctrine of the Incarnation made impossible the belief that the material and the divine are in ultimate opposition, and so now evil appeared as the absence of the good, which belongs to the nature of all created things.[3]

In rejecting all forms of a dual origin of the world, Christian theologians maintained that the universe was created *ex nihilo*,[4] and thereby affirmed that all things owe their existence to God and are dependent upon Him. Nevertheless, by granting a measure of freedom to man they allowed for the relative independence of human

---

[1] *Ad Simplic.* I, q, 1, 2, 4, 10, 16; *De Peccat. Meritis*, I, 29; *De Nuptis et Concep*, I, 1, 22.

[2] *Retract*, II, 42; *Ep.* CLXVI, 3, 4.

[3] Cf. Aquinas, *De Malo* Q, ii, 4, 2; *Contra Gentiles*, III, ix, x.

[4] Irenaeus, *Haer.* IIx, 3, 4; Anselm, *Monolog.*, ix, Denzinger *Enchiridion*, 428 (355).

action and choice absent in Oriental dualism and the conception of emanation. Similarly, the Platonic distinction of body and soul, although recurring in a modified form in the Pauline differentiation of flesh and spirit, was resolved when the Aristotelian principle of body and soul constituting one personality was adopted by St. Thomas in the thirteenth century. By introducing into the physical organism an individual substance divinely created *ex nihilo*, the Scholastic doctrine made the soul intrinsically independent of the body but extrinsically dependent on it in the sense that the divinely created spiritual essence was so inseparably related to the material integument as to constitute one substantial unity, or personality, under the conception of form and matter.[1] This Thomist anthropology raises its own problems, but it avoided a fundamental dualism.

The growth of asceticism, however, under the powerful influence of monasticism, not only made a rigid distinction between the secular and the sacred, interpreted in terms of life in "the world" and in "religion," but gave a new emphasis to the overwhelming power of the Devil and his agents in time and space. The Pauline precept that he who would walk in the Spirit "must turn away from the works of the flesh,[2] became regarded as a battle with the body and its lusts in which demons strove to destroy the soul. The biographies of the medieval monks are full of such dualistic combats, and of the means adopted to mortify the physical appetites and crucify the body in order to save the soul from the assaults of its enemies. The Biblical opposition of the earthly and the heavenly was transformed into a gigantic struggle with Satan as the lord of the world, whose power was so absolute that, in the opinion of Wycliffe, the earth must obey him.[3] Luther regarded him as the most potent force on earth; a belief that continued for at least two centuries after the Reformation.

As pagan deities were regarded as demons, it was believed that they were able to incite men to practise magic, and from the fourth century there were instances of a deliberate pact being made with the Devil. Popular notions of this kind, borrowed from paganism, which included aerial flights of women with Diana, Herodias and other diabolical figures, including *incubi* and *succubae*, developed into an organized cultus (e.g. the Cathari, Luciferians or Palladists)

[1] *Summa Theol.* I, q, 4, 12; *Contra Gentiles*, II, 80.
[2] Gal. v, 10ff.
[3] *De Domino divino*, 1375.

in which Satan was worshipped as a god of light, as a reversal of the normal dualism. In the later Middle Ages an esoteric ritual was established with its Sabbaths, Black Masses and Festivals, characterized by sexual perversions, and every imaginable species of debauchery, which in the form of witchcraft lingered on as an underground movement into the eighteenth century. Although the Church endeavoured to discountenance and suppress these superstitions, the existence of demons who incited men to evil was officially recognized. Bull after bull was issued by the Papacy against sorcery as an established custom, but the Scholastic theology gave support to many of the beliefs on which the movement rested. Indeed, it was not until the seventeenth century that scepticism became general,[1] and in the next century Wesley was still a firm believer in witchcraft.

The conditions that prevailed in medieval Europe—hunger, plague, war, heresy and a low moral standard among the illiterate—constituted a fruitful soil for the growth of demonology, supported by confessions extracted under torture, and the genuine hallucinations of overwrought monks. Miss Murray has overstated her case in trying to prove that the witch-cult in Western Europe was a Dianic religion which was superseded by Christianity and then revived as a rival hierarchy with its own divinities, church and worship,[2] since it was not until the fourteenth century that the Church branded the practice as a heresy punishable by death. But while it is difficult to believe that an organized secret society of the kind she describes ever existed, medieval Satanism doubtless was of pagan origin and owed much to the dualistic doctrines of the Gnostics, the Manichees and the Albigenses,[3] before it was incorporated in the demonological systematizations of such writers as John of Salisbury, Gervase of Tilbury and the Schoolmen. From the days of the Apostles to those of the Curé d'Ars, a personal malign power had seemed to be rampant in a perverse world in perpetual conflict with Christ and His spiritual allies,—St. Michael and later the Virgin, with their angelic hosts. Thus, Satan became a serious rival to the Deity, and, as Mr. C. S. Lewis has remarked, hardly less powerful and much more interesting than God.

[1]Cf. J. Glanvill, *Sadducismus Triumphatus* (1681), Hutchinson, *Historical Essay Concerning Witchcraft* (1718).

[2]M. A. Murray, *The Witch-Cult in Western Europe* (Oxford, 1921). For a recent somewhat fantastic application of the theory, cf. H. R. Williamson, *The Arrow and the Sword* (London, 1948).

[3]R. L. Thompson, *History of the Life of the Devil* (1929), p. 86ff; L. Coulange, *Life of the Devil* (London, 1929), p. 143ff.

Black Magic in the Middle Ages, however, was regarded as fundamentally anti-social and as such was condemned equally by Church and State. Both institutions made every effort to discountenance and suppress diabolical heresies and pagan practices, not because they represented a rival religion but on account of their repellent nature and characteristics. If there was a dualistic strain in the popular mind which found an outlet in the cult of demons, care was taken to subordinate the diabolical forces to those of the Lord and His saints, and to reduce their rites to blasphemous parodies and perversions of Christian worship, like those of the Waldenses, the Templars and other heretical sects. Ultimately all things were grounded in the one, infinite, self-existent, righteous and beneficent Creator beside Whom a rival eternal world could have no rightful place except as a lower order of derivative creation. But a living personal God upon Whose sovereign Will all things depend, cannot be confined in His creative activities to a universe of time and space and history. We know the Infinite, St. Thomas Aquinas declared, in and through finite beings, and the existence of one kind of created personality makes reasonable the supposition that other personal spirits, equipped with a relative independence and freedom, have their place and function in the divine scheme. Therefore, behind the naïve mythological speculations of apocalyptic and medieval angelology and demonology there lies an unexplored and mysterious domain of spiritual reality which, rightly understood and kept in proper proportions, does not conflict with the conception of divine unity; though admittedly it may readily become a crude dualism when assigned a position co-existent with God.

The theist must insist that all creation is due to the will of the sole Creator Who is the single ultimate Ground of the universe so that all existence—the evil as well as the good—falls within His jurisdiction. But when to this is added the conviction that the Ultimate Reality constituting the unifying principle is essentially ethical and beneficent, the presence of evil as an integral element in the phenomenal order becomes a riddle that has tortured the mind of man ever since it first began to reflect upon the problems of existence. The dualistic solution conflicts with the unity of the universe and with the ethical character of its theistic ground, since if evil is the work of some rival god or spirit who was responsible for making and ordering the material world, or the malevolent element in it, there cannot be a single almighty, all-good Creator. Similarly, Plato's conception of God as the will for good limited on the one hand by rational principles of order (cf. *Philebus*), and on the other by "discordant and disorderly motions" (cf. *Timaeus*) in the Ideas or Pattern out of which He fashioned the cosmos, leaves us with only a good God Who desires "that, so far as is possible, all things should be good and nothing evil."[1]

Or, again, Descartes's unqualified dualism of mind and body, with their irreconcilable attributes of thought and extension, led to a principle of causality from which even the penetrating intelligence of Kant failed to produce a cohesive Ultimate Reality behind phenomena in the noumenal world of "things-in-themselves." All he could postulate was "a world-architect who would always be greatly limited by the suitability of the stuff with which he works."[2] The inward law of goodness required, he felt, a Power behind the universe Who is essentially righteous and complete in Himself, but since this "necessary Being" lay beyond human knowledge, it left the problem of evil unsolved.

Nevertheless, both Plato and Kant recognized that evil is a complex phenomenon made up of a great variety of qualities and conditions ranging from physical disorders and catastrophes, through pain and suffering, to moral wickedness. Furthermore, they were agreed that of all the different forms it may take, the only aspect which is fundamentally bad in itself is that described by the theist as "sin," proceeding from perverse volition. Moral evils ought not to be because no rightful place can be found for them in an orderly and beneficent universe. Many of the other ills of life can be shown to have some useful and even edifying purpose, either as warnings of imminent dangers, disciplinary measures, aids to higher ethical ends, or (in the language of the absolute Idealists) as "incomplete goods." In short, most of the things regarded as "physical evils" are good for something, whereas moral evil is good for nothing, and, therefore, contrary to the mind and purpose of an ethical Creator.

Where, then, is its source to be sought? If, following St. Augustine, it be relegated to the human will and the endowment of freedom of choice as an essential quality of moral beings, some limitation is thereby imposed on divine activity. But inasmuch as it is a self-imposed condition it does not presuppose divine finitude. When the material universe was called into existence and moral beings were created within it, equipped with intelligent wills and

[1] *Tim.*, 30A.
[2] *Critique of Pure Reason*, E.T. by N. K. Smith (New York, 1929), A627.

the power of free choice, the possiblity of the emergence of evil could not be avoided in the very nature of the case. Things were liable to occur which were not and are not directly ordained by the Creator, however much they may be under His supreme control, so far as ultimate ends are concerned. But being contingent upon that which was created fundamentally good and essentially ethical, evil can only be imputed to Deity in the sense that by creating a moral order under conditions of time and space, with good as the positive category, inevitably He opened the way for its negative quality to arise. But this does not suggest the existence of an Evil Being or Principle co-equal and co-eternal with the primal Good. On the contrary, evil being contingent upon good and capable of transmutation into good, cannot be on the same level of reality and permanence. Therefore, notwithstanding its power and influence in the world of experience, the prevailing conviction of reflective mankind has been that it exists to be overcome in a teleological moral order, fundamentally ethical and beneficent, grounded in a single God Who is good.

CHAPTER VII

THE PHILOSOPHY OF THEISM

FOR our present purpose the term 'theism' will be used as a convenient designation for a philosophical conception of Deity as the single, personal, ultimate Ground of the universe and Source of all existence, distinct from polytheism, pantheism and dualism, and also from the more specifically prophetic interpretations of monotheism. Thus understood, theism is opposed to a plurality of independent gods, or rival divine principles, to a metaphysical Absolute, to a limited, finite, emerging Deity, and to a deistic First Cause existing outside and alongside the world and its processes and affairs. Standing between the two extremes of a wholly transcendent, extramundane, unconditioned Being, and an equally completely intramundane, immanental principle, essence or substance in which God and the world are emerged in a pantheistic unity, theism represents the Creator as the sovereign Ruler of all things, and yet at work in the universe He has called into being, ordering the course of events in accordance with His will and purpose. As the most real Being, the ground and unity of all that is other than Himself, He is distinct from the phenomenal order. As the intelligent self-conscious Will and the highest good, He is the living unity of existence and value, in vital relationship with His creation.

The first serious attempt to establish a philosophical theology was made when Plato and his immediate predecessors broke away from the Olympian tradition in Greece and postulated God as the ultimate reality responsible for the orderly motions of the universe. But, as we have seen, it was not until the Christian era that the Platonic supremely "good Soul" was transformed into a genuinely theistic conception of Deity, under the influence first of Plotinus and his school, and more specifically by the Christian Platonists and St. Augustine. The foundations having been laid by the Alexandrian and Cappadocian Fathers, St. Augustine, with his Neoplatonic background and a metaphysic of personal religious experience, based his philosophy on the fact of self-consciousness, "existentially," as might be said to-day. "It is beyond question," he affirmed, "that I exist, and that I know that existence. In these truths there is nothing

130

to fear from the argument of the academies: what if you are mistaken? Even if I am mistaken, I am. One who does not exist cannot possibly be mistaken."[1] From this presupposition he argued that this is not a consciousness of the self alone. It carries with it an immediate apprehension of an external Creator because it is the self-consciousness of a creature limited, created, dependent and finite.

It was this self-knowledge of God that Anselm regarded as an absolute concept which all rational minds must believe by virtue of their rationality, once the fact of Deity is realized. Since Plato had already demonstrated that the apprehension of Being is the proof of Being as a necessary condition of valid metaphysical thought, it remained for Anselm to postulate in the mind the idea of a Being than which nothing greater can be conceived, to establish an onto-logical argument for divine existence.[2] Either God is the Ultimate Reality or a self-contradictory idea, inasmuch as it was not for the Abbot of Bec a question of an idea in the mind having its counter-part in reality, as Gaunilo and Kant imagined, but that this *unique* concept is an essential apprehension of the mind—a profound inward mental experience. Doubt about the existence of Deity is possible, it was argued, only so long as the true meaning of the term was not understood, the idea of Deity being different from all other ideas in its perfection. But, as Dr. Collingwood has pointed out, "what the ontological argument proves is not that because our idea of God is an idea *id quo maius cogitari nequit* therefore God exists, but that because our idea of God is an idea *id quo maius cogitari nequit*, we stand committed to belief in God's existence."[3] To define the concept of Deity does not solve the problem of the metaphysical reality, or in the idiom of Anselm, that He exists *in re* as well as *in intellectu*.

Thus, St. Thomas Aquinas did not hesitate to deny *a priori* the possibility of the non-existence of God,[4] notwithstanding the weight of the evidence he himself produced to prove divine existence *a posteriori* by reasoning from effect to cause. Starting from the Aristotelian principle of a Prime Mover required by a changing world which is not a self-contained system, he arrived at a First Cause—i.e. from motion to a First Mover. Similarly, in the world of sense the connexion between the present, the past and the future is only intelligible on the principle of efficient causation—i.e. from

[1] *De Civitate Dei*, IX, 26.
[2] *Proslogion seu Alloquium de Dei existentia*, Chap. 2, 3.
[3] *An Essay on Metaphysics*, p. 47.
[4] *Contra Gentiles*, i, 11.

causal movements to that which produces them in a sequence that cannot be infinite, and so must lead eventually to the ultimate Cause, "and this every one understands to be God." Thirdly, the contingency of the world, as Plato and the Jewish philosopher Maimonides had recognized, presupposes a cause, and if infinite regress be rejected, the existence of necessary Being must be asserted. Moreover, in a world exhibiting grades of perfection and "degrees of reality," by which the existence of greater and lesser goods are inferred, there must be something supremely good; while the orderly government of the universe suggests a teleological principle as the "final cause."[1]

If these "Five Ways" are not singly or collectively wholly convincing, and, as will be considered later, rest on an interpretation of causality which requires very considerable modification in the light of present day knowledge of the working of natural processes, nevertheless, they constitute an impressive rational demonstration of the existence and attributes of God. The subsequent Cartesian attempt to remove all presuppositions which were not either self-evident or demonstrable by the rules governing human experience, was a return to an "existentialist" apprehension of ultimate reality in self-consciousness by reducing all knowledge to a subjectivist knowledge of the mind's own ideas. This left belief in God, and the possibility of divine revelation, without any foundation in objective reality. By resting the intellectually unprovable Deity on a basis in the moral consciousness—the categorical imperative—Kant, substituted the shifting sands of experience for the firm ground of reason. Thus, divorced from rationalism in a *philosophia perennis*, religion in general and the idea of God in particular were at the mercy of the emotional reactions to the universe and its laws and processes at a time of intense intellectual ferment and unstable speculation.

The emancipation of the physical sciences from the dead hand of Aristotelian cosmology at the end of the Middle Ages was followed immediately by a search for principles as certain as the axioms of mathematics, in terms of which natural philosophy could be restated. Kepler's work in the elucidation of the physical connexion between the planets and the sun in the new Copernican solar system, pointed the way to an entirely new conception of time and space in which the Aristotelian interpretation of motion and causation was abandoned in favour of the Cartesian theory of extended and

[1] *Summa Theol.* la, q, 2, art. 3.

thinking substance. It only remained for Newton, following the lead of Gassendi (1592-1655), to regard space as having a reality of its own (instead of being a plenum, as Descartes surmised) to represent the universe as a self-contained system. In this world of Newtonian imagination, material particles and events occupied their respective places, and exercised their proper functions, according to certain fixed but imperfectly understood laws. Light appeared to consist of minute waves moving in a subtle hypothetical "ether," filling all space, though their nature and the properties of the medium that conveyed the vibrations at an enormous velocity, could not be determined. This grand generalization embraced the entire physical phenomena of the universe in a vast deterministic self-contained mechanism which admitted no extramundane influences or factors, as in the Aristotelian-Scholastic cosmology. Given time and space, the rest followed.

In such a natural order the concept of Deity, as Laplace recognized, seemed to be superfluous, if not wholly irrelevant. All that was required was a Deistic initial "First Cause" to start the mechanism working and it would then continue to function according to its own inherent laws and processes. This indeed became the predominant view of nature from the seventeenth century onwards until the Newtonian universe proved to be almost as fallacious in some respects as its Aristotelian predecessor, and the philosophy based upon it infinitely more inadequate than the Scholastic metaphysic. With the growth of empiricism, metaphysical interests, began to wane, and although the most outstanding figures in the scientific renaissance did not cease to be men of religious faith, the eighteenth century was the age of reason based on faith in the order of nature as a closed mechanistic process explained in mathematical terms.[1] To know the ultimate ground of the universe seemed to be a hopeless quest, and, in any case, there was more than enough to discover about the "secondary qualities" of the knowable world to keep the mind of the inquisitive occupied for generations. So transcendental inquiries were abandoned in favour of empirical investigation.

Such was the spirit that pervaded the Enlightenment with its critical intellect, its lack of imagination and profound thought, its emphasis on moral conduct and ethical theory, and its distrust of all enthusiasm. In reaction to the prevailing materialism, the absolute idealism that had found its champion in Berkeley at the commence-

[1] Cf. A. N. Whitehead, *Science and the Modern World* (Camb., 1928), p. 71ff.

ment of the epoch, represented an attempt to stem the tide by the enunciation of a philosophy with its objectivity grounded in the mind of God. But, as Kant recognized, the achievements of science could not be dismissed in the manner proposed either by Berkeley or his opponent Hume, though his own defence of empiricism, as we have seen, left the concept of Deity merely a necessary postulate of the practical reason beyond human experience and knowledge. If the categories of the pure reason are only valid within the sphere of sense-experience, they are inapplicable to transcendental and divine realities. Therefore, on this view, the essence of religion is reduced to an emotional reaction resting on the moral law divorced from reason. But to separate the world of space and time from the eternal order of purpose, meaning and value, cannot solve the problem of the universe or bridge the gap between matter and spirit, Creator and creation. A more radical approach to the situation was demanded and this the nineteenth century produced when, under the influence of the Romantic reaction and the Darwinian revolution, it substituted a philosophy of organism for that of mechanism.

The new interest in and appreciation of nature found expression in due course in the landscape painting of Turner, Constable and the Norwich school, and in the poetry of Wordsworth and Shelley. A kinship between man and nature was recognized enfolding within them the same eternal spirit of life and goodness proceeding from a common spiritual source. The former sceptical rationalism and intellectualism gave place to an emotional imagination which became a creative power in human life, and produced a sense of the mysterious in man's nature and the natural order. In Coleridge the feelings of awe and amazement were combined in revolt against the assumption that the relation of the Creator to the universe was that of a mason to his work. The Deistic conception of God which placed Him outside the world and beyond the sphere of natural law, now underwent a fundamental change. The transcendentalism of the "absent God," not uncongenial to the Calvinistic theology of divine sovereignty and irresistible grace, moved in the direction of an immanentism in which the feeling of sympathy between man and nature tended towards a Spinozan pantheism couched in the language and symbolism of Romanticism. It only remained for the biologists to bring the entire order of organic life under the reign of natural law to complete the transformation.

In the opening years of the nineteenth century the harmony of nature that was made the basis of an apologetic energetically pursued

by Paley and the authors of the Bridgewater Treatises in terms of a
"Natural Theology," represented the cosmic processes as a teleological
scheme perfectly adapted to its purpose by a beneficent Creator.[1]
The examples quoted in the Bridgewater Treatises in support of
the "argument of design"[2] were carefully chosen to illustrate "the
beautiful adjustments and adaptations of nature"[3] regardless of the
dysteleological side of the picture. But the attack upon this conception
of creative intelligence manifest in the organization of the universe
came from biological rather than philosophical considerations.

At the beginning of the previous century Georges Leclerc,
Comte de Buffon (1707-1788), had detected organs of little or no
use in the bodies of animals. The Miltonian doctrine of "Special
creation," however, was firmly entrenched in the scientific thought
of the period. Thus, Linnæus (1707-1778), the foremost botanist,
declared that plants and animals were endowed by the Creator with
their peculiar characteristics and distinguishing features, while the
French comparative anatomist Cuvier (1769-1832) maintained that
a divine re-creation of the flora and fauna occurred at the end of
each of the periodic terrestrial cataclysmic upheavals which he
postulated in the formative period of the earth's history. Nevertheless, against this generally accepted belief in the "fixity of species,"
Erasmus Darwin (1731-1802) and Lamarck (1744-1829) urged that
the more complex organisms were developed from pre-existent
simpler forms, modification, growth or atrophy in the use or disuse
of organs being due mainly to physical conditions, crossing and the
stress of necessity. Since the changes effected in these ways were
transmitted to the offspring, they became permanent features.

Despite the sustained opposition of the leading scientists, this
evolutionary hypothesis gained ground. In 1827 von Baer published
his account of the development of the chick, and eventually showed
the remarkable resemblance between the early embryos of the
vertebrates. Schleiden and Swann reduced all plants and animals to
a complex cell organization, and in 1844 Barry showed that certain
protozoa are unicellular organisms, thereby opening the way for
the derivation of all organic evolution from a single cell. Meanwhile,
in 1830, Charles Lyell, in his *Principles of Geology*, had disposed of
Cuvier's theory of cataclysmal changes in the earth's surface, and
established a genetic connexion between the fossils brought to light

[1] Paley, *Natural Theology* (London, 1802), p. 456ff.
[2] W. Proud, *Chemistry, Meteorology and the Function of Digestion* (1834); W. Whewell, *Astronomy and General Physics* (1833), pp. 3, 381.
[3] Cf. Prout, op. cit., p. 14.

by palæontological investigation and excavation, and their continuity with modern forms of life. But it remained for Charles Darwin and A. R. Wallace to formulate the revolutionary hypothesis of 1859 in which Natural Selection was made the key to the interpretation of the evolution of species, destined eventually to change the whole outlook on the organic universe and its processes.

The flash of inspiration which gave Darwin the clue to his far-reaching solution of the problem came from his accidental reading of Malchus's *Essay on Population*, published in 1838. If the tendency of the human race to outrun its means of subsistence can only be kept in check by famine, pestilence and war, it occurred to the trained mind of the naturalist that a similar struggle for existence among animals and plants explained in terms of natural selection "the cause of variation and survival in organic evolution." Species that developed the best natural equipment to engage in the conflict with their environment were able not only to survive but also to leave behind more descendants to inherit the useful novelties they had acquired. Those that lacked these safeguards and advantages tended to become extinct in course of time, since they had less offspring and were more readily eliminated.

Although the idea of evolution was inherent in the Copernican astronomy, and Newton as Kant recognized, had revealed a mechanism which seemed to be able to explain the operation of natural laws without reference to supernatural agencies, it was not until Darwin showed the effects of the selective action of external conditions on the development and elimination of species in relation to variation, heredity, struggle and isolation, that the world of organic life was brought under the reign of natural law. This revolutionary hypothesis inevitably had repercussions on the theological situation since it rendered untenable the doctrine of special creation understood in terms of the fixity of species. Nevertheless, the opposition was led by Richard Owen, the leading anatomist, who with more bitterness and personal prejudice than wisdom and justice, dismissed the theory as "nothing but guesswork and speculation." The distinguished geologist, Adam Sedgwick, was even more scathing and violent in his review of *The Origin of Species* in *The Spectator*. Indeed, Darwin himself affirmed that "all the most eminent palaeontologists, and all our greatest geologists, have unanimously, often vehemently, maintained the immutability of species."[1] Even the

[1] *Origin of Species* (First edition, p. 310, cf. A. R. Wallace, *Darwinianism* (London, 1889), p. 8.

unfortunate intervention in the dispute on the part of the Bishop of Oxford, Samuel Wilberforce, during the meeting of the British Association held in his cathedral city in 1860, was inspired by Richard Owen. That Wilberforce was ill-advised in his action, and lacked the technical biological knowledge and philosophic insight to pass a reasoned judgment on the issue, is obvious, but in consulting the recognized expert at that time, he at least was following the most authoritative scientific opinion of the day. Moreover, it must be admitted that the evidence was very incomplete at this initial stage in the enunciation of the Darwinian hypothesis. That the ecclesiastics had their own axe to grind in ranging themselves on the side of the opposition is beyond question, and therefore it is the more remarkable perhaps that the first zoologist publicly to accept the Darwinian contention was Canon Tristram, and he was followed on more general grounds by Charles Kingsley. Indeed, even so jaundiced an anti-clerical as T. H. Huxley was surprised at the lack of opposition among the "white cravats."[1]

Although, as Darwin recognized and admitted, the theory was not incompatible with "belief in God as a philosophical doctrine," that with which it did collide, and with which it seemed to be absolutely inconsistent, was the theological conception of creation based on the opening chapters of the book of Genesis.[2] At first it appeared that the evolutionary process was a mechanism operating according to certain fixed laws which pursued their course in complete independence of divine guidance, though admitting possibly the existence of a transcendent Deity as a remote First Cause. As knowledge increased, however, and interest centred more and more upon nature as a dynamic process, or organism, the emphasis shifted from divine transcendence to divine immanence regarded as a quasi-pantheistic principle.

In the ascent through millions of years of continuous life on the earth, the origination of new species by a creative adaptation in either stable or changing conditions of environment, suggested that every structure in an organism had a definite function to fulfil in the production of greater efficiency. The mode of life determined the form of the species since natural selection was the cause of change and the secret of survival. Therefore, on this hypothesis, if teleology was to be maintained at all, it could only be in relation to the evolutionary process itself. The former conception of God

[1]Huxley, *Life and Letters*, Vol. II, pp. 205n, 236, 323.
[2]Huxley, op. cit., Vol. I, p. 307. *Report of the British Association*, 1878, p. 575.

K

which placed Him outside a world He only influenced through sporadic interventions, could not be reconciled with an internal selective operation revealing no indication of requiring any external interference, or betraying any signs of divine "design," in the sense in which the term was understood by Paley and the Bridge-water writers. Arctic animals have not been equipped with fur by a beneficent Creator to protect them from cold, but having them-selves developed this device, they have been able to survive, while those who failed to acquire adequate means of protection, have succumbed. Similarly, the eye is to be explained genetically by reference to the development of the organism as a whole. Thus, the emphasis was on immanence rather than on transcendence.

In the second half of the nineteenth century the progressive sequence which seemed to be established from the amoeba to man had its counterpart in the cultural and political spheres. Indeed, no phase of human activity appeared to lie outside the domain of "evolution". Everything was marching in an orderly manner to its goal by virtue of an inner ceaseless "urge" towards higher and more complex forms, independent of any transcendent extramundane Controller of the process. This was in line with the naturalistic Positive Philosophy of Auguste Comte (1798-1857) which had reduced all knowledge to that of "the laws of phenomena" and the facts of experience, leaving no room for any "unknown reality."[1] But the evolutionary process is not so easily explained in terms of mechanistic development, or immanental dynamism, as it appeared in the full blush of an epoch-making discovery.

The more intensively the process is studied, the clearer it becomes that specifically new qualities and values are constantly coming into existence which are not merely "resultants" of previous conditions. These mutations, such as life, reflective thought and self-consciousness, appear as novelties in an unpredictable manner; creative occurrences modifying what has already existed and raising it to a higher level of complexity and potentiality. They stand over and above the regrouping of pre-existing events, and have appeared to such an observer as Lloyd Morgan to constitute a progressive unfolding in time of revelations of a creative "activity" which is universally enfolded *sub specie aeternitatis*.[2]

[1]Comte, *Cours de philosophie positive* (Paris, 1877), fourth edition, Vol. IV, p. 317ff, Herbert Spencer, *First Principles* (London, 1862, new edition, 1910), Vol. II, p. 321.
[2]*Emergent Evolution* (London, 1923), p. 19ff, 67.

Similarly, Henri Bergson saw in the flow of events a surging of an *élan vital*, or spontaneous urge of life akin to consciousness, which finds its outlet in variation and new forms. To exist is to change, to change is to produce novelty, and to produce novelty is to create something which did not already exist. "The central radiation of life is God." And God is "unceasing life, action, freedom."[1] This, of course, does not necessarily imply a personal Creator and providential ordering of creation. Reality, on this hypothesis, is a never-ceasing flow which assumes a vast variety of experimental forms as the primal urge finds this or that creative outlet. This reaches its climax in man with his powers of choice and freedom, though eventually Bergson was led to conclude that the *élan vital* either is or comes from God, Who can be known only in mystic intuition.[2] But while he substituted an organic conception of the universe for the former static materialism, it is only "chance," or "accident" which makes the creative impulse behave as though it were a teleological process. The human organism, however, adjusts its environment to itself by virtue of its self-consciousness, instead of adapting the organism to the environment.[3] In this differentiation between instinct and intelligence Bergson sees the development of conscious thought capable of reflecting upon its surroundings and utilizing them for its own ends and purposes. The mind is essentially free, or creative, in its activity.

Now, as Whitehead maintains, "consciousness pre-supposes experience and not experience consciousness."[4] Within the process of which it is conscious consciousness arises, the mind being simply a special organization of the system of events that constitute the body. Actual experience, it is argued, is always an experience of concrete events, or "organisms," in which the character of the whole influences the characters of the subordinate parts that constitute it. "The whole point of the modern doctrine is the evolution of the complex organisms from antecedent states of less complex organisms," the term "organism" being used to include all reality without any distinction between inorganic and organic entities. So conceived, the organism is "a unit of emergent value, a real fusion of the characters of eternal objects, emerging for its own sake."[5]

In Whitehead's complex system of thought nature is essentially

[1] *Creative Evolution* (London, 1911), p. 93ff.
[2] *The Two Sources of Morality and Religion* (London, 1935), pp. 197, 216.
[3] *Creative Evolution*, pp. 152, 155.
[4] *Process and Reality* (Camb., 1929), p. 72.
[5] *Science and the Modern World* (Camb., 1928), new edition, p. 135.

a process in which "events," or passing elements, are non-recurring units continually in process of motion yet exhibiting continuity because they overlap. "In the inescapable flux there is something that abides; in the overwhelming permanence there is an element that escapes into the flux." In the elements that remain—the "eternal objects" or universals—creativity manifests itself as "the ultimate principle by which the many, which are the universe disjunctively, become the one actual occasion, which is the universe conjunctively."[1] "Objects," as the permanent elements in the universe, are continually entering into "events," as the passing units of evolving process. The reality is in the process itself—the "prehensions" or "events" in nature, in Whitehead's terminology.[2] Objects enter into space-time relations mediately through their relation to events, or at least require space and time for their "situation" or "duration."[3] The "ultimate limitation," and the ground of all "concrete actuality" is God, regarded as the "Principle of Concretion."[4] But since "He does not create eternal objects; for His nature requires them in the same degree that they require Him,"[5] He is not the Ground of all existence in the theistic sense of the concept of Deity. Although God is postulated as "that non-temporal actuality which has to be taken account of in every creative phase"; the one systematic, complete fact, which is the antecedent ground conditioning every creative act,"[6] He is not *before* all creation but *with* all creation."[7] If He "transcends the temporal world because He is an actual fact in the nature of things,"[8] it is as true to say that the world is immanent in God, as that the world transcends God; the world and God having "equal claim to priority in creation."[9]

In short, for Whitehead, Deity is "the primordial creature," not generically different from that of other actual entities in any other respect, and, therefore, a finite evolutionary Deity.[10] Both God and the world are "in the grip of the ultimate metaphysical ground,"[11] so that there is a causal factor beyond the Principle of Concretion

[1]*Process and Reality*, p. 28.
[2]*Science and the Modern World*, p. 90.
[3]*Principles of Natural Knowledge* (Camb., 1925), second edition, pp. 152, 202.
[4]*Science and the Modern World*, p. 216ff.
[5]*Process and Reality*, p. 363, cf. 333.
[6]*Religion in the Making* (Camb., 1930), p. 81.
[7]*Process and Reality*, p. 486.
[8]op. cit., p. 139.
[9]op. cit., p. 492f.
[10]op. cit., pp. 42, 103.
[11]op. cit., 493f.

(i.e. God), though how "the non-temporal actuality" is absorbed in the temporal process of creativity is not explained. Thus, the "philosophy of organism" is resolved into a system of divine immanence realizing itself in the "principle of novelty" in the world as the valuation, ideal and power of creativity. "God adds Himself to the actual ground from which every creative act takes its rise,"[1] but, for practical purposes, nature, as Whitehead interprets it, creates itself very much as in Samuel Alexander's scheme creation is regarded as "a forward movement with a *nisus* towards deity"—the name he gives to the higher type of being awaiting to be evolved.[2]

In the curious reversal of theism suggested by Alexander the evolutionary process is made to transcend its source in a higher empirical quality than mind as an ideal at once non-existent, unknown and incapable of realization. Starting from a four dimensional space-time of pure motion as the concrete reality, "experienced features" or "categories" emerge in space and time, such as existence, universality, substance, order, quality, number and motion. These form patterns to produce materiality as a new quality in which infinite grades of existence have come into being, including life, mind and consciousness. The whole universe is "the body of God," "deity" being a nebulous "higher quality of God" towards which the *nisus* of evolution is tending as a process of becoming. At most this can be but an ideal which will always remain elusive since it is essentially an emerging quality beyond the reach of the eternal present.

For Alexander, religion is "the sentiment in us that we are drawn towards Him (God), and caught in the movement of the world to a higher level of existence. The vocation of the religious man is that of doing his part in advancing the world towards its goal in the ideal order to be established when the evolutionary process has attained its end."[3] But, as Dr. C. C. J. Webb has pointed out, "the religious consciousness demands not merely a prospective but an actual God, already possessing all to which we can aspire."[4] "The vision of something which stands beyond, behind and within, the passing flux of immediate things," visualized by Whitehead as "something which is real, and yet waiting to be realized—something which is the ultimate ideal, and the hopeless quest,"[5] does not fulfil

[1] *Religion in the Making*, p. 156.
[2] *Space, Time and Deity* (London, 1920), Vol. II, p. 419.
[3] op. cit., p. 429.
[4] *God and Personality* (London, 1918), p. 203.
[5] *Science and the Modern World*, p. 238.

these conditions. Nevertheless, his idea of Deity, unlike that of Alexander, transcends both the "eternal objects" and the "concrete occasions" of which he thinks nature consists.

But in all these evolutionary immanental philosophies it is difficult to escape the conclusion that Deity is regarded as an emerging quality in a cosmic system in which self-creativeness is a fundamental principle independent of any extramundane "efficient cause." In a "hierarchy of qualities" emerging from below, within the organic series, that is to say, the highest spiritual realizations are built upon and emerge from that which has gone before. Divinity thus becomes either an *élan vital*, or an unconscious striving and perpetual re-creation, as Bergson contends; or, as Whitehead maintains, the Principle of Concretion and Source of limitation; or, as Alexander imagines, the quality which is next to emerge; or, finally, as Lloyd Morgan would say, "the *nisus* through whose activity emergents emerge, and the whole course of emergent evolution is directed." But in none of these interpretations is the concept of Deity compatible with that of the living God of theism, inasmuch as each conflicts with the recognition of a real distinction between the eternal source and ground of all existence and the dependent created existents.

Causal connexion, it is true, is only one of many types of relations between objects, and to-day a single "world-function" seems to be taking the place of the idea of a causal nexus. As the quantum theory has revealed, the time of the break-up of a radium atom is unpredictable, and electrons pass from one state to another in a series of scintillations at irregular intervals, thereby introducing a principle of *discontinuity* in the path of the electron. The orbit of an electron can be regarded now as a series of detached positions, and not as a continuous line. This would seem to indicate that some theory of discontinuous existence is required by the ultimate data of mathematical physics. Within the atom, at any rate, the old mechanistic Newtonian laws do not appear to be obeyed so far as the path of the electron is concerned, since, in radiation electrons jump from one orbit to another, or even outside the orbits altogether, rather than move in an orderly continuous process like the flow of waves. Moreover, in the emission and absorption of quanta, as packets of energy (i.e. radiation), there is a break in the causal chain, which negatives the Kantian postulate that the law of the connexion between cause and effect is a necessary postulate of the pure reason.

An atom now may be regarded more in the nature of a complex organism possessing many interrelated parts and exhibiting many properties—radiation, vibration and creativity—the precise functioning of which is not completely understood. Physical phenomena no longer rest ultimately on a scheme of completely deterministic laws. The electron has no clearly defined starting point, or regulated mode of behaviour, with the result that the causal nexus between objects has now been abandoned in favour of a single cosmic function governing the whole of existence, with new creations, or novelties, emerging within the evolutionary process in a series of discontinuous intrusions.

If relations are all "universals" so that separate objects have no independent existence, as Lotze maintained and some exponents of the new physics surmise, all elements of reality are comprehended in a universal scheme capable of interpretation as an immanental world-ground. Furthermore, if, as Bertrand Russell argues, all existents really exist at a mathematical instant, the whole world is composed of a multiplicity of events.[1] But whether these have causes is by no means clear. The ultimate stuff of reality is neither mental nor material, on this hypothesis, and so he arrives at a "neutral monism" which is inconsistent with his postulated logical pluralism, since monism is qualitative whereas the pluralism is substantival—one kind of "stuff" with a multiplicity of "events," or entities, which have various relations to each other. Philosophy, it is maintained, cannot determine the end of life, but out of the intellectual contemplation of eternal logical forms belonging to all possible worlds, Lord Russell endeavours to create a practical ideal of life. The metaphysical quest, however, must be abandoned as useless, and even though belief in God may "happen" to be true, for the logical positivists the word "Deity" is without meaning, and the concept incapable of verification. Thus, the idea of God having lost its original meaning and significance in terms of theism, it is finally eliminated altogether as ceasing to be a logical necessity in a world of "subsisting" characters and relationships, with the result that the universe and its processes are left without any ultimate ground.

To-day, then, the philosophical theist is confronted with a very different cosmological situation from that which formerly obtained. The conception of radiation as a discontinuous process has changed fundamentally the idea of causation. Motion and force have been

[1] *The Principles of Mathematics* (London, 1937), new edition, p. 449ff; cf. *A History of Western Philosophy* (London, 1947), pp. 692ff, 695.

replaced by cosmic events and processes, radiation and energy; and cause by "predictability," with a very deeply laid principle of indeterminacy in the ultimate constitution of nature. Similarly, it can no longer be held that the contingency of finite things depends upon the concept of "necessary Being," in the manner suggested in the Thomist Cosmological Argument. Apart from the contention of Kant that contingency and necessity are mental constructions devoid of any essential objective reality, the data within time and space are not contingent, leave alone the entire universe in its extramundane relations. Moreover, the denial of the possibility of infinite regress now has to contend with the notion of a multiplicity of relations between events in the physical order, each minimal event, according to Lord Russell, being logically a self-subsistent entity. A causal nexus at most is only one of these relationships in an elaborate network of uniform sequences, and cannot be regarded as a fundamental principle, as in the Platonic-Aristotelian-Thomist philosophical schemes.

Nevertheless, it can be argued that a network of entities, however complicated it may be, does not eliminate what are virtually causal sequences in a vast system of inter-connected operations.[1] But if such a sequence be recognized for the purposes of the Cosmological Argument, it must be made secure against re-entry into the chain of events, as in the case of a mathematical monotonic relation, each sound being a semitone higher in pitch than the note before it. In the Aristotelian cosmology the system of spheres secured this succession, and in modern physics the velocity of light *in vacuo* being a theoretical absolute limit, whether measured from a system in motion or at rest, no moving object can exceed it in speed, and, therefore, in time it precedes all effects. However fast an observer may be moving, the same value for the velocity of light is always a constant, while matter increases in mass the faster it travels. At the speed of light this is infinitely great and constituted the ultimate velocity. Here, then, we have something in the nature of an absolute entity in the physical universe giving rise to a monotonic type of relationship between cause and effect.

The aim of physics being to discover the pattern of events which controls the phenomena scientifically observed, how the pattern originates lies outside the range of scientific inquiry. Nevertheless, the cosmic order, its laws and processes, must have had a beginning since the phenomenal world can be resolved into primary entities—

[1]Cf. E. L. Mascall, *He Who Is* (London, 1943), p. 50ff.

e.g. electrons, protons, photons, neutrons—which have no permanent existence, no shape and no location, capable only of symbolization in mathematical formulæ. Matter in the last analysis becomes a symptom of the curvature of space losing itself in discontinuities which at present defy explanation. Lindemann regards energy as a statistical concept meaningless unless averaged over a finite time,[1] while Jeans has been led to conjecture that matter has been "poured into our universe from some other, and entirely extraneous, spatial dimension, so that to a denizen of our universe the centres of spiral nebulæ appear as points at which matter is being continually created."[2] Therefore, if these conclusions are correct, it would seem that the cosmos has had a beginning through creative activity outside and beyond itself. In other words, that it was created in time by some extramundane agency. Moreover, the uniformity and mathematical construction of the cosmic process are indicative of transcendental Mind as the ultimate ground of creation.

Mathematical law being a concept of the mind valid throughout the cosmos, it is reasonable to infer that behind the entire process there is a single supreme Mind directing all things to their appointed ends. A teleological principle is discernible in the adaptation of inanimate nature to the realization of good and beneficent purposes. In laying the stress upon final causation rather than on evidence of "design" in evolutionary mechanisms, Aquinas was on firmer ground than Paley. By adopting this line of argument he avoided the damaging criticisms which the Darwinian hypothesis engendered in the latter part of the nineteenth century, and in the light of the present revelations of a continuity which is characterized by novelty—the sudden and unpredictable emergence of new types adapted to higher functions and purposes—the teleological principle becomes more apparent. As Dr. Tennant says, "the discovery of organic evolution has caused the teleologist to shift his ground from special design in the products to directivity in the process, and plan in the primary collocations. It has also served to suggest that the organic realm supplies no better basis for teleological argument of the narrower type than does inorganic Nature."[3]

The schemes of evolutionary philosophy recently put forth to interpret the creative character of the process, being primarily concerned with the cause of the changes and the conditions that

[1] *The Physical Significance of the Quantum Theory* (Oxford, 1932).
[2] *Astronomy and Cosmology* (Camb., 1928), p. 352.
[3] *Philosophical Theology* (Camb., 1928), Vol. II, p. 85.

accompany them, throw little light on the ultimate causes of emergence. It is when what lies behind the *élan vital*, the *nisus* towards perfection, the holistic principle, or the principle of concretion, is interpreted in terms of a finite God realizing Himself in the world, that this approach becomes a challenge to theism. Deity is then represented as "the last irrationality," "the ultimate limitation," or "the whole world as possessing the quality of deity," so that "God is seen God in the stone, in the star, in the flesh, in the soul and the clod," as an immanental principle of creativity. Such a conception of divine activity is manifestly incompatible with that of the self-existent infinite Being standing over against creation in a relation of personal sovereignty, behind history as well as above nature, transcending both the historic and natural order.

Dr. Tennant sees in a purposiveness beyond itself emerging from nature a strengthening of the case for theism inasmuch as the evolutionary process is capable of being regarded as instrumental to the development of intelligent and moral creatures.[1] The moral status of man is thus, on his interpretation, "the coping-stone of a cumulative teleological argument."[2] rather than, as Kant maintained the only sure ground for believing in the existence of an ethical Deity. The moral consciousness, it was argued, demands the realization of its ideal of the highest good, regarded as a union of the right condition of the will (virtue) with its complete satisfaction (happiness). This can only be achieved in a moral order in which the moral law is a categorical imperative binding upon the universal conscience of mankind. The sense of duty cannot be explained on any naturalistic basis. Therefore, unless Deity is accepted as a practical postulate necessitated by the moral reason, moral obligations are without motives, and moral ideas are as unrealizable as the moral ideal is unattainable in nature or man. Since goodness is an ultimate concept, the practical reason gives the right to affirm the dependence of the world on a Supreme Being Who is the ground and source of the moral order, combining in Himself perfect wisdom, power and holiness.

To this Tennant replies that "if the *summum bonum* has its possibility of realization guaranteed by the concept itself, Kant in principle employs the ontological argument in ethics after demolishing it in theology." God as "a regulative idea for the theoretical

[1] op. cit. Vol. II, p. 103.
[2] op. cit. Vol. II, p. 100.

reason" is made "a postulate for the practical reason."[1] If what ought to be is to be, God must exist. But the moral argument is not without significance quite apart from the difficulties raised by the Kantian ethics and metaphysics taken as a whole. If the intelligible world is an objectively valid moral order so that moral values belong to the nature of reality, the moral ideal can only claim validity in so far as it is grounded in an absolute good.

The demand of the moral consciousness to find the realization of the idea of the good, suggests that the natural universe is adapted to ethical ends, but while the moral life is progress towards an ideal, ethics as such can give no assurance of ultimate attainment. The end of civilization is cosmic destruction so that mundane values must terminate in defeat. Yet ultimate good must exist if ethical aspiration is not a delusion. If values are to be eternally valid they must have objective reality independent of their existence in finite minds and consciences, or in a material environment that is gradually "running down" to its own extinction. All intrinsic values transcend the temporal and spatial conditions in which they are manifested as conscious experiences, and themselves give an ultimate meaning to the evolutionary process and its finite existences. If they are not verifiable in sense perception,[2] and so lie outside the empirical sphere of the logical positivists, they are, nevertheless, integral elements in the ethical and religious experience of mankind, and they bear witness to a transcendental order of reality independent of nature and the objects and events of space and time contained therein.

That this source and ground of value is a supramundane unity is suggested by the coherence and interrelation of cosmic processes and the adaptation and co-ordination of the several parts as vital elements in a composite whole working towards specific ends. But the single unifying Mind required to give cohesion to the entire universe, is neither synonymous with creation nor "wholly other" than anything in the world. Spinozan pantheism and Barthian transcendentalism equally fail to supply what the evidence demands. Mind and matter are not merely two aspects of one underlying divine reality, as Spinoza contended, with extension as one of the infinite attributes of Deity, nor is God dependent upon the existence

[1]op. cit. p. 96ff.

[2]This also applies to scientific induction inasmuch as a similar "intuitive" insight and "act of faith" prior to experimental verification are required in the interpretation and evaluation of natural phenomena.

of a world with which He is coeval, as Tennant affirms.[1] But if the available data indicate a single unifying Mind and personal Will external to the cosmos with its coherent, selective and creative purpose, and its orderly organization of laws and processes combined with a certain freedom of action in the production of novelties, this Ultimate Reality is not "wholly other" lying entirely outside the grasp of human reason and experience.

In its Deistic form, absolute transcendence reduces Deity to the "pure Form" of Aristotle, for ever separated from the material and mutable order—just a thinking of thought and an Unmoved Mover—or, in its eighteenth century guise, the non-interfering eternal First Cause completely unconcerned with the government of the world He created and then left to its own resources. Similarly, in the Neo-Calvinistic movement of Karl Barth and Emil Brunner, God can only be known through revelation quite independent of reason or experience. He is the living, active Spirit, choosing, laying hold of and possessing man, coming to him from without, that is to say, from beyond knowledge and beyond history, and speaking in an oracular 'Word of God' from His sublime and solitary heights in eternity, interpreted by the inner witness of the Holy Spirit. He is "the one and only One and proves Himself to be such by His being both the Author of His own Being and the source of all knowledge of Himself. In both these respects He differs from everything in the world. A God Who could be known otherwise than through Himself, i.e. otherwise than through His revelation of Himself, would have already betrayed, *eo ipso*, that he was not the one and only One and so was not God. He would have betrayed Himself to be one of those principles underlying human systems and finally identical with man himself."[2] Therefore, it is not because man seeks God that he finds Him in faith, but because He has first of all found man that human beings seek Him. To set about proving the existence of such a *Deus absconditus* is as blasphemous to Barth as it was absurd to his predecessor, Kierkegaard.[3]

This revival of transcendentalism in its most extreme christocentric form has been somewhat modified by Dr. Brunner to allow for the fact that divine knowledge, so far from being confined to regenerated Christians, is the common possession of all rational

[1]op. cit. Vol. II, p. 128ff; cf. Whitehead, *Process and Reality*, p. 486.
[2]*The Knowledge of God and Service of God according to the teaching of the Reformation* (E. T., London, 1938), p. 19.
[3]T. Haecker, *Sören Kierkegaard* (E. T. by A. Dru., London, 1937), p. 47.

beings, prior to and independent of any acceptance by faith of the Christian revelation. If this were not so, evangelization by human agents would be seriously at a discount, to say the least. To meet this difficulty Dr. Brunner grants some measure of "general" knowledge of God to mankind as a whole, and that the *form* of the divine image has not been completely obliterated by the Fall, as Barth declares. Therefore, man is responsible to his Creator though incapable of making a right response to Him except through the Divine Word "which addresses us and calls us into existence."[1] But for Brunner as for Barth the Christian conception of Deity, and the relations of nature and grace, remain fundamentally "a different thing from every philosophy" because "the complex of grounds and consequences developed by natural reason has been broken into by revelation," regarded as "the breaking through of the unconditioned into the world of the conditioned."[2] Only a personal encounter with God, a total surrender to Him in Christ as mediator, can enable man to have any genuine knowledge of Deity, independent of either reason, philosophy or theology. It is a divine gift in the real person of God present in His Word, Who as such is also the creative presence of the Holy Spirit.[3] The most that the human intellect can hope to do is to discover the inner significance of natural and human events, and to speculate concerning the structure of the universe, though it is granted that it may explain and elaborate the truths made known by revelation.[4]

This theocentric revolt against the whole empiricist tendency and the repudiation of Schleiermacher and Ritschl, with the substitution of a theology of crisis for a dialectical philosophy, represented the modern counterpart of the reaction in the sixteenth century against the intellectualism of medieval scholasticism with its reasoned arguments for the existence of God. To-day, against the complacent immanental subjectivism of an over-confident age, a tired, disillusioned and frustrated generation has set an absolute transcendentalism and existentialism of an experienced ever-present person, to give a new assurance in a disintegrating world, intellectually confused and economically bankrupt. The Kierkegaardian-Barthian theism at least supplies a dynamic answer in the affirmative to the question, "is God dead?", though it completely fails to

[1]Brunner, *Natur und Gnade; Zum Gesprach mit Karl Barth* (1934), p. 18; cf. P. Fraenkel, *Natural Theology* (London, 1946).
[2]*Philosophy of Religion* (New York, 1937), p. 13.
[3]Brunner, *The Divine Human Encounter* (London, 1944), p. 73f.
[4]Brunner, *Revelation and Reason* (London, 1947).

reconcile the religious and philosophic approaches to the problem common to both disciplines; viz. the nature and relation to the universe of the Ultimate Reality, which in the refrain of St. Thomas Aquinas, "all men speak of as God." The fact that this concept of Deity is of universal occurrence shows the futility of centring the entire problem of revelation in a single Judaeo-Christian tradition, and of dismissing as of no account the rational theology of Plato, Aristotle, the Scholastics, and the remarkable spiritual insight of Oriental mysticism, together with the whole body of philosophical, scientific and theological knowledge brought under review in our present inquiry. Nevertheless, the Barth-Brunner reaction calls attention to the importance of bringing philosophical theism into relation with the *religious* conception of God as the sovereign personal Creator, Sustainer and Ruler of the universe.

CHAPTER VIII

THE GOD OF RELIGION

THE traditional arguments for the existence of God, to which in the last resort the philosophy of theism points in its attempt to discover the Ultimate Reality in the universe, cannot hope to reach a degree of finality comparable to the precise demonstration attainable in a mathematical theorem dependent solely upon logical propositions universally accepted, or to the conclusions of experimental science established under conditions that admit of complete empirical verification. "We can no more *prove* God's existence," as the late Professor de Burgh has said, "than we can *prove* that of our fellow men: our knowledge of the one as of the other is founded on the experience of their presence."[1] It is here that there is substance in the "existential" approach to an understanding of the concept of Deity. And in the face of the challenge of the logical positivists, doubtless much is to be gained from the shifting of emphasis to language and experience. Nevertheless, so far as actual proof is concerned, the idea of God must remain outside our present range of absolute theoretical certainty.

This limitation, however, is not confined to the data of theistic consciousness and religious experience. Principles such as those of causality carry us beyond the sphere of direct observation and experiment into the realms of metaphysics, while, as we have seen, the hypotheses of mathematical physics admit an element of uncertainty and incompleteness—sometimes even of logical inconsistency—in relation to ultimate concepts, entities and conditions. In short, there can be no absolute proof or finality in a world of relativities in which the nearer we get to ultimate reality the more apparent it becomes that we only "know in part". Thus, Epistemological arguments for the existence of God cannot be expected to establish more than a justification for the use of the term Deity to explain certain features of spatial abstractives which are not self-explanatory within human experience. But for the practical purposes of religion the concept must contain a certain content other than that of a probable existence. In the last analysis the test of all theoretical

[1] *Towards a Religious Philosophy* (Lond., 1937), p. 169.

reasoning and philosophizing on the subject is whether or not it produces a God Who is adequate to the demands made upon Him by His worshippers, both for their own inmost needs and urgent necessities, and for the ultimate purposes of the universe at large.

From the earliest and most rudimentary attempts of the human spirit to establish effective relations with a transcendent Power manifesting itself in time and space, controlling natural processes and determining the destinies of man, the interpretation of Deity that has made the most ready appeal has been that of a supramundane Providence, at once above and within the world He sustains. This, as we have seen, embraces a very great variety of forms and aspects, but to fulfil the essential conditions of religion, it must be the affirmation of a supernatural Reality responsive to human needs, the objective ground and sovereign moral ruler of the universe, the personal source and conserver of value, the ultimate standard of conduct, a worthy object of worship, the guide of man from the cradle to the grave and the hope of immortality.

To a greater or less degree this idea of God occurs in almost every religious system from primitive polytheism to personal theism. It not infrequently happens, however, that one or other of these elements is lacking, or given undue emphasis, thereby modifying the efficacy of the concept as the religious interpretation of ultimate reality. Thus, in the case of primitive polytheism, while the recognition of many gods supplies a providential background of events in the natural world and in human society by assigning divine attributes to inanimate objects, arresting occurrences and abstract or moral entities, such as wisdom, truth, will and mind, apart from the naïve mythological setting of the beliefs and the cultus, and its crude anthropomorphisms, the reduction of all existence to a multiplicity of independent beings raises serious metaphysical and scientific issues.

Although pluralism has never lacked its advocates among thinkers from the days of Democritus to those of Leibniz and William James, an underlying fundamental unity and wholeness are not in doubt. Little room is left for a primitive polytheistic interpretation of natural phenomena in atomic speculation, the doctrine of monads and similar philosophic attempts to reconstruct a pluralistic cosmic order. Nevertheless, it has to be remembered that Plato did not hesitate to attribute divinity to the heavenly bodies,[1] and the Stoics

[1]*Tim.*, 41A.

found no difficulty in blending their pantheistic conception of Providence with the traditional polytheism of Graeco-Roman mythology.[1] Similarly, in the later Vedic hymns in India, the personification of the physical universe was closely related to the mystical pantheism of philosophic Hinduism.

Conversely, neither monism nor monotheism has been able to escape from a tendency to the endless multiplication of lesser divinities, spirits, angels or saints as objects of veneration. Thus, just as in primitive society the remote Supreme Being is obscured by the multiplicity of the more accessible animistic spiritual beings, so in India the people as a whole worship the Shining Ones rather than Brahman, the One eternal Spirit pervading the universe and immanent in the souls of men. Indeed, Brahman has his consort, Sarasvati, just as Shiva and Vishnu, are associated with Kali and Lakshmi respectively. These are regarded as goddesses like the the thousands of other deities incorporated in Hinduism from a variety of sources. To the subtle minds of the sophisticated this plurality of gods appears only as so many manifestations of one and the same transcendental pantheistic unity. In religion, however, human nature requires something more than an abstract philosophy to satisfy the cravings of the heart. Therefore, for the majority the unmanifested Deity reveals Himself not only in the trinity, Brahman, Vishnu and Shiva, and their consorts and avatars, personifying the principles of creation, preservation and dissolution, but in innumerable gods and goddesses, each of whom represents a separate being to be approached, supplicated and propitiated as occasion demands.

So in Iran, although Zarathushtra gave Ahura Mazdah a unique position as the Lord of Creation, the one and only Master and Ruler of all things immune from all change, six divine intelligences, originally regarded as abstractions or attributes of the Supreme Being, in course of time assumed an independent existence and function in the divine ordering of the universe. In the heavens they held their celestial councils, ruled over the seven zones assigned to them, and were responsive to the requests of their votaries on earth. Below them were the *Yazata*, or beneficent ones, who conferred numerous boons on humanity, notably Mithra the harbinger of light and herald of the dawn from whose all-seeing eye nothing was hidden, and whose radiance dispelled all darkness, physical and moral. To him men turned with prayers and offerings for health and offspring, alike for themselves and their cattle. Thus, while Ahura

[1]Cicero, *De Natura Deorum*, ii, 23, 60.

L

Mazdah was the source and ground of all beneficence, his providential bounty was bestowed through personified attributes as distinct personalities in whom his essence dwelt. It was in this way that he exercised his functions as a God of religion.

In pre-exilic Israel, as we have seen, the localized worship of the baalim and elim always proved to be a powerful counter attraction to the monolatry of the desert tradition[1] because it satisfied the practical requirements of an agricultural community by providing a vegetation cultus through which the crops and the seasons were brought under supernatural control. The prophetic movement endeavoured to relate the God of Israel to the everyday life of the people by insisting on the ethical demands of Yahweh in a practical morality. But the attempt to give religious expression to the ideals of the eighth century prophets in a centralized worship at Jerusalem, widened the gulf between Yahwism and the nation inasmuch as it meant in practice that Israelites living at a distance from the capital only visited the temple three times a year; viz., at the great festivals. It was not until after the Exile that this gulf was bridged. The determined effort that was then made to organize the greatly reduced community as a theocracy resulted in the establishment of ethical monotheism on the basis of an elaborate sacrificial worship referred back to a Mosaic revelational origin under priestly influence in the manner that has been considered.[2]

The success of this achievement gave Yahweh the status of a special Providence, or personal God, transcendent as the sole ethical Creator and sovereign Ruler of the universe, and immanent as the Lord of history Who by His mighty aid and intervention had revealed His care for His chosen people, and through them for mankind as a whole. Polytheism was rigidly excluded (though apparently it lingered on in the Jewish colony at Elephantine in the Nile valley), but a link was retained with the former régime by the retention and reinterpretation of the pre-exilic agricultural festivals.[3] The Abrahamic covenant was made efficacious in an objective worship in which a new emphasis was placed on atonement and reconciliation, and the ethical ideals of the prophetic movement. The synagogues, which apparently were first instituted during the Exile, were made to serve the spiritual needs of Jews in Palestine

[1]Cf. p. 102.
[2]Cf. p. 103.
[3]Oesterley, *Myth and Ritual* (Oxford, 1933), p. 113ff; A. R. Johnstone, *The Labyrinth* (London, 1935), p. 85ff.

living at a distance from Jerusalem, and also those of the Diaspora farther afield. Though the liturgical non-sacerdotal offices of these local assemblies were independent of and subordinate to the daily offerings of the temple, they followed the sequence of the central sanctuary so closely in idea and intention that when the temple was destroyed in A.D. 70 they carried on the post-exilic institutional tradition in the hope and conviction that eventually the worship of Zion would be restored in its fulness.

By these means the nation was weaned away from the pre-exilic polytheistic cults to the acknowledgment of the one supreme ethical Creator Who hears and responds to the cry of sinful man, and Who alone is worthy of worship. It was not denied that other supernatural beings existed, but by comparison with Yahweh they were only demons, or "idols," however that term might be interpreted. For the purposes of religion there was but one God of Israel, and He was in truth the supreme and sole Lord of the universe. This, however, did not exclude a whole hierarchy of other personal spirits, good and evil, possessing a measure of relative independence and freedom. In fact, when Yahweh was enthroned in heaven as the transcendent Creator, He was surrounded with a host of ministering angelic agents who were represented in the post-canonical Jewish literature not only as delivering His messages on earth and executing His commands, but also as presiding over natural phenomena—the motion of the stars, rain and hail—acting as patrons of nations and guardians of individuals.[1] Nevertheless, God alone as "King of the universe" sustained all things, and in Jewish thought He was never excluded from the world and its operations like the Unmoved Mover of Aristotle, or the First Cause of Deism.[2] The omnipotence and majesty of Yahweh did not conflict with His accessibility any more than belief in a "special presence" in the Holy of Holies was incompatible with His omnipresence.

Thus, by the beginning of the Christian era religious thought and practice in Judaism had reached a stage in which divine transcendence and immanence were brought into conjunction. The God Who stands over and above the world is He in Whom "we live and move and have our being," for Israel was proud to be called "the sons of the living God."[3] God was in heaven but He was also everywhere—in His temple and in the entire world, and He "is

[1]*Ber.*, 51; *Sanh.*, 38; *Yeb.*, 16b; *Yom.*, 36; *Pes.*, 118.
[2]*Ecclus.* xlii, 15, xliii, 33; Rest of Esther (LXXXV), xiii, 9-11.
[3]*Hos.* i, 10.

nigh unto all them that call upon Him."[1] In the conception of divine Fatherhood His exaltation and nearness were united, and it only remained for the Founder of Christianity to reveal this relationship in terms of love and grace to open a new chapter in the history of theism.

While it is certainly not true to say with Dr. McGiffert that "at no point did Jesus go beyond his people's thought about God,"[2] it is, nevertheless, a fact that the Fatherhood of God was a belief as characteristic of the Old Testament as of the New Testament.[3] Where Christ made a genuine departure from the accepted belief of Judaism, as Dr. Montefiore admits, was in his insistence on the constraining love of God in seeking the sinful and giving them a place in His kingdom, not of right or merit but solely as an act of grace.[4] This goes beyond the merciful kindness of the Lord as conceived by the Hebrew psalmist,[5] and it inaugurated a new idea of redemption as self-giving on behalf of the sinner involving suffering and complete surrender, even of life itself.[6] In the Johannine interpretation of the Synoptic tradition this is further emphasized.[7]

It was not, however, what was said about redemption and the Fatherhood of God that introduced the new era in the history of religion. It was rather the seal placed upon the teaching of Jesus by His actual act of self-renunciation on the Cross that made Christianity the revelation of a new conception of divine love and forgiveness which lies enshrined in the heart of God at the very centre of the universe. This has remained ever since the proof of the love of the Father for erring humanity. "God commendeth his own love towards us, in that, while we were yet sinners, Christ died for us."[8] And love constrains because it has a stimulating magnetic effect in drawing the one loved towards the lover. Therefore, a God Who is love cannot be remote and disinterested in His creatures. Consequently, His grace and personal favour, or kindliness, to man is represented in the New Testament as mediated through Christ as redeemer.[9] This gives an assurance of salvation inasmuch as in the

[1]Ps. cxlv, 18.
[2]*The God of the Early Christians*, (Ed. 1924), p. 21.
[3]Cf. Montefiore, *Some Elements in the Religious Teaching of Jesus*, (Lond. 1919), p. 93.
[4]op. cit., p. 97f, *The Synoptic Gospels*, (Lond. 1927), Vol. I, p. cxviii.
[5]Ps. ciii.
[6]Mk. xiv, 24–7; Mk. x, 45; cf. Lk. xii, 50.
[7]Jn. xiv, 13, cf. xii, 24.
[8]Rom. v, 8.
[9]Rom. v, 15; I Tim. ii, 5; Heb. viii, 6, ix, 15, xii, 24.

idiom of St. Paul, no power in heaven or on earth can separate the new humanity from "the love of God which is in Christ Jesus our Lord."[1] Thus, the transcendent Creator was regarded as reconciling the world to Himself in the Incarnate Lord from heaven[2] Who raised mankind to a new status of sonship with the Father, thereby enabling the human race to gain access, as never before, to the inmost nature of the divine.[3]

This religious conception of the Fatherhood of God involving intimate personal relations as of those existing between a parent and his offspring, was altogether different from the philosophic use of the term 'Father' applied to Deity in the Platonic sense of the *fons et origo* of human life.[4] Moreover, the transcendental ultimate ground of existence easily passes into a materialistic pantheism, as in Stoicism, unless the conception of Fatherhood embodies the idea of paternal love and care calling forth a filial response and devotion. It is here that Judaeo-Christian theism parted company with Graeco-Roman thought. For Plato God was a particular Soul Who stands in a purely transcendental relation to the temporal order He sustains, and not until later, mainly under Alexandrian influence, did He become the Source of all knowledge and being (i.e. the good). It is not surprising, therefore, that Platonism did not in fact prove to be quite the handmaid of Christianity that some modern writers have supposed, though unquestionably it provided the general conception of theistic thought into which Christian theology had to be fitted.

The failure of Philo's attempt to interpret the Jewish doctrine of ethical monotheism in terms of a Platonic metaphysical Absolute by means of a series of lesser and more intelligible forms, or *logoi*, is but an illustration of the difficulties incurred in establishing communion with the divine in a religious personal relationship when Deity is regarded as wholly transcendent, ineffable and inconceivable. As a mystic, Philo's belief in the possibility of immediate union with "the first God" was genuine enough, but, so far as is known, he had no disciples and exercised no influence on Judaism; at any rate until the Middle Ages. His importance lies in the atmosphere he played his part in creating in which the Fourth Gospel and the Epistle to the Hebrews were written, and Neoplatonism subsequently developed. The Apostolic Church, like orthodox

[1] Rom. viii, 39.
[2] II Cor. v, 19.
[3] cf. Pringle-Pattison, *The Idea of God* (Oxford, 1917), p. 157.
[4] Plato, *Tim.*, 28C.

Judaism, was not philosophically-minded, and when the Faith spread in the Graeco-Roman world, Tertullian[1] and the Early Fathers especially in the West, did all in their power to discourage the encroachments of metaphysical speculation. But this was a position which could not be maintained indefinitely. The religious appeal of Christianity brought many converts from among those who had been trained in the philosophic schools—Stoics, Peripatetic and Pythagorean—and who, therefore, had adopted the Greek rather than the Jewish approach to the religion the Church offered.

Thus, Justin Martyr (c. A.D. 100-165), a native of Flavia Neapolis, began his search for truth first under a Stoic who affirmed that a knowledge of God was unnecessary. Gaining no satisfaction from this negative impersonal attitude, he applied next to a Peripatetic philosopher, then to a Pythagorean with no better results. Finally he went to a Platonist with whom he made progress towards the attainment of a knowledge of God, until he was led from Plato to faith in Christ and found Christianity to be what he described as "the only philosophy that is sure, and suited to man's wants."[2] Having become a Christian, he retained his philosopher's cloak and propagated the Faith in terms of a Logos doctrine in which the divine Word was represented as instructing the world not only through the Jewish patriarchs but also through those Greek philosophers who lived according to reason.[3] In Christ alone, he maintained, the All of reason dwelt in full perfection, whereas in the philosophers it was only partially revealed.[4] The Logos was the sole means by which the Father could be known, and in isolating God from the universe Justin sometimes identified the world with Deity, and by way of reaction virtually made the Word a distinct personality (ὑπόστᾰσις), thereby destroying the unity of the Godhead.

With the rise of the Catechetical School at Alexandria in the second century a systematic attempt was made to combine Platonism, Stoicism and the religion of the Old Testament in a Christian setting. But while Clement was more religious and less metaphysical in his Logos-doctrine than Philo, he did not wholly escape from a Sabellian tendency in making the Trinity virtually a threefold

---

[1] De Praescript, 7.
[2] Dialogue cum Trypho, CC, ii, iii.
[3] Apol. i, p. 83B.
[4] Apol., ii, 8, 10, p. 48B.

revelation of God as the "First Monad" known only to the Son as a subordinate Logos. Nevertheless, he maintained that no man cometh unto the Father except through Christ as the Logos, Who was also the instrument in creation and "the lover of mankind."[1] For Origen the Incarnate Christ was the supreme revelation of God, one stage removed from and so inferior to the Absolute, rather than the Word made flesh. The Holy Spirit was less than the Son being the eternal image of God, a second stage removed from the Father.[2]

This difference of essence (ἑτερότης τῆς ὀυσίας) paved the way for Arianism, but the Alexandrian Christian Platonists succeeded not only in giving Gnosticism its quietus but in presenting Christianity in a manner that satisfied both the religious and the philosophic instincts of the age. They offered a cultus in which objective worship and the personal needs of salvation were met in a manner that was intellectually, spiritually and ethically infinitely superior to anything the Graeco-Oriental Mystery Religions could produce. The catholic appeal of the Faith, based on the universal claims of Jesus, was not subject to the nationalistic limitations of Judaism, while the contemporary desire for a mystical *gnosis* was met by the interpretation of the Incarnation in terms of a Platonic logos-doctrine in which Christ as the divine Word was represented as the source of all true knowledge, intelligence and morality; enlightening all men according to their capacity. Thus, the needs both of the serious thinkers and the unsophisticated were supplied. For the simple believers all that was necessary for the Christian way of salvation was made available in the institutional faith and practice of the Church. For those who could rise to a more profound knowledge of divine things there was the Christian *gnosis* to enable them to live on a higher plane like good Platonists. To this in due course was added a higher mysticism as a discipline for rare souls devoted to the contemplative life.

Adopting this constructive policy, the Alexandrians continued to use the positive material of traditional Christianity in a manner which appealed to the common sense and deeper understanding of intelligent men without destroying its religious value and significance for the unlearned. But if this position was to be maintained, it was essential that the Church should definitely formulate its creed and firmly establish its ecclesiastical organization. In vindicating

---

[1] *Protrept*, 6.
[2] *De Prin*. i, 2, 3, ii, 6, 7, iii, 5; *In Joh*. ii, 6.

ing its teaching and practice during the succeeding centuries it was careful to safeguard at its most vital points its *religious* conception of divine transcendence and immanence as revealed in its central doctrine of the Incarnation. Its way of salvation differed fundamentally from that offered by Neoplatonism in terms of a mystical metaphysical redemption—"the final utterance of the speculative genius of Greece"—just as it was compelled to combat the various attempts to dissolve the unity of the Deity into a Tri-theism; or, conversely, to reduce the Saviour of the world to the level of an inspired human being. On the philosophic side, the Alexandrians incorporated the best of Platonism and Stoicism, while theologically the protracted Christological controversy ended in the affirmation of the incarnational conception of Christ as of "one substance with the Father," against the Greek and Gnostic emanational view of the generation of the Logos and the Nous. Jesus was the Logos become man of the same nature (ὁμοούσιος) with the Father in His divinity, and of the same nature with us in His humanity.

If the Chalcedonian definition of the Incarnation did little more than declare in plain terms that the Godhead and manhood were united in One Christ, without attempting any reasoned philosophic interpretation of the controversial issues, it at least preserved the essential elements in the Christian conception of God in His redemptive relation with the world and mankind. Arianism cut at the heart of the doctrine of the Atonement by making the Saviour a created being distinct from the Creator and at the same time not truly man, being devoid of a human nature, as in Apollinarianism. Nestorianism, again, set the Godhead and Manhood in such complete opposition that the human race virtually was left unredeemed. Finally, the Eutychians in maintaining that the humanity of Christ was lost in His divinity, fell under the same condemnation as the Apollinarians, who made the divine Logos in Christ replace His human soul. If the controversy as a whole represents "the bankruptcy of Greek patristic theology,"[1] the outcome safeguarded the Christian conception of God and His relation to mankind at a number of strategic points.

The Nicene faith as defined by the Chalcedonian Fathers constituted the final issue of a long struggle to formulate a doctrine in a manner that preserved the essential unity and transcendence of the Deity while allowing at the same time for His incarnational union with the human race in the Person of Jesus Christ, without denying

[1] Cf. W. Temple, *Foundations* (London, 1912), p. 230.

either the perfect divinity of God or the true humanity of the Word made flesh. This definition, stated in the paradoxical language of Western thought, provided the theological basis the Church needed to carry on its work as a unifying spiritual dynamic in an age in which a syncretistic religious culture was in process of disintegration. A distinction between the Creator and the creature had to be maintained if polytheism was to be avoided and incarnational worship made secure in an institutional religion grounded in a carefully balanced conception of divine transcendence and immanence. Where Cæsar was worshipped as God, Jesus had flung down His challenge, and when the glory of the Roman Empire had crumbled into dust, His Church remained because it had been built upon a rock.

By representing Christ as the spiritual head of a new humanity and a new world order, the Church became a transforming leaven renewing a dying age by offering the power of God in justification and sanctification through the redemptive relationship Christ established between man and the eternal God, Who transcends the natural and the historic order. The Infinite and the Finite were brought together as an interpenetrated whole sacramentally united; the temporal becoming the channel of the life of the eternal world. Thus, the State was prevented from becoming a self-contained all-embracing omnipotent political entity exercising supreme and undisputed sway over its members. Equally the Church, while it claimed universal jurisdiction over the whole of life in its spiritual aspects, allowed abundant scope for independent human activities initiated and exercised by the secular authority. A large measure of personal freedom was granted to the individual who could render his own life explicit under the control of two masters. In this way Christian civilization was built up on a tension of dualties in a pluralistic society unified by the underlying conviction that it was God Who transcended all things in a world in which He was working out His purposes in a realm of ends.

While in Eastern Christendom an abstract mysticism led the hermits of the Nitrian desert and the Thebaid to live in complete detachment from all social obligations and rational knowledge to attain "a static absorption in an unconditioned Reality,"[1] in the Latin West this conception of the *via negativa* was never adopted. In the Benedictine monasteries the lamp of learning and culture was kept burning during the Dark Ages, and if the Augustinian Christian

[1] K. E. Kirk, *The Vision of God* (London, 1931), p. 303.

counterpart of the Platonic ideal Republic was never realized, the medieval Church was the dynamic centre of European civilization.

For good or ill, it created a Christian society in which every aspect of life and culture was pervaded by a religious motive under the control of a two-fold hierarchy of spiritual and temporal authority transcending political and racial allegiances. Thus a great spiritual commonwealth of divers ethnological and cultural traditions was welded into a composite whole under one sovereign head who exercised universal jurisdiction as the Vicar of Christ on earth. Abuses abounded, but there was a sense of a real community with every aspect of life regarded as the means to the attainment of the true end of man in God's world. And it cannot be denied that at the height of its achievement in the thirteenth century, the medieval synthesis produced one of the most splendid ages in history, despite so much that was radically wrong with the system and its institutions. To it we are indebted for such masterpieces of architecture as Westminster Abbey in its present form, and the magnificent cathedrals of Amiens and Chartres, of Salisbury and the angelic choir at Lincoln. Among men of learning, letters and genius St. Thomas Aquinas, Grosseteste, Dante and Roger Bacon are outstanding figures, while in St. Francis of Assisi the new spiritual culture of Western Europe reached its climax in devoted service to God and his fellow men for Christ's sake. The universities, established in the previous century, made their influence increasingly felt, as did the grammar schools attached to cathedrals and collegiate churches under the jurisdiction of their chancellors, together with the friars' schools belonging to the religious houses.

Bad as conditions were in many aspects of secular and ecclesiastical life, the thirteenth century stands out as a notable example of a great cultural achievement which derived its inspiration from its theistic presuppositions acting as a spiritual dynamic. During the centuries that followed the fall of the Empire, the widespread distrust of learning and philosophy, outside the narrow range of current theological thought and practices, left the Church ill-equipped to meet the new intellectual stirrings aroused by the Crusades and the Moorish conquests. But from the ninth century the intellectual movement began by John Scotus Erigena (c. 810-880) and carried on by Anselm and Abelard, prepared the way for the remarkable Scholastic synthesis after the re-discovery of Aristotle. Thus, while a free use was made of Aristotelian principles, especially by St. Thomas, the Augustinian and Neoplatonic traditions were not without their influences in the medieval attempt to combine into a single system all available knowledge as the handmaid of Christian faith and practice.

In a graded scheme of Reality the Universal Church unified in the Papacy became the Absolute which absorbed the part in the whole. Therefore, in spite of the opposition of Duns Scotus and the Nominalists, and the Franciscan reaction against the Dominicans and their Thomism. the scales were weighted heavily on the side of Realism against the Nominalist contention that particular things alone are real. This, theologically interpreted, conflicted with the transcendental sovereignty of the spiritual authority and its universal jurisdiction, and eventually opened the way for the growth of a new scientific spirit and principle of individualism, when ecclesiastical control and the cultural hegemony of the Church ceased at the end of the Middle Ages. So long as this domination was maintained, the only sphere that was left to the "unaided" reason was the natural order. St. Thomas, it is true, was prepared to grant that it was theoretically possible to think rationally about God and the universe in the terms of the Aristotelian categories apart from faith, but beyond this limited range of knowledge the human mind could not penetrate by its own efforts. Indeed, he affirmed, "mankind would remain in the deepest darkness of ignorance if the path of reason were the only available way to the knowledge of God."[1]

The delimitation of the spheres of natural knowledge and revealed theology led eventually to the Deistic disregard of what reason admittedly could not discover, and its concentration upon what remained of the historical religion of Europe, "confined within the limits of the mere reason."[2] This "cardinal mistake" of the Thomist dualism opened the way for a rationalism destined to end in scepticism and disillusion when the restoration of classical studies in the fifteenth century freed the mind from its absorption in theological speculation and the tyranny of Aristotle. Philosophy and natural science claimed more and more to be independent quests of knowledge, and human reason appeared to be perfectly adequate to arrive at truth without any external divine aid. The centre of interest shifted from the sacred to the secular, and God was left relatively or absolutely remote from human affairs and natural processes. In this new humanistic philosophy the God of religion

[1] *Contra Gentiles*, Bk. I, chap. iv.
[2] C. C. J. Webb, *Studies in the History of Natural Theology* (Oxford, 1915), p. 231, 289.

became either a transcendental First Cause, or an immanent Life principle in the universe.

Thus, in a natural order in which impersonal laws were the enduring realities the idea of a self-sufficing metaphysical Absolute reappeared as the transcendental Cause of the universe and its orderly processes, and the Ground of the absoluteness of moral obligations as "the Power that makes for righteousness." But it was not easy to identify this Deistic Deity standing apart from creation and having little or no personal intercourse with man, with the God of religion. The Hegelian attempt to bridge the gap by a dialectical process of thesis, antithesis, and synthesis, in which the Absolute externalized in nature realized Itself in spirit, dissolved religion in metaphysics. It only remained for Marx to substitute matter for the idea on its way to self-knowledge as the sole reality, to transform the dialectical process into a materialistic interpretation of history in which religion was represented as "the opiate of the people"; the shadow cast by a defective economic system, destined to pass away as soon as the classless state is established.

Neither an absentee Deity nor an atheistical determinism, however, meets the deepest needs of struggling humanity as its strength and stay in the mastery of its environment and in the solution of the manifold problems of everyday life and experience. Even an intelligent Mind and Will guiding and fashioning cosmic mechanism does not suffice. The God of religion must be a genuine Providence, the extra-mundane universal Good and Source and Ground of all that is, standing in a personal relation to man and creation. "Other" He must be, but not "wholly other" lest He be regarded as so transcendent that He becomes an abstraction like Aristotle's Unmoved Mover. Equally if He be so absorbed in the universe as to be virtually a part of nature, or of the process of history, He ceases to exercise sovereign rule over the order of objects and events in space and time, or to be in possession of a consciousness analogous to that of human beings, or intelligible to the human mind. Similarly, a God creatively realizing Himself in the world as "the ultimate fact of the universe,"[1] or as an immanental finite emerging principle, cannot be the living God standing over against creation in a personal relationship.

The very idea of the Absolute, monistically or pantheistically conceived, implies the absence of external relations to other things, leaving the Deity either as the non-interfering external Creator

[3]A. S. Pringle-Pattison, *The Idea of God* (London, 1920), p. 312.

completely dissociated from the universe He has made, or as the whole reality of which nature and man are partial manifestations lacking permanence and individuality, or even independent existence when the phenomenal order is regarded as illusory. While such a conception of divinity finds expression in a mystical experience of impersonal unity with the All, the distinctions of rational consciousness are absorbed in a pantheistic essence beyond good and evil. As on this hypothesis everything proceeds from the One, so everything leads to the Source of all reality, but only by way of emancipation and absorption, precluding a personal relationship with a living, active God Whose sovereign will has called into existence the created universe in its entirety. It is here that the doctrine of the Absolute, be it conceived deistically or pantheistically, fails to provide an adequate basis of religion.

In the light of our present day understanding of the evolutionary process in its manifold forms, phases and operations, the conception of an ever-present, ever-active Ground of finite existence, not merely its beginning, has gained a new significance, emergence being linked with purpose in a realm of ends in which the "final cause" seems to be the realization of values of definite worth. Within and throughout the cosmic process this Ground transcends the natural order and directs it towards that which is best in the physical, intellectual and spiritual spheres. Inasmuch as it is a principle of perpetual adjustment to environmental conditions revealing itself in variation and mutation yet sustaining all things by unchanging volitional activity, the ultimate creative energy of the cosmos reasonably may be regarded as that of intelligent personal will with Whom communion is possible on the part of beings equipped with human personality and spiritual consciousness. Moreover, Deity so conceived, at once transcendent and immanent, becomes related to His creation in a manner that brings its processes and events under His immediate control in the working out of His purposes for the world as the scene of divine creative activity.

In nature and history the principle of variation is fundamental, and if the universe is sustained at every moment by the energy of the conscious rational will of its Creator, its processes and events may be expected to manifest His guiding hand, just as those whom He has created in His own image and likeness may be regarded as having been endowed with the power of establishing personal relations with Him, and of responding to His promptings and disclosures in time and space. Thus, a God of religion, Who is at once the transcendent and immanent Creator and Sustainer of the universe, is distinct in idea from the conception of an ineffable unconditioned Absolute, or a pantheistic principle in constant evolution. While He is continuously present and all things are held to be in direct dependence upon His will, He is not identical with them, or in any sense dependent upon them. If by the activity of His will He has given being and unity to the spatial and temporal order of which He is the transcendent Ground, the control of the adaptability and variability which characterize nature and history, must lie within the sphere of divine Personality so conceived.

Therefore, religion is justified in its fundamental presupposition that the living God, Who is the object of its veneration and devotion, is actively at work in the world, in the course of history and in human experience. That this activity often has been and is interpreted in an arbitrary and capricious manner, at variance with the principle of uniformity observable in the behaviour of natural law, is hardly surprising in view of the naïve conceptions of the unsophisticated mind concerning cosmic processes. The same is true in the ethical sphere. "Every religious standpoint," as Höffding maintained, "gathers up into its conception of God the highest known values,"[1] but these are conditioned by the general level of moral and social attainment at a given stage of cultural development. The function of religion is always to provide standards and sanctions in accordance with that which is highest and best, as these qualities are evaluated at a particular time and place, however much they may fall short of the absolute good and the ultimate truth. The existence of a spontaneous element in the human consciousness of the divine, transcending man's search for and apprehension of Deity as the *summum bonum* and ultimate ground of all things, has led to the idea of a self-disclosure in the form of revelation. This has been variously interpreted, ranging from infallible divine oracles to the minds of individuals, or ready-made theologies vouchsafed to a particular community, nation or church, to the unveiling of the living God Himself through events. But however the process be understood, it presupposes the religious conception of Deity as a personal Being and self-conscious Will with Whom man is capable of being in vital intercourse, and Whose beneficence is manifest in His creation as a teleological order perpetually under His control.

[1]*Philosophy of Religion*, E.T., p. 61.

CHAPTER IX

DIVINE REVELATION

THE confusion that has arisen on the subject of divine revelation is the result in great measure of a dualistic separation of the sacred and the secular issuing in a sharp distinction between natural and revealed religion. In primitive states of culture and in ancient society no such differentiation is or was contemplated. As Marett has said, "the savage has no word for 'nature'. He does not abstractly distinguish between an order of uniform happenings and a higher order of miraculous happenings. He is merely concerned to mark and exploit the difference when presented in the concrete."[1] The natural and the supernatural are so interwoven that Providential activity is recognized in each and every occurrence that lies outside the normal sequence of events directly under human control and the range of human experience. As the two spheres have become more clearly defined and differentiated, Providence either has assumed a more independent role as an external transcendent Deity or has become merged in the universe and identified itself with its processes in a manner that leaves little or no room for the exercise of sovereign rule, creative guidance and revelational self-disclosure or communication. Man may claim an immediate mystical knowledge of the Absolute within the soul, but an impersonal pantheistic or monistic Ultimate Reality cannot reveal itself like the living God in a personal relationship with His creation.

From the most rudimentary inklings of Providence to the highest conceptions of personal theism, revelation has been a feature of all religions in which the divine Power manifesting itself in the universe has been thought to exercise transcendental control over natural events and human destinies. The gods, ancestral spirits or culture heroes who create and mould the world communicate their will and power to man through divine kings, concrete events, ecstatic experiences, the practice of divination, the reading of omens and auspices, and by astrological lore, until at length Deity is thought to unveil Himself as a Person to persons through events rather than to reveal supernatural truths in the form of hidden wisdom, credal

[1] *Threshold of Religion* (London, 1914), p. 109.

dogmas and theological propositions dictated by a divine oracle, or made known through an infallible book or Church, or by signs, portents, prodigies and augurs. In primitive society all this is essentially a temporal process, a sequence of divine activities and manifestations ordering and controlling the course of nature and history by a series of interventions and prescriptions expressed in the established sacred tradition as myth, ritual and cultus.

In order to ascertain the will and directions of Providence a special technique has had to be devised ranging from visionary experience and shamanistic occult methods to prophetic illuminattion and objective self-utterance and self-disclosure in the unveiled life of God Himself. In the arctic region from Bering Straits to the borders of Scandinavia, where shamanism is widely practised as a developed cult among the Eskimo and Palaeo-Asiatic tribes, no one, as Miss Czaplicka has pointed out, becomes a shaman of his own free will; it comes to him *nolens volens*, like a hereditary disease.[1] First he must show the proper symptoms—excitability, fainting, irritability, moroseness, love of solitude, hallucinations, trance and similar abnormal neurotic predispositions. He then undergoes an intensive and rigorous course of training under the guidance of an experienced practitioner to increase his suggestibility and learn the lore of the spirits with whom he is destined to become *en rapport*, together with the technique through which be receives communications from them.[2] This accomplished, he is able to summon the spirits by beating the sacred drum, or assemble them in his tambourine, penetrate to the heights of heaven and discern its deepest secrets in ecstatic visions, utter prophecies, discover whether sacrifices have been accepted, forecast the weather and other future events, the prospects of harvest, and even recover wandering souls. But his principal function is to reveal the mind and will of the gods and spirits with whom he has direct intercourse. Thus, he is the agent of a divine revelation acquiring supernatural knowledge through ecstasy, visions and occult ritual methods, calculated to produce a highly neurotic state of frenzy.

It was this shamanistic tradition that found expression in the Thraco-Phrygian tumultuous worship which lay behind the Dionysian and Orphic mysteries in Greece and the cult of the

[1] *Aboriginal Siberia* (Oxford, 1914), p. 169ff, cf. 177ff.
[2] V. M. Mikhailowsky, *Journal of Royal Anthropological Institute*, XXIV, 1895, p. 85ff; W. Jochelson, The Koryet, *Jesup North Pacific Expedition* (New York, 1905–8), Vol. VI, p. 47.

Nebi'im, or "sons of the prophets", in Israel. In the Thracian orgies held by night on the tops of mountains, characterized by wild music and dancing and the free use of wine, the votaries, or maenads, became god-possessed as "Sabazoi" or "Bacchoi" (i.e. spiritual beings), and in this condition of hieromania they attained a shamanistic insight into, and communion with, the god (Dionysos) whose invisible presence they thus discerned and whose life they shared.[1] Under the sobering influence of the Delphic Apollo and the Orphic movement, these unearthly longings of the mystically-minded Greeks for ecstatic revelation, and the breaking down of the barriers separating man from the supernatural order, were transformed into healthier if less thrilling experiences.

From very early times Delphi was a centre of inspiration and divination associated with the god Apollo, who was supposed to have superseded Dionysos at the shrine, where a vapour rising from a cleft in the ground is said to have inspired the prophecies.[2] There the priestess, or Pythia, seated in the inner shrine, perhaps over the vaporous cleft, after drinking water from the sacred spring Kassotis, became inspired and prophesied.[3] Her words, though not improbably actually unintelligible, were interpreted by the προφῆται, and written down in hexameters as the oracles of Zeus given through Apollo with whom the Pythia was *en rapport*. But Apollo was not an ecstatic figure, his function being that of divination rather than of telling the will of his father (Zeus) at specified seasons. The prophetess, therefore, seems to be an innovation in his cultus, derived from the Dionysian background of the shrine. But if her presence made the Delphic oracle instrumental in the propagation of the worship of Dionysos, its Apolline connexions modified the Thraco-Phrygian orgiastic rites, and brought them under the sobering influence of divination. Since Orpheus apparently was also an Apolline figure before he was incorporated in the cult of Dionysos,[4] the movement that derived its inspiration from him had a similar effect. Thus, in Greece the wilder forms of shamanistic practice were never established as a Hellenic tradition. At Eleusis, as we have seen, the esoteric revelation to the initiated centred apparently in a sacramental mystery drama in which the goddess and her child

[1]Farnell, *The Cult of the Greek States* (Oxford, 1909), Vol. V, p. 88ff; J. Harrison, *Prolegomena to the Study of Greek Religion* (Camb., 1922), p. 363ff; R. Rhode, *Psyche* (London, 1925), p. 256.

[2]Cf. Plutarch, *de Defect. Orac*, 43.

[3]Farnell, op. cit., Vol. IV, p. 188.

[4]Guthrie, *Orpheus and Greek Religion* (London, 1935), p. 43ff.

M

were disclosed in the symbolism of sacred objects, sounds and lights to effect a fundamental change in the spiritual condition of the neophytes. In this there was no idea of the escape of a divine element from a hampering body, as in the Dionysian-Orphic tradition, or the Platonic soma-sema relation and the doctrine of reincarnation.[1]

When the Orphic imagery, however, found a place in Plato's conception of the heavenly origin of the soul, it became a vision of eternal truth, beauty and goodness in the world of pure ideas of which the world of time was only a reflection. Nevertheless, the dualism of body and soul was fundamental in the Platonic theory, and as each belonged to a different world, the soul could not attain the true wisdom so long as it was hampered by its fleshly integument. The real philosopher, it was affirmed, is "in every respect at enmity with the body and longs to possess the soul alone"; "to fly away from the earth to heaven as quickly as he can." This is to become like God, and "to become like Him is to become holy and just and wise."[2]

In this quest divination played its part notably in the case of Socrates who attributed his pursuit of truth to a supernatural gift bestowed by an 'inward voice', or Daimonion,[3] who warned him of undesirable actions. Again, it was to the Delphic oracle that he turned for guidance on more than one occasion,[4] the Pythia having declared him to be the wisest of men. Henceforth he regarded himself as in the service of Apollo and under his protection, so long as he lived perpetually in accordance with his divine direction. But notwithstanding the vision of reality vouchsafed to the philosopher, however much he might be aided by oracular revelations and the right use of the noblest senses,[5] true knowledge, as in Orphism, was only attainable after death when the soul had been freed from the body.[6] This later led Plotinus to develop a doctrine of ecstatic communion with the Absolute Who could not be known directly by reason. The soul was attuned to the divine in active contemplation by a long process of internal quietude, of abstraction from sense and absorption in reason.[7] Passivity led to divine intoxication and full communion with God in the beatific vision. But so deeply

[1]*Cratylus*, 400C; *Phaedrus*, 247ff.
[2]*Phaedo*, 64, 66ff; *Theaetetus*, 176.
[3]Plato, *Apol.*, 40A, 41D.
[4]*Apol.*, 19A.
[5]*Symposium*, 210, 211.
[6]*Phaedo*, 66.
[7]Enneads, VI, ix, 3.

laid in the Graeco-Roman world was divination that in the fourth and fifth centuries A.D. Neoplatonic mysticism readily degenerated into a means of communicating with the ancient Olympian gods by oracles, and receiving revelations from them,[1] very much as in Babylonia questions were addressed to gods from whom answers were received through intermediaries purporting to be directly inspired.[2]

In Assyria letters were written by kings to Ashur and the rest of the pantheon reporting the fortunes of battle,[3] and in Egypt correspondence with divinities was of common occurrence.[4] Indeed, even to this day notes are written to the Virgin and the saints at shrines in peasant Europe, but since the eighth century A.D. there are no records of written replies having been received.[5] In the ancient world the king was the ordinary means of communication with the gods by virtue of his office and function,[6] and in Assyria the invention of divination was attributed to an ante-diluvian ruler, Enmeduranki.[7] Henceforth it became part of the royal prerogative to seek divine guidance through extispicium (the inspection of entrails), oracles, dreams and visions in the conduct of military campaigns and on all other occasions where an incalculable element was present. As divination and astrology developed into a systematized "science" the king collected round him an order of inspired men to inspect the liver, interpret the stars and other heavenly phenomena, determine the omens and utter prophetic warnings. But, as Sir William Halliday has pointed out, "of the seer or mantis is demanded not only knowledge but a wise and understanding heart, or at least something of the genius of successful opportunism."[8] It is, however, in the realms of magic and the domain of the medicine-man that the antecedents of divination are to be sought.

---

[1]In Ancient Rome the introduction of the Sibylline oracles in the fifth century B.C. increased the belief in the direct communication of the divine will through inspired seers inherent in the widespread practice of divination by auspices. Ecstatic communion, or revelation, was also fostered by the extraneous worship of the Magna Mater which persisted at Thebes and Delphi to a late period notwithstanding the efforts made to regulate the orgiastic cult in the late Republic and in the Empire.

[2]*Cuneiform Texts*, xxxix, 41; F. Nötscher, *Orientales*, Nos. 51-4, p. 218.

[3]F. Thureau-Dangin, *Une relation de la huitième campagne de Sargon*. R. Labat, *Le caractère religieux de la royauté*, p. 273; C. J. Gadd, *Ideas of Divine Rule in the Ancient East* (Schweich Lectures, 1945, O.U.P., 1948), p. 27f.

[4]J. Cerny, *Bulletin de l'institut francais d'archéologie orientale du Caire*, xxxv, 42.

[5]F. Mader, *Revue des traditions populaires* (Paris, 1905), p. 65ff.

[6]Prov. xvi, 10.

[7]Zimmern, *Beiträge zur Kenntnis der babylonian religion*, No. 24, ll, 74ff.

[8]*Greek Divination* (London, 1913), p. 55ff.

In Israel the idea of revelation developed along different lines. The covenant relationship between Yahweh and his Chosen People presupposed a divine self-disclosure to and intervention on behalf of the nation in which the kings of Israel played a very inconspicuous part (I Sam. xxviii, 6; xiv, 41). The God who walked in the garden and talked with Adam at the dawn of creation continued to reveal himself to the patriarchs at the tamarisk of Beersheba and its sacred well, at the terebinth of Mamre and Ophrah, and at the megalithic sanctuary at Bethel, just as he disclosed his presence to Moses at the theophany in Midian, or on the Holy Mount. Sometimes he was alleged to have appeared to men in dreams and visions as in the case of Abimelech, Jacob, Joseph and Pharaoh, to impart knowledge of future events.[1] When his earthly abode became the sacred ark of the covenant, this numinous object, which carried on the desert tradition of the tent of meeting, was the centre of divination. Charged with his divine personality as a kind of miasma clinging to "the mercy seat" overlaid with gold, it was addressed and treated as if it were Yahweh himself.[2] From it oracles were obtained, and before it, in all probability, the sacred lots (*tora, urim* and *thummim*) were cast to obtain information concerning the divine will.[3] The methods employed in Hebrew divination are obscure as are the contents and construction of the ark, but they included the use of the ephod,[4] the divining cup,[5] the divining rod[6] and the shooting of arrows.[7] The stars were regarded as having been created as 'signs'[8] for man and eclipses were thought to have a sinister significance.[9]

The function of the seer (*kohen*) was to ascertain the divine will by means of oracles and such special insight and knowledge as he possessed by virtue of his daily contact with the deity. In addition to these official diviners there were men endowed with unusual occult and superhuman powers who by ecstatic inspiration were able to become god-possessed like shamans. These Nebi'im, or "sons of the prophets," were grouped round certain sanctuaries, such as Gibeah, Rama, Bethel, Gilgal and Jericho, and worked themselves

[1] Gen. xx, 3ff, Gen. xxviii, 12ff, Gen. xxxvii, xl, xli.
[2] Num. x, 35; I Sam. iv, 5, 8.
[3] Jos. vii, 16f; I Sam. x, 20f; cf. Prov. xvi, 33.
[4] II Sam. vi, 14, 16, 20f; Jud. viii, 24ff, xvii, xviii.
[5] Gen. xliv, 5.
[6] Hos. iv, 12; Num. xxi, 18.
[7] Ezek. xxi, 26; I Sam. xx, 20ff; II Kgs. xiii, 18f.
[8] Gen. i, 14.
[9] Joel, iii, 3f.

into a frenzy by the aid of the timbrel, pipe, harp and psaltery, as in the case of the Dionysian votaries. In this condition of divine intoxication they gave utterance to prophetic oracles unintelligible until they were interpreted.[1] The contagion spread with great rapidity and affected all who came under its influence,[2] if they had the right disposition. The seer's personality was heightened so that he became "another man," or god-possessed,[3] i.e. Yahweh dwelt within him and the divine efflatus, or *ruach*, moved him to give vent to revelations.

The relation of these Nebi'im to the great Hebrew prophets of the eighth century B.C. is a matter of dispute.[4] The term "prophets" (*nabi*) is used in the Old Testament in three connexions. Prior to 800 B.C. it refers either to the groups of inspired men associated with sanctuaries, such as Saul encountered, or to outstanding individuals, e.g. Samuel, Elijah and Elisha, and a few isolated figures like Nathan, Gad and Ahijah. From 800 to 550 B.C. outstanding spiritual personalities come into great prominence as the proclaimers of a divine message which was emphatically ethical. They too believed that they were invaded by a transcendent power which they called "the word of Yahweh," under whose pneumatic influence they were inspired to give utterance to his imperative commands[5] and to bear witness to the mighty hands of God in the control of the course of history. "Thus saith Yahweh" was their constant refrain. It was the character of the prophecy rather than the manner of its reception and deliverance that differentiated the great prophets from their predecessors. Both employed signs, symbolic gestures, inspired words (often couched in poetic rhythmic form) spoken with the directness and violence of an oracle coming from without and endowed with supernatural efficacy calculated to bring about the results pronounced.[6] But the words of the great prophets, although received in visions and ecstatic experiences,[7] were stamped with genuine originality and opposition to contemporary thought to a greater degree than in the previous period. They were conscious of the contrast between their own feelings and ideas and the purpose of God Who constrained them to give verbal expression

[1] I Sam. x, 5ff, I Kgs. xxii, 11f.
[2] I Sam. xix, 20-4.
[3] I Sam. x, 6.
[4] Cf. A. Guillaume, *Prophecy and Divination* (London, 1938), p. 142ff.
[5] Amos iii, 7, 8; Jer. xxiii, 18, 22; Is. xxxvii, 1, xlii, 1.
[6] Jer. li, 59-64, xix, 11f, xx, 1-6.
[7] Cf. Is. vi; Ezek. iii, 22ff.

to His divine decrees, regardless of the consequences to themselves.

As Edouard Meyer says, "the step forward which Amos, Hosea and Isaiah took denotes one of the most momentous changes in the history of mankind. The all-subduing force of conscience, or, more exactly, of the conscience of a single individual in opposition to the whole surrounding world, came into action and made itself felt for the first time. The consequences of the struggle fought out in the eighth and seventh centuries B.C. within the small area of Palestine are still felt throughout the whole range of civilization."[1] They were themselves politicians in the sense that they tried to shape the policy of the country in accordance with what they believed to have been the divine will made known to them, but unlike their rivals, they were not fanatical nationalists. The Day of Yahweh for them was a time of judgment and disaster rather than of victory and success, of darkness not of light, because the absolute righteousness of Yahweh had been violated by His people.[2] Punishment was inevitable, culminating in the exile.

At length, however, out of the darkness of captivity came a voice from an anonymous poet, the Deutero-Isaiah, declaring that the sufferings of the nation had atoned for its iniquities and the approaching victory of Cyrus the Persian would secure the release of the remnant of Judah.[3] A new Exodus was at hand because Yahweh, the sole Creator of the universe and the absolute Ruler of its destinies, had ordained that His servant Cyrus should be the means of restoring Israel's glory as part of His instrument for the gathering together of the peoples of the whole earth, and the establishment of His righteous rule to the ends of the world. This conception of universal monotheism was proclaimed more explicitly and controversially than by any of his predecessors, and it marks the beginning of a new epoch in theistic revelation.

In the post-exilic period although prophecy in the former sense ceased to function,[4] and the prophetic office fell into considerable disrepute owing to the failure of the more optimistic predictions, the influence of the movement lived on in the organization of the religious and social life of Judaism. The words of the great prophets were held in the highest regard[5] as the utterances of the will of God,

---

[1] *Kleine Schriften zur Geschichte theorie und zur wirtschaftlichen und politischen Geschichte des Altertums* (Halle, Niemeyer, 1910), p. 213.

[2] Amos v, 20; Jer. xxviii, 6, 12–16.

[3] Is. xl.

[4] Cf. Ps. lxxiv, 9.

[5] Zech. i, 4ff; II Chron. xxxvi, 21.

so that the prophetic oracle of Yahweh remained side by side with the priestly ascription of the Law to Moses in its all-embracing entirety. Haggai and Zechariah may have been members of a definite company of prophets attached to the temple at Jerusalem which they were instrumental in restoring,[1] and if Zechariah was a visionary, his summary of ethical duties was in line with the doctrine of divine righteousness proclaimed by Amos. The concluding chapters of Isaiah (lv-lxvi) show that two generations later the prophetic spirit still survived and, as in the case of the anonymous writer called Malachi and the liturgical apocalyptist Joel, devotion to the cultus did not diminish zeal for the truths of ethical religion.

It was, however, primarily the Law, or Torah, which for the Jew constituted the Word of Yahweh. All that He had spoken to Moses on the Holy Mount must be done,[2] for they were nothing less than divine oracles given as an integral part of the covenant and sealed by a solemn blood-rite. Moreover, scholarship may have demonstrated that much of the legislation which hitherto was thought to have been handed down from the days of the wilderness is in fact the product of later ages, but as represented and interpreted in the Deuteronomic code and the post-exilic community, the Torah and the cultus were claimed to have been directly revealed by God to the founder of Israel as a nation in the desert. That some of this literary material does belong to a time long before the Exile is now generally conceded, and if the earliest laws refer to an agricultural rather than a nomadic culture, the resemblances between the Hebrew Book of the Covenant (Ex. xx. 22-xxiii. 19) and the Babylonian Code of Hammurabi are too intimate to be unconnected with each other. Since the Deuteronomic Code (Dt. xii-xxvi, xxviii) is based on the Book of the Covenant, its antecedents are deeply embedded in the foundations of Israel, and it has many points of contact with the Levitical Code (Lev. xvii-xxvi). It only remained for the post-exilic priests to complete the work of codification towards the end of the fifth century B.C., to refer back to Moses the sacrificial system and all the institutions of Judaism as divine revelational ordinances. Thus, through the Deuteronomic priestly legislation the holy will of Yahweh was made known, and the first requirement of His people was that of obedience to His commands. It was this which constituted holiness.[3]

[1] A. R. Johnston, *Expository Times*, XLVII, 1936, p. 316.
[2] Ex. xiv, 3.
[3] Num. xv, 40.

One of the chief functions of the priests was to give *toroth*, or oracular decisions, and these included ethical as well as ritual teaching respecting the will and purposes of God.[1] Since like the *Toroth* of the prophets, they were ascribed to Yahweh,[2] the priests became His mouthpiece, and as an elaborate system of legalistic and allegorical exegesis—*Midrash, Targums* and *Haggadah*—was developed to adapt the written Torah to current needs, revelation acquired a new character in Rabbinical Judaism. Proceeding on the assumption that God's activity in the world in general, and in Israel in particular, is a continuous process manifest in His divine control of history, He was represented as the guardian of the Law. In and through it He made known His will in respect of each and every concrete situation as it arose, and He revealed Himself in the priestly oracle, or the casting of the lot given by the numinous Urim and Thummim, and by the words of the prophets.[3] The Pentateuch, however, became the norm as the Word of Yahweh to Moses, and was and is regarded by Jews as the most sacred and authoritative revelation of all divine disclosures and interventions, embodying in a homogeneous and perfect code the will of Yahweh for Israel. This being the revelation *par excellence*, it embraced all the fundamental beliefs, doctrines and decrees of Judaism. Therefore, it only remained for the rabbis to interpret and supplement what had been given once and for all in order to enable the revealed principles to be applied to everyday life and changing conditions in each successive generation. These commentaries, it was alleged, were written down in the Talmuds (i.e. Mishnah and Gemara) and Midrashim under a measure of divine inspiration, though the charismatic influence was not of the same intensity as in the case of Moses and his prophetic successors. The rabbis were merely teachers and judges, not priests, prophets or seers, and they never claimed to 'divide the Word of God' like a living Church. The Law had been given: the final utterance had been declared, and for good or ill Israel had to accept and act upon what had been revealed and applied to human needs in the authoritative scriptures. Therefore, like Islam, Judaism is a revelational religion of a Book, consisting in the first instance of the narratives attributed to Moses but also including the Prophets, the Writings and the Rabbinical literature.

On a lower level of authority the experience and ethical teaching

[1]Hag. ii, 11; cf. Jer. xviii, 18, Mal. ii, 6f.
[2]Zech. vii, 12; Is. i, 10-17, xlii, 4.
[3]Jos. xviii, 6, 22; Dt. xxxiii, 8-10.

of the "wise men" is accorded an indirect revelational value, but only as practical counsel concerning conduct.[1] The Hebrew Wisdom movement appears to have been dependent upon its prototype in Ancient Egypt where the "Teaching of Amen-em-ope" is identical in form with Proverbs xxii. 17-xxiii. 11, and earlier in date. As a divine attribute wisdom is personified in this literature and becomes a manifestation of Yahweh, thereby emphasizing an essential element in the Biblical conception of revelation as the disclosure of God Himself, and not merely of truths concerning Him and His doings among men. From Him all morality was derived so that by Him "princes decree justice"[2] and the inner secrets of the hearts of man are discerned by the conscience illuminated by Him.[3]

Since the words of the wise are the words of God, they acquired a revelational significance as part of the divine direction of human life.[4] It is Yahweh Who giveth wisdom and out of His mouth proceedeth knowledge and understanding,[5] revealing Himself by His Spirit, but transcendentally rather than immanently in the soul of man. In Judaism all revelation comes from God and is part of the Torah as an inspired whole, so that, however imperfectly perceived by the human instrument may be the divine truth disclosed, the disclosure is independent of the spiritual experience and understanding of the recipient. It was God Who spake to Moses and satisfied His covenant with Israel,[6] Who gave the Law and used the prophets as His mouthpiece. It was He Who demonstrated His power and purpose in history by mighty acts and signs and the control of natural events, renewing His covenant with His people and establishing His kingdom. The writers of this record of revelation, therefore, were not displaying their own inspirational insight, though it may be argued that their minds were divinely illuminated to discern the purposive activity of God in the process and events they interpreted.[7] In everything they believed themselves to be His instruments impelled to declare what they dimly perceived, if indeed they understood at all the message they felt they had received.

This transcendental conception of revelation is not confined to Judaism. It recurs with equal insistence in the New Testament. As

[1] II Kgs. xviii, 20; Is. xix, 3; Prov. i, 8, iii, 1, iv, 2, vi, 20, 23; Job xxii, 22.
[2] Prov. viii, 15.
[3] xx, 27.
[4] Prov. viii, 14f, xx, 27; Ecclus. xxxix, 6; Job xxxii, 6ff.
[5] Prov. ii, 6.
[6] Ex. vi, 2-7.
[7] cf. W. Temple, *Nature, Man and God* (London, 1934), p. 314f.

Yahweh was alleged to have manifested Himself to Moses, so in the Christian dispensation the fundamental dogma was that the Word had been made flesh and dwelt among men who beheld His glory full of grace and truth.[1] Thus, the mystery of faith was rooted and grounded in the doctrine of a personal God breaking into the world of time and space in a stupendous incarnational intervention. This constituted more than a "progressive revelation." It was rather, as Professor C. H. Dodd has said, "a cutting across of purpose by events; the entry into history of a reality beyond history."[2]

Upon the unique interpretation of the vicissitudes of Jewish history which characterized the message of the Hebrew prophets, Christian tradition built up a theology in which the historical reality of the life, death and resurrection of Christ was the event *par excellence*. In it all that had gone before found its climax and fulfilment. The action of God in history described in the Old Testament as "the mighty acts of Yahweh," in the New Testament was represented as having attained its consummation in a supra-historical Personality Who gave meaning and significance to the Hebraic revelation. The prophets claimed to deliver a personal message from the living God, unique and unpredictable, while the Torah was alleged to be the disclosure of the divine will to Moses. Jesus, according to the Synoptic record, went beyond this when He affirmed that the Messiah had come, "the reign of God had begun. Repent ye and believe the Gospel!"[3] This was the challenge that turned the world upside down and introduced a new era in civilization as well as a new epoch in revealed religion. It is open to argue that the claims were unfounded in fact, but that they were made and accepted by many cannot be denied.[4] The crucial question is whether or not the Kingdom which came in Christ came from God. If it did so come it fulfilled the Jewish conception of revelation inasmuch as it bore witness to the advent of One Who was Himself the Incarnate Lord from heaven and the personification of divine redemptive activity. In that case, God had visited and redeemed His people. The Covenant had been renewed, the Kingdom established and the Mystery "kept silence through times eternal now was manifested."[5]

The revelational event was represented as final and absolute, constituting a complete break with the past. It was, therefore, more

[1] St. Jn. i, 14.
[2] *History and the Gospel* (London, 1938), p. 181.
[3] St. Mk. i, 14f.
[4] Mk. iv, ii; I Cor. ii, 1, 2, 7; Rom. xi, 25–36, xvi, 25f; Ephes. iii, 5.
[5] Rom. xvi, 26.

than a sequel to a "progressive revelation." Eternity, it was claimed, had entered the time-process through the Incarnation, whereby the temporal order had acquired an eternal significance it did not formerly possess. The Kingdom had come with power, and although its consummation belonged to the future, "the life of the age to come" was an experienced reality here and now.[1] The omnipotent Deity Who in times past had made Himself known by His mighty acts in Israel, in this visitation had created a new humanity by a fresh epiphany of divine power and love.[2] This was revealed at first as the Messianic secret to the apostolic company of believers;[3] then later it was proclaimed as a catholic Gospel in an ever-widening range of contacts.[4]

The "mystery of the Kingdom," as Schweitzer has maintained, was the power of God which from so small a sowing has produced such an abundant harvest.[5] It was a "realized eschatology" in which those who were initiated into the Church were the recipients of the new revelation and partakers in its power and grace which flowed from the death and resurrection of Christ as the culmination of His Messiahship.[6] The esoteric disclosures of the pagan Mystery cults became in Christianity a revelation foreshadowed in the old dispensation and made known in its fulness in the New Israel as the Kingdom of God wherein the Gospel is proclaimed[7] and its hidden meaning perceived.[8] "The mystery of the Kingdom" on which such emphasis was placed in the New Testament centred in the particular interpretation given by Jesus to His Messiahship. For Judaism the very idea of a suffering and humiliated Christ was as foreign as it was anathema.[9] For Christianity it was the core of the Gospel; the revelation of revelations, summed up in what may be a pre-Pauline hymn incorporated in Philippians ii. 6-11. There Christ is declared to have laid aside His divinity in order to take the form of a slave and to be born in the likeness of man. Having thus emptied Himself "He became obedient even unto death on a cross,

[1]St. Mk. i, 15.
[2]Mk. i, 24, iii, 11, v, 7.
[3]Mk. iv, 11f.
[4]Acts x, 38; Mt. xiii, 11; Lk. viii, 10.
[5]*Quest of the Historical Jesus* (E.T. London, 1911), p. 106ff.
[6]Cf. Dodd, *The Parables of the Kingdom* (London, 1936), p. 79; A. E. J. Rawlinson, *St. Mark* (Westminster Commentary, 1926), p. 51f.
[7]Ephes. vi, 19.
[8]Mk. iv, 11.
[9]Targum on Is. lii, 15-liii, 12; Driver and Newbauer, *Jewish Interpreters of Isaiah LIII.*

wherefore God exalted him exceedingly, and gave him a Name above every name (i.e. κύριος, "Lord"), that in the name of Jesus the knee of every created being in heaven and on earth and in the nether regions should bow and every tongue confess that he is Lord to the glory of God the Father."[1]

This equation of Jesus with the Messiah and the Isaianic Suffering Servant exalted as the Lord in glory, differentiated the new dispensation from the whole of previous history. The relation of the historical Jesus to God was one of subordination. This safeguarded the Jewish fundamental doctrine of the supremacy of Yahweh, but, nevertheless, he was κύριος, whether or not this title carried with it a cosmic significance.[2] As the Incarnate Lord He stood between God and man, and by his death and resurrection He had wrought a mighty deliverance,[3] incomparably greater than anything that had been accomplished by any previous divine intervention in the course of history. Therefore, as interpreted in Christian theology, He was established for ever so that the glory of God is seen for all time in the face of Jesus Christ.[4] Human history was viewed as a single and unique process of events, in which, as Professor C. C. J. Webb has said, "every past happening has its position and date, and no part of which is wholly unrelated to any other."[5] The establishment of the Kingdom was not merely a future event but a present reality based on the new revelation of the fatherhood of God with its demands of filial love and self-giving.[6] This was exemplified supremely in the perfectly surrendered will and life laid down on the Cross, which became the crucial factor in the Christian mystery of redemption, and the point to which all divine revelation and intervention in the temporal order converged.

Henceforth, as Edwyn Bevan has maintained, "the great dividing line is that which marks off all those who hold that the relation of Jesus to God—however they describe or formulate it—is of such a kind that it could not be repeated in any other individual —that to speak, in fact, of its being repeated in one *other* individual is a contradiction in terms, since any individual standing in that relation to God would *be* Jesus, and that Jesus, in virtue of this

[1]Lightfoot, *Epistle to the Philippians* (1868), p. III; H. Lohmayer, *Philipper, Kolosser und Philemon* (Göttingen, 1930), p. 90ff; W. K. L. Clarke, *New Testament Problems* (London, 1929), p. 145ff.

[2]Bousset, *Kyrios Christos* (Göttingen, 1913), p. 5; Lohmeyer, op. cit., p. 97.

[3]Rom. v. 9.

[4]II Cor. iv, 6.

[5]*The Historical Element in Religion* (London, 1935), p. 80.

[6]T. W. Manson, *The Teaching of Jesus* (London, 1931), p. 89ff.

relation, has the same absolute claim upon all men's worship and loyalty as belongs to God. A persuasion of this sort of uniqueness attaching to Jesus seems to me the essential characteristic of what has actually in the field of human history been Christianity."[1]

The delay in the Parousia gave increasing significance to the Church as the divinely appointed sphere in and through which this absolute Christian revelation was vouchsafed to mankind. As the Kingdom of God on earth it regarded itself as commissioned to carry on the sovereign rule of the Creator in the world, and to bear historical witness of the truths committed to its care from generation to generation, as an integral part of a *living* tradition. Therefore, it maintained that what it taught officially and dogmatically had been revealed as an ingredient of its own life through the Holy Spirit. To doubt this revelation would be to doubt the veracity of God Himself. For all time it remains the apostolic fellowship because it has been raised up to bear witness of the resurrection of the Incarnate Lord from the dead, and to perpetuate for ever the sacrifice once offered on which the redemption of mankind depends. The apostolic ministry, sacraments and faith all hang together as a living witness to a primeval reality which expresses, enhances and codifies a divine revelation that governs faith and controls conduct.

This conception of the office and work of the Church arose quite naturally from the idea of a spiritual society united by a common faith and worship and committed to a particular way of life grounded in certain fundamental beliefs about its Founder, with Whom it enjoyed a spiritual union and felt itself permeated and sustained by the Holy Spirit. It was this connexion with the Holy Spirit that gave it its divine authority, just as its apostolic fellowship preserved in the episcopate provided the assurance that it was still the community founded by Christ.[2] Being above all things a revealed religion and the inheritor of the promises made to Israel, Christianity claimed to be the recipient of the disclosure of the divine truths made to certain individuals, and corporately to the society as a whole in its official capacity. Since the Incarnation was a new creative act which set the seal on the long series of divine interventions by which God had made known and worked out His purpose in human history, all that proceeded from it gained a new spiritual and redemptive significance.

[1] *Hellenism and Christianity* (London, 1921), p. 271.
[2] Cf. F. J. Bethune-Baker, *Introduction to the Early History of Christian Doctrine* (London, 1932), p. 356f.

The sacred records of the apostolic age, embodying the original oral tradition, teaching and preaching material expanded into the Gospel narratives and supplemented by the letters of St. Paul and others to local communities, were assigned a revelational status as an integral part of the proclamation of the Kingdom of God and the Mystery of divine grace and purpose completed in Christ and fulfilled in the Church, which was His Body. The literature that eventually emerged as the New Testament became the common Rule of Faith and in due course received the official imprimatur of revelation. As the historical text-book of the Church it has remained throughout the Ages the ultimate criterion of orthodoxy, containing the first-hand testimony of the apostles and their converts.

In the light of our present day knowledge of this literature as revealed by modern criticism, the trustworthiness of most of the books is firmly established. The attempt of the Tübingen School in the middle of the last century to reduce them to second century pseudepigrapha arising out of a hypothetical conflict between St. Peter and St. Paul, has long since been abandoned. "That time is over," as Harnack remarked at the turn of the century, and the discoveries of the last fifty years would seem to have made the traditional position in this matter quite secure. The Chester Beatty papyri, brought to light in 1931, contain fragments of most of the books of the New Testament and have reduced the gap between the earlier manuscripts and the traditional dates to negligible proportions. The prevalence of variants in the second century versions shows that manuscripts were being copied freely everywhere, and the fragment of the Fourth Gospel from Egypt, published in 1935 and now in the John Rylands Library at Manchester, is dated about A.D. 130-150, contemporary with the three leaves of a papyrus codex secured for the British Museum by Sir H. I. Bell and Mr. T. C. Skeat in the same year, containing incidents in the life of Christ in the language of the canonical Gospels. Taking this evidence collectively, Sir Frederick Kenyon seems to be justified in his claim that "no other ancient book has anything like such early and plentiful testimony to its text, and no unbiased scholar would deny that the text that has come down to us is substantially sound."[1]

By the end of the second century all the books of the New Testament with the exception of the Epistle to the Hebrews, the two shorter Epistles of St. John, the second Epistle of St. Peter, the

[1] *The Bible and Modern Scholarship* (London, 1948), p. 20.

Epistles of St. James and St. Jude, and the Apocalypse, were acknowledged as apostolic and authoritative throughout the Church. These disputed books were subsequently declared to contain the inspirational quality of scripture and so were labelled as canonical. Thus, through a selective process the Church determined which should be given the status of the revealed Word of God from among the very considerable number of documents current about the middle of the first century relating to the life and teaching of Jesus (of which that known as Q probably is an example) That the choice was well founded has been borne out on the whole by modern scientific examination of the literature.

Thus, it now appears that between A.D. 65 and 70 John Mark compiled the first synoptic account of the message of salvation from the material in circulation in the Christian community at Rome. As the oral tradition centred in the story of the Passion and Crucifixion of Christ, this apparently was the earliest continuous narrative to take fixed form. To it St. Mark added the account of the controversies which led up to the final event (Mk. ii. 1-3, 6; iii. 22, 30; vii. 5-13; viii. 11f; ix. 11-13; x. 2, 12; xi. 27, 33; xii. 13-34), together with a series of incidents, parables and a Jewish-Christian apocalypse (xiii. 6-8, 14-20, 24-27) partly perhaps derived from Q. In this material many of the Sayings of Jesus had been recorded, and some of the "popular" stories handed down orally, like that of the Gerasene demoniac (v. 1), or the walking on the sea (vi. 45, 52). The author's task was that of selecting, arranging and editing the data, supplying introductions, summaries and transitions, and drawing the moral from the various incidents. In all this he seems to have organized his material in order to make it conform to a general pattern, beginning with the Galilean ministry (i-viii. 29) and leading up to the recognition of the Messiahship of Jesus and its sequel (viii. 30-xvi. 8).

It was this Marcan narrative that St. Luke used as a source of his fuller evangelic tradition, supplementing it with material drawn from the hypothetical collection of discourses known as Q, and his own special information (L), which represents about half of the entire Gospel bearing his name, collected perhaps at Caesarea and other centres in Palestine. From Judaea he derived the story of the births of John the Baptist and Jesus (i. 5-ii. 52), whether or not the events came originally from Mary herself or those to whom she confided her intimate domestic secrets (ii. 51). Finally, he composed the prefatory dedication to a Roman official Theophilus in which he explained how and why he had embarked upon this ordered statement of the things most surely believed among the Nazoreans.

To this narrative he added, with the same dedication, an account of what happened immediately after the resurrection appearances, describing in the Acts of the Apostles the formation and organization of the Church commissioned to carry on the work begun by Jesus. There can be little doubt that the author or compiler of both records was one and the same writer, though possibly some extraneous material has been incorporated in the Acts borrowed from contemporary sources, including, it has been suggested, the writings of Josephus. It is also possible that he may have used the diary of a fellow-traveller of St. Paul, and this would explain some of the inaccuracies in the account of the Apostle and his movements. But against this is the employment of the first person plural in the "we passages," and St. Paul's own references to St. Luke in the Epistles. Therefore, if the Lucan authorship is not certain, the balance of probability is in its favour, and the date falls most conveniently some ten years after the Gospel according to St. Mark.

Rather later, a teacher, traditionally known as Matthew in the little Jewish Christian community at Jerusalem, after the fall of the city in A.D. 70, retold the Marcan story with certain variations, abbreviations and additions for the purpose of setting forth Jesus as the fulfilment of Messianic prophecy in accordance with the hopes and aspirations of his nation. He too had access to the document Q, and he drew largely on a collection of Old Testament passages, written perhaps in Hebrew, to emphasize the Messianic claims of Jesus and the Catholic conception of the Kingdom as an organized community of redeemed humanity.

The Fourth Gospel clearly belongs to a different tradition, and its date and authorship have long been matters of acute controversy. The Rylands fragment, containing portions of chapters xviii. 31-33, 37, 38, shows it was in circulation at the beginning of the second century, and this is supported by the Bell-Skeat leaves in the British Museum in which phrases from John v. 39, 45, ix. 29, vii. 30, x. 39. occur. It is not improbable, therefore, that it was compiled at the end of the previous century as a theological interpretation of Jesus as the transcendent Son of God tabernacled in human flesh, based on historical reminiscences of a writer who claimed to have been an eye-witness of the events he described. At the end of his life he may have felt himself compelled to add his testimony to that of the Synoptic tradition, having in the intervening years reflected deeply upon the inner significance of the light that shined in the darkness of a world that comprehended it not.

St. Paul's correspondence, so far as it has come down to us, is different in character from the Gospel tradition and the Acts. A good deal of it consists of fragments, and represents an attempt to express in current theological language and Hellenistic thought-forms the Apostle's personal experience of "the life that is hid with Christ in God." But in one of the earliest and most authentic letters, the First Epistle to the Corinthians, written probably in the spring of A.D. 55 or 56, he appealed to the teaching which he had received from the Church after his conversion respecting the death, burial and resurrection of Christ as a redemptive act.[1] Therefore, unless he is to be discredited as a witness, his testimony stands as evidence of the things most surely believed among the earliest disciples in line with that of the rest of the New Testament. If it was he who formulated Christian theology, he did so in accordance with the established tradition, summarizing its contents in what has been considered to have been the earliest form of the preaching of the Gospel in apostolic times.

It was the conviction that a reconciliation had been achieved through the moral perfection of Christ sealed in the atoning act of His death and resurrection, that constituted the centre and core of the Christian Faith. To it the New Testament bears witness as a unique event in history and a revelation of the invisible God. In course of time this sacred literature took over the character of inspired scripture comparable to that which formed the basis of Judaism. If in fact it was the message that was inspired and the events that disclosed the revelation, rather than the books in which they were recorded, what was written and taught came to be regarded as "of faith." The words of the writers might be their own,[2] but inasmuch as they came from God they were exempt, as it seemed, from all erroneous beliefs and ideas, since the writers "had perfect capacity for knowledge."[3] Nevertheless, the Church reserved to itself the right to interpret Scripture in accordance with its own official formularies and decisions, thereby maintaining the standard of doctrinal orthodoxy. So while appeal was made at councils to the supreme and infallible authority of the Bible as, in the words attributed to Constantine, possessing "the teaching of the most

[1] I Cor. xv, 3.
[2] Justin Martyr, *Apol.* i, 36; Tertullian, *Apol.*, 18.
[3] Irenaeus, *Adv. Haereses*, iii, 1, 5; Origen, *De Princip*, iv.

N

Holy Spirit committed to writing,"[1] it was to confirm the faith that had been established once and for all by divine revelation.

This, however, tended to make inspiration oracular and to reduce the Church and the Bible almost to the level of the Delphic Pythia, especially in the fourth century A.D. when ideas of divination were still current in the Graeco-Roman world. This conception of revelation has persisted throughout the ages and as recently as 1893 Pope Leo XIII in his encyclical *Providentissimus Deo* affirmed that "all the books which the Church receives as sacred and canonical, are written wholly and entirely, with all their parts, at the dictation of the Holy Ghost; and so far is it from being possible that any error can co-exist with inspiration, that inspiration not only is essentially incompatible with error, but excludes and rejects it as absolutely and necessarily as it is impossible that God Himself, the supreme Truth, can utter that which is not true." Similarly, the Protestant *Westminster Confession* maintained that "the authority of the Holy Scripture, for which it ought to be believed and obeyed, dependeth not upon the Testimony of any man or church: but wholly upon God (Who is Truth itself) the Author thereof; and therefore it is to be received, because it is the Word of God."

In both these statements the Scriptures are represented as the actual revelation rather than the record of God's self-disclosure, very much as in Islam the Qur'an is regarded as the speech of Allah, written in the sacred text, preserved in the memories of believers, recited by their tongues and revealed in its fulness to the Prophet. It is uncreated and only the ink, paper and writing are the work of men for human needs. "The speech of Allah is self-existing, and its meaning is understood by means of these things" yet never dissociated from Him.[2] Whatever He quotes in it "from Moses or other prophets, from Pharaoh or from Satan, is the speech of Allah" inseparable from Him, sent down from heaven complete and revealed to Mohammed, either by the angel Gabriel, in a series of visions or dreams, or through an actual appearance of God Himself.[3]

Thus, both for Islam and Christianity the conception of revelation raises crucial issues. Is the divine disclosure *revelatio*, an act of revealing, or *revelatum*, a reality revealed? Considered as a record of a revelation the New Testament and the Qur'an have a beginning

---

[1]Gelasius *Hist. Conc. Nicaea*, III, 7.

[2]*Wasiyat Abi Hanifa*, Art. 9; *Fifth Akbar* II, Art. 3, 26.

[3]Sura II, 91, LIII, 5. The eternity of the Qur'an was denied by the Mu'tazilites but has been firmly maintained by orthodox Moslems as an infallible pre-existent oracle.

in time and history, and belong to a particular society or tradition. The *revelatio* began with historical persons, Jesus or Mohammed, and continued in the respective religious communities, it is alleged, through either the Holy Spirit, in the case of Christianity, or the omnipotent power of Allah, in Islam. But as a *revelatum* the revelation is eternal, being a self-disclosure of God Who is without beginning or end, or any limitations. In Christian theology, the Deity having spoken of old to the fathers by the prophets, "at the end of the days has spoken to us by a Son Whom He appointed heir of the universe."[1] In Islam, the revelation was not in Mohammed but in the message disclosed to him which he gathered together in a book for the guidance of man, freed from all error.[2] Nowhere, however, in the Christian Scriptures is a doctrine of revelation formulated or defined.

As the record of a revelation the primary instrument of the disclosure has been inspired persons who have confronted their own day and generation with absolute demands and commands which they have declared in the name of God and in relation to particular events and occurrences, especially to spiritual processes (e.g. redemption, judgment). Thus, in the New Testament the Incarnation is represented as the supreme divine act whereby God's eternal nature and His purpose for the world and mankind have been revealed both as a *revelatio* and a *revelatum*. But in neither case is the dictation of infallible oracles implied, or the communication of theological systems of doctrine and articles of faith. The apprehension of the revelation, of course, is dependent upon the human mind perceiving and interpreting the significance of what has been disclosed, and this involves a subjective element. An act of faith is required to evaluate correctly the event and its record, but since the human mind is fallible, room is left for finite and even erroneous judgments in matters of interpretation and of historical detail. Therefore, no hard and fast distinctions can be drawn between the objective and subjective aspects of revelation, or between natural and revealed religion.

Revelation must always be a realized reality on the part of its recipient, and this is neither wholly objective nor entirely subjective. Prophetic insight is required if concrete situations are to be evaluated in relation to their deeper significance as divinely guided events. Thus, in the eighth century B.C. the Hebrew prophets by

[1]Heb. i, 1f.
[2]Qur'an V, 3, XCVIII, 2-3.

their spiritual illumination proclaimed a revelational message to
their nation in and through its own history, just as the Christian
Church later found in the life and work of its Founder a divine
intervention having momentous consequences for the world. At a
moment when the Empire seemed to be at the height of its power
and glory, its sun in point of fact had touched its zenith. The clouds
had not yet begun to gather, and no shadows crept across the fair
landscape, with peace at home and triumph abroad. It was only in
an obscure and struggling community of spiritually alert minds
that the truth had dawned that among the hills of Galilee a Figure
had appeared Who was destined to shake the entire Empire to its
foundations, and to lay the whole fabric of ancient civilization in the
dust. They had come to realize that they stood at the very centre
of history, and so felt themselves compelled to noise abroad the
glad tidings they had heard, and make known the things they had
seen and could testify by their own first-hand knowledge and
experience of the events they had witnessed and perceived. Thus,
the Biblical revelation is always represented as a divine encounter
in and through historical situations, issuing in practical results for
the world at large as well as for the individuals immediately
concerned.

Now, as Dr. Hodgson has pointed out, theology is the study
of Christian history with a view to determining the exact nature
and meaning of its content.[1] Consequently, it has to take account
of both the historical situation out of which the Faith arose and
the beliefs and teachings of the persons concerned in it. For instance,
the doctrine of the Trinity represents rational reflection upon and
interpretation of a series of events which actually occurred in time
and space, and upon which the dogma ultimately rests. The divine
disclosure was of God Himself and of His purpose for the world
and mankind as consummated in Christ. But this could only be
understood and made intelligible to others through the thought-
forms and expositions of those who, as they believed, had seen
God in the face of Jesus Christ.

Therefore, the function of the Church was and is that of interpreting the mysteries of faith which it claims to have received,
and of which, according to its credentials, it is the custodian. The
protracted controversies which characterized the process of credal
formulation bear witness to the absence of a revelation of systematized doctrines, and even when a settlement was reached in

[1] *The Doctrine of the Trinity* (London, 1944), p. 24.

451 at the Council of Chalcedon, it was in the nature of a com-
promise. The Church set its seal on certain propositions of Cyril
of Alexandria (though its key-word did not come from Alexandria)
and those of the *Tome* of Leo, but however useful for practical
purposes the definition may have been, the inconsistency latent in
the Christology of Cyril was unresolved.[1] Therefore, it was not as
a formulated doctrine that the Trinity in unity of the Godhead
was presented to the world or to the Church for authoritative
acceptance in the beginning. The Deity Who had disclosed Himself
as the ultimate ground of all existence was recognized to be the
Father of mankind Who was leading all things to their appointed
ends through a divine intervention in the process of history in the
Word made flesh. To this event the apostolic company and their
successors bore witness by their teaching and the reproduction of
the life of Christ in themselves, in the power of the Holy Spirit
dwelling in them and leading them to all truth.

   Though the doctrine of the Trinity appears in embryo within
the New Testament itself,[2] regarded by the Church as the inspired
record of a unique self-revelation of God Himself, it does not
depend on any theory of the mode of the composition of the
various books of which the literature is composed. The metaphysical implications of the nature of the Godhead originated in
Christian experience of the traditional conception of ethical monotheism in Judaism combined with that of the Person of Christ,
interpreted in terms of the risen and ascended Incarnate Lord, and
the work of the Holy Spirit realized in the lives of His followers
as a divine afflatus. Each of these three modes of experience was
distinct yet they were experiences of the One Living God, Creator,
Redeemer and Sanctifier. It was this apprehension which was given
theological formulation in the language and thought of the fourth
century, and the affirmations have stood the test of time because
they expressed the fundamental concept of Deity which Christianity had made its own particular revelational interpretation of
the Divine Being.

   It was in this way that a systematized body of Christian tradition
took shape, based on the Biblical record and subsequently set forth
in the creeds and confirmed in the spiritual experience of the

---

[1]L. Hodgson, *Essays on the Trinity and the Incarnation* (London, 1928), pp. 359ff,
387.
   [2]Cf. St. Mt. xxviii, 19; II Cor. xiii, 18; I Cor, vi, 11, xii, 3; Gal. iv, 6; Ephes. iv,
4–6; St. Jn. xiv, 16f, 26, xv, 26.

Church. The life, death and resurrection of the Christ were held to be the manifestations of God in these historical events which revealed the divine nature in its triune majesty in selfless love and the conquest of evil. The manner in which the Incarnation was effected, and what actually happened on the "third day" after the Crucifixion, are questions for rational inquiry in the light of the available evidence, and must be judged accordingly.

The doctrine of the Virgin Birth, for example, though very intimately associated with the Incarnation regarded as a revealed truth, actually is an interpretation of the event to be validated or rejected in relation to the documentary evidence and the other relevant data. A literary and critical examination of the Scriptural narratives in which the tradition is embodied yields very uncertain results.[1] The Lucan and the Matthaean accounts raise too many critical difficulties conclusively to prove the tradition, and there is nothing to show that either St. Mark or St. Paul was aware of the virginal conception of Mary. On the other hand, it is not easy to account for the belief except on a basis of fact,[2] especially as clearly it was not invented for apologetic purposes since it is not mentioned in the apostolic expositions of the Incarnation. Even in the First Gospel the descent of Jesus is traced through Joseph back to David.

In the absence of any convincing and conclusive historical judgment, the issue becomes one for theological investigation. Here again opinion differs. To some theologians it seems that the doctrine is inconsistent with the true humanity of Christ, while others regard it as an absolutely essential and integral element in the whole conception of the Incarnation. That it was affirmed and given credal authority by the general consensus of the Church from the second century onwards is unquestioned, and despite the absence of evidence that such a claim was made for the belief in apostolic times, it may be reasonably contended that an event of such unique occurrence and significance as the Incarnation is represented to have been, requires a special operative cause produced "neither by the will of the flesh, nor the will of man, but of God."[3] Granting the premises, if the Ultimate Reality of the universe is personal Will it would be incongruous if He were not able to act in special ways to meet the needs of particular occasions of unique

---

[1] V. Taylor, *The Historical Evidence for the Virgin Birth* (Oxford, 1920).
[2] J. G. Machen, *The Virgin Birth of Christ* (New York, 1930), p. 271f.
[3] St. Jn. i, 13f.

significance in His ordering of His creation to its appointed ends. The only question at stake, therefore, for those who accept the advent of Christ to have been an inauguration of a new era in the process of history, is whether or not the evidence for a virgin birth is sufficient to justify this interpretation of what actually occurred.

Very different is the situation when what is alleged to have happened at the coming of Jesus into the world is extended to His mother. For the dogma of the immaculate conception of Mary there is no clear and convincing warrant in Holy Writ. The so-called *Proto-evangelium* of Genesis iii, 17 has no bearing upon the supposed immunity from original sin on the part of the instrument of the Incarnation by a miraculous intervention, any more than has the angelic salutation recorded in the Lucan account of the Annunciation.[1] Although the Christian Fathers and their successors generally held the Virgin to be a specially sanctified vessel—"a tabernacle exempt from corruption"[2]—this was only in respect of actual or personal sin. It was not until the twelfth century that the question of her exemption from original sin was raised when a controversy arose in connexion with the observance of the Oriental Feast of the Conception, which had been held in the East on 8th December, probably since the seventh century. If this festival was brought to England from Tarsius by Theodore when he became Archbishop of Canterbury in 668, it explains the prominence it attained in the British Isles in the Early Middle Ages, whence it spread to Normandy. In France, however, it encountered determined opposition from Bernard of Clairvaux on the ground that it was a superstitious novelty in the West and foreign to the old tradition of the Church. Moreover, it was said to give emphasis to sexual generation which, according to the Augustinian theory, involved concupiscence. The English monks replied by asserting the miraculous exemption of Mary from defilement. Thus the way was opened for the Feast to be transformed into that of the Immaculate Conception to reconcile it with St. Augustine's doctrine of original sin. But both the observance and its theology were refuted by the Scholastics, including Albert Magnus, Bonaventura, Hugh of St. Victor, Peter Lombard and St. Thomas Aquinas, who recognized that the doctrine could not be reconciled with the Pauline declaration that the whole race required redemption because it was infected with the sin of Adam. If Mary had been an exception, it

[1] St. Lk. i, 28.
[2] Cf. Hippolytus, *in Gallandi; Bibl. patrum*, II, 496.

was argued, she would have been excluded from salvation and Christ would not have been the Saviour of all men.[1]

In the next century Duns Scotus and the Franciscans, in opposition to their rivals the Dominicans, took up the cause of the protagonists of the Feast and its theological implications, aided by the modifications that had occurred during the thirteenth century in the Augustinian theory of concupiscence. Under Franciscan influence the doctrine of the Immaculate Conception of Mary was adopted by the universities despite Dominican opposition, and in 1476 the Feast on 8th December was acknowledged by Pope Sixtus IV without official recognition of its associated dogma. The Council of Trent expressly exempted from original sin "the Blessed and Immaculate Virgin Mary, Mother of God," but refrained from defining what it affirmed. So the controversy continued until, with the powerful aid of the Jesuits and the Ultramontanes in the seventeenth and eighteenth centuries, bolstered up by spurious legends, the ground was prepared for the promulgation of the doctrine in the bull *Ineffabilis*, issued by Pius IX on 8th December, 1854. Four years later a series of apparitions to Bernadette at the famous grotto on the banks of the River Gave at Lourdes, during which the figure is alleged to have proclaimed *Je suis l'immaculée conception*, appeared, as it seemed to some, to give supernatural confirmation to the dogma by the miraculous cures effected at the renowned Pyrenaean shrine.

For our present purpose the history of this doctrine is illuminating inasmuch as it shows how readily interpretation passes into speculation, legend falsifies history and hallucination is made the medium of divinely guaranteed theological propositions and formulated beliefs, usually appealing to the emotions at the expense of the reason, regardless of the nature of the evidence on which they are based. When this is accomplished "pious belief" becomes *de fide* revealed dogma so that in a recent Papal encyclical it could be affirmed "all who are truly Christ's believe, for example, the conception of the Mother of God without stain of original sin with the same faith as they believe the mystery of the August Trinity, and the Incarnation of Our Lord, just as they do the infallible teaching of the Roman Pontiff." It is no part of our business in this inquiry to pass judgment on revealed truth in the abstract in any religion, but surely to put on the same revelational level all these very diverse and unequally substantiated interpretations

[1]*Summa Theol.* III, Q. xxvii, a, 2.

of theological doctrines, is untenable. This, however, is always liable to occur when revelation is sought in theological systems and propositions rather than in divinely ordered events apprehended in the illumination of faith and the self-evidencing authority of truth itself, verified at the bar of history, reason and spiritual experience.

The function of reason in relation to revelation is that of subjecting the alleged divine disclosures to a strictly rational inquiry as against the claims of all external and oracular guarantees of inspirational and revelational truth. Reality must be capable of verification within the limits of its own subject-matter. Because the finite mind is incapable of knowing in all its fulness the essential being of the Infinite, is no excuse for assuming with Schleiermacher that religion has nothing to do with knowledge,[1] or with Barth and the neo-Calvinists that "truth comes in the faith in which we begin and in the faith in which we cease to know," and depends solely upon God's self-unveiling.[2] Such an antithesis of revelation and reason is as indefensible as the traditional distinction between natural and revealed religion.

The objective study of religion as an empirical science along the lines indicated by Dr. Henry Wilde in the Statutes governing the Lectureship he established in the University of Oxford,[3] acts as a corrective of ill-founded *a priori* assumptions based on supposed doctrinal disclosures in conflict with ascertainable and verifiable knowledge. For the religious mind the purely rational approach to the problem of the divine ordering of the universe will always be too coldly serene and intellectual to meet the needs of the spirit; and, as Professor Laird has pointed out, "natural theology could never be the whole of Christian theology, even if it uniformly supported that theology. It must always be less than Christian, and would seem to be narrower in principle than the theologies of many other religions. That in itself is not an objection to natural theology; but there would be serious reason for complaint if the limitations of the sphere of natural theology were sedulously and not quite candidly concealed."[4]

Thus, it cannot pass judgment on the doctrine of the Trinity,

[1] *On Religion; Speeches to its Cultured Despisers* (London, 1893), p. 101.
[2] K. Barth, *Doctrine of the Word of God* (E.T. by G. T. Thomson, Edin., 1936), pp. 14, 368ff.
[3] As this volume owes its origin to lectures given on the Wilde Foundation, its scope and aims are discussed in the Preface.
[4] *Theism and Cosmology* (London, 1940), p. 38f.

or the historicity of the Incarnation and Resurrection of Christ, except in so far as the data with which it is concerned bear upon these theological propositions. Yet the validity of these articles of faith as statements of fundamental truth are of vital concern for Christianity as a religion, for without them it could not be what it is. Revelation, therefore, cannot be lightly dismissed in the study and evaluation of particular creeds, or in religious inquiry in general. But just because it is of such crucial importance, the evidence on which it rests must be investigated in relation to the observable facts and verifiable knowledge and experience correctly interpreted.

To exempt alleged divine disclosures from such a test as self-contained systems of truth beyond the natural capacity of the human mind, is to remove them from the life and thought of the world altogether and leave them at the mercy of unrestrained speculation and fantasy. Moreover, to make a fundamental distinction between what can be known about God by "the unaided reason" and "the saving knowledge" bestowed by Him from without, opens the way for a disastrous dualism in the quest of truth. On the other hand, theologians may reasonably contend that any theory of "natural religion" or "progressive revelation" that does not take account of the dissimilarities as well as the affinities between a religion like Christianity which rests its claims on revelation, and other faiths, does not meet the observable facts. There are, for example, as we have seen, certain unique features in the Christian conception of Deity which require explanation. This has led some apologists to differentiate a "general revelation" common to the universal religious consciousness of mankind from a "special revelation" mediated through particular historical episodes, persons and situations as the means by which the truths of "general revelation" are apprehended.[1] This hypothesis avoids the former dualism based on revealed propositional truths contrasted with unaided natural knowledge and leaves room for the interpretation of the peculiar contribution of Christianity, or indeed of any other religion, in terms of divine self-disclosure. If, as St. Augustine affirmed, all knowledge of truth is in fact revelational,[2] the idea of "natural" and "unaided" knowledge becomes superfluous, but

---

[1]For a recent statement of this position cf. A. Richardson, *Christian Apologetics* London, 1947), p. 116ff.

[2]*De Civ. Dei.* Bk. x, chaps., ii, iv.

even so there may be degrees of disclosure and illumination in the giving and perceiving of higher truth.

Whether or not any specific tradition can maintain its claim to be in possession of an absolutely unique and final "special revelation" is a matter for independent inquiry in the light of the evidence available for the purpose. So far as the comparative study of religion is concerned, its contribution towards the elucidation of the problem is mainly in providing carefully collected and properly assessed data analysed and evaluated in a genuinely scientific, philosophic and sympathetic spirit.

INDEX

ABSOLUTE, The, 57ff., 83, 97, 164ff., 167, 170
Adonis, 36, 48
Aeschylus, 41, 96
Agni, 53f., 60
Ahura Mazdah, 111, 153
Alexander, S., 141f.
Aleyan, Sky-god, 38f., 40
Al-Ghazali, 107
Allah, 106, 186
All-Father belief, 4, 26f., 80
Amida, Worship of, 66
Amon-Re, 93ff.
Amos, 78, 104
Analogy, Principle of, 71, 84f.
Animism, 25, 30
Anselm, St., 131, 162
Anthropology and the study of religion, xi
Anthropomorphism, 72ff., 81ff.
Apollo, Oracle at Delphi, 47, 169, 171
Aquinas, St. Thomas, 31, 72, 84, 131, 144, 150, 163
Arian controversy, The, 161
Aristotle, and motion, 31, 99, 117, 131, 144, 148
——and theism, 98, 131, 154
Ark of the covenant in Israel, 172
Atman, Conception of, 57, 60, 63f.
Atomic structure of the universe, 142ff.
Aton, Worship of, in Egypt, 94
Attis, Cult of, 48, 50
Atum, Cult of, 32
Augustine, St., 123, 128, 130
Avatars in Hinduism, 61, 65, 153
Avesta, The, 112
Axe, Cult of the Double, in Crete, 42

BACCHANALIA, The, 48
Barth, K., 148f.
Bergson, H., 139
Berkeley, George, 85, 133
Bevan, E., 180

Bhagavad-gita, The, 59, 61
Bodhisattvas, Conception of, 63f.
Brahma, 62
Brahman, 56ff., 153
Brahmana texts, 56f.
Brahmins, 53, 91
Bridgewater treatises, The, 135, 138
Bruhl, Lévy, 18, 26
Brunner, E., 148f.
Buddha, The, 63
Bull-roarer, The cult of, 28
Butler, Bishop, 85

CALVINISTIC THEISM, 134
Causation, Conception of, 133f., 142 (cf. teleology)
Christ as Messiah, 104f., 178, 180
——Divinity of, 105f., 156, 158, 160f. (cf. Incarnation)
Church, The, and society, 162f.
Cleanthes, 100
Codrington, R. H., 19
Collingwood, R. G., 131
Comte, A., 138
Confucius, 69
Cosmological argument for theism, The, 131ff., 143f.
Covenant, Idea of, in Israel, 79f., 154
Cow, Sacredness of, in India, 53
Creation, Conception of, 26f., 77, 81, 123
Creator, The, 26ff., 77, 130, 154, 165
Cybele, Worship of, 48

DARWIN, C., 136ff.
Davids, Mrs. Rhys, 63
De Burgh, W. G., 151
Ded column, raising of, in Egypt, 50
Deism, 133f., 148, 154, 163
Deity (cf. God, Theism, Absolute, Revelation)
Demeter, Worship of, 44ff.
Descartes, R., 128, 132f.